na al
Er sh

intermediate teacher's book
Ruth Gairns & Stuart Redman

OXFORD
UNIVERSITY PRESS

contents

introduction

how we wrote this course

Before we established the language syllabus for the **natural English** course, we wanted to be sure that what we set out to teach intermediate learners corresponded to what they actually needed to learn at that stage in their language development. We started by planning a series of communicative activities with certain criteria:

- they should be achievable, engaging, and purposeful
- they should be language rich in that they would push learners into extensive and varied language use, and could not be accomplished with a very limited range of expression
- they should range across different time frames (past, present, and future)
- they should have different topics and themes
- they should include different activity types, e.g. role play; discussion; giving, justifying, and reacting to opinions; planning and negotiating; exchanging information; presenting ideas; sharing experiences; telling stories, etc.
- finally, they should each be different in tone: fun, business-like, factual, nostalgic, etc.

We then wrote the activities. Initially, we produced more than we needed, and after trialling, we eliminated those which did not work as well as we had hoped, or that overlapped with others which were richer in language or more successful. Those that remained became the extended speaking activities and role plays which you will find in the **student's book**, in a much refined and reworked form, thanks to the learner data and feedback from teachers received during piloting of the material (see below). Here are two examples:

you're going to:	you're going to:
collect ideas plan your holiday complex: who it's for, where it will be, and what facilities it will have	**collect ideas** read a true story about a couple who have to make an important decision
prepare a presentation decide exactly how to present your complex to another group	**reach a decision** discuss the advantages and disadvantages of the options they have and decide on the best one
present your ideas give your presentation and decide which group has designed the best holiday complex	**listen** find out what the couple's decision is
role play act out a role play at the complex	**but first ...** Look back at the **extended speaking** boxes in this unit. You can use this language in the activity.
but first ... Look back at the **extended speaking** boxes in this unit. You can use this language in the activity.	

from **student's book unit two** p.30 and **unit six** p.78

trialling and recording the activities

We asked teachers to use the material with their intermediate classes and record small groups doing the activities. We also piloted them ourselves with small groups. In all, we recorded over two hundred learners who came from more than twenty countries in Europe, South America, and South East Asia. We had planned to record intermediate learners doing the activities and then compare them with recordings of native speakers of English doing the same activities. However, it soon became obvious that a native speaker model alone would not lead us to a satisfactory syllabus; it was often too colloquial and idiomatic, and in some cases, too idiosyncratic. (See **what is natural English?** below, for more detail on this.)

Instead, we turned to learners themselves. We realized that a more realistic goal for intermediate learners could be provided by those who had already broken through the intermediate barrier: upper intermediate and low advanced learners of English. Our research therefore changed at an early stage, and we and the teachers involved in the project piloted and recorded the activities with separate groups of intermediate and higher level learners.

analysing the learner data

Finally, we transcribed the recordings. This data enabled us to look at the differences between intermediate and higher level learners. We examined how each group performed, what the language differences were, and what achievable goals we could set for intermediate learners in terms of language and performance strategies. This data influenced our selection of language in preparation for the role plays and extended speaking activities, although we also decided to include other language suitable for the level to ensure that the syllabus was as comprehensive as possible. At that point, we were able to start writing the **student's book**.

To summarize, the development of the course involved the following stages:

1 devise the extended speaking activities / role plays for trialling
2 trial and record intermediate and higher level learners
3 transcribe and analyse the data
4 select appropriate language for the syllabus
5 write the learning materials in each unit leading up to the extended speaking and role plays (and refine them)

what is natural English?

As we have already said, native speaker talk did not provide us with a model of English that was necessarily the most appropriate for intermediate learners. In a nutshell, the gap between the two was just too great, and the native speaker model represented a target that was unattainable for intermediate learners of English. One of the features of native speaker talk, especially with native speaker to native speaker, is its highly idiomatic nature. Native speakers can use *at the end of my tether* or talk about *getting their head round a problem*, and when they do, it sounds perfectly natural. Transferring that language and trying to integrate it within an intermediate learner's current interlanguage often has the opposite effect; it sounds very unnatural.

There are, however, degrees of idiomaticity. At the extreme end are the more picturesque but often opaque expressions such as:

He's got a finger in every pie.
She's full of beans.
When all's said and done.
They're thick as thieves.

But at the other end are much lower levels of idiomaticity in expressions such as:

He's changed his mind.
I'll let you know.
We've got nothing in common.
Did you have a good time?

This second group contains phrases that are very natural for native speakers and, in most cases, much more frequent than the more opaque idiomatic expressions above. For intermediate learners of English though, they have a further benefit; being less idiomatic and more neutral in style, they are more accessible and easier to use alongside the rest of their current interlanguage. This lead us to a general principle for language selection: choose language proficient speakers and native speakers use naturally, which intermediate learners could incorporate into their evolving language and also use naturally. Hence, **natural English**.

the natural English syllabus

How does anyone decide exactly what language will fulfil this criteria? It is, of course, highly subjective. As yet, there isn't a readily available core lexicon of phrases and collocations to teach intermediate learners on the basis of frequency, let alone taking into account the question of which phrases might be most 'suitable' for learners at this level. Our strategy has been to use our own classroom knowledge and experience to interpret our data of intermediate and higher level language use, in conjunction with information from the *Longman Grammar of Spoken and Written English*, a range of ELT dictionaries and data from the British National Corpus. In this way, we arrived at a useful and relevant language syllabus for intermediate learners.

On the one hand, we have steered away from highly idiomatic language. On the other, we have also tried to avoid modified and stilted forms of language that can arise from using a traditional written grammar as the model for teaching spoken English, which tends to produce slightly unnatural English, for example:

A: Do you have a car?

B: Yes, I do. OR No, I don't.

While the focus on the correct manipulation of the auxiliary is understandable, it would be more natural to use *have got* (in British English) to ask about possession, and allow a wider range of possible answers. For example:

A: Have you got a car?

B: Yes (a Golf / but I want to get a new one, etc.) OR No (not at the moment / afraid not / I don't drive, etc.)

what else did we learn from the data?

These are some of the general findings to emerge from our data, which influenced the way we then produced the material.

general communication needs

- Intermediate learners had far more difficulty sustaining conversation than higher level learners. Their utterances and interactions were far shorter. Our approach was, therefore, to try to boost learners' confidence to 'keep going'.
- We give them time to plan and even rehearse what they want to say in longer activities.
- We provide frameworks and checklists to help them to structure their speaking, in order to free them from worrying about how to organize their discourse.
- We teach them language and give them practice in extending what they say, for instance, giving reasons, giving examples to support their opinions, and so on.
- Many intermediate learners had shortcomings in conversation strategies, such as initiating and closing conversations, involving the listener, and moving conversation on. Sometimes when they did initiate, they sounded very direct and even unintentionally rude. We set out to give them ways of introducing what they want to say or achieve with natural English phrases:
- learning initial phone greetings, e.g. *Is that …?*
- introducing a request, e.g. *There's something I wanted to ask you …*
- inviting someone to speak, e.g. *How about you, Tomoko?*
- moving the conversation on, e.g. *Shall we go on to the next question?*
- Learners at this level are more concerned with what they have to say themselves than with listening and responding to others, as they would normally do. Again, planning and rehearsal time gives learners more confidence in speaking more fluently, and this in turn frees them to respond to others. We focus throughout the course on ways of responding when you are listening, i.e. asking follow-up questions, responding with interest or sympathy, asking for clarification, etc. This is achieved by:
- the selection of phrases we have focused on in the **natural English** boxes
- learners themselves selecting appropriate natural language by using the transcripts for listening activities.

Want to know more? Go to **how to …** teach listening (use of transcripts) *p.154.*

- The role plays proved to be a very useful source of data. They often illustrated some of the weaknesses above, and it became obvious that as they required a different form of transactional language (especially in 'service encounters', such as phoning to make arrangements, buying things in a shop, etc.), they were essential for more rounded language skills. The data also showed that learners improved dramatically in achieving their aims in these activities when they were given considerable language preparation, help in structuring the activity, listening models, and planning and rehearsal time.

language needs

- Modal verbs appeared frequently in the data of our recordings of upper intermediate learners, but were notably absent in intermediate data, especially *will, would, might, could, should*.

- Tenses were still generally problematic at intermediate level, a fact that will not surprise any teacher. Indeed, we saw many very predictable problems with traditional grammar areas such as articles, determiners, word grammar, adjectives and adverbs, etc.

- Learners at this level seemed to shy away from adverbs. *Very* appeared everywhere, but not some of the high frequency adverbs we found in the upper intermediate level data, e.g. *extremely, slightly, occasionally, fortunately*, etc.

- When we analysed the data of learners doing the different activities, we found many examples of awkward or incorrect English that resulted not so much from traditional grammar mistakes, as from learners not being familiar with or able to produce common native speaker chunks of language such as these:

  I don't know much about (football).
  The most important thing is (good weather).
  I'd find it very difficult to (drive on the right).
  No, I'm afraid not.
  Have you got any left?
  I don't like that sort of thing.
  It doesn't really appeal to me.

  What is interesting about most of these lexical phrases is not the number of new words they contain, but in fact, the familiarity of most of the words, even for intermediate learners. The problem is knowing when and how to assemble these largely familiar words into the natural native-speaker-type utterances above.

  Most of the phrases and language input presented in **natural English** arose out of perceived learner needs and shortcomings picked up during the trialling of the role plays and extended speaking activities.

how to use the key features of natural English

- life with Agrippine / do you get it?
- **natural English** boxes
- wordbooster
- test yourself!
- language reference and cover & check exercises
- the listening booklet
- workbook

life with Agrippine / do you get it?

Alternate units in the course (1, 3, 5, etc.) begin with a section including a Bretécher cartoon called **life with Agrippine** while the other units (2, 4, 6, etc.) begin with a recorded, illustrated joke called **do you get it?** Each of these sections begins with personalized speaking practice, followed by the cartoon or joke, with natural English features derived from the reading or listening input highlighted in the **natural English** boxes. Both have a glossary, and the jokes also include a vocabulary development activity.

why cartoons and jokes?

They provide a light-hearted and engaging lead-in to the theme of the unit through listening or reading for pleasure. The Bretécher cartoons raise recognizable and universal issues to do with contemporary life, and although aimed at adults, they are also appealing to younger adults. The jokes have been chosen to be linguistically and culturally accessible – and, we hope, amusing for a wide audience.

how to ... use the cartoons

With the Bretécher cartoons, there will be a temptation for learners to read ahead to the next cartoon strip if they like them. If they do so, at least it will mean that learners are very motivated.

- You could do the first speaking activity in the cartoon section with books closed, either by telling learners orally what to do or by writing the questions / prompts on the board. This will prevent learners from reading the cartoon before you want them to. The speaking activity can be done in pairs, groups, or as a whole class.

- You can then tell learners to look at the pre-set questions and read the cartoon. In the early units, point out the glossary so that learners can read quickly and understand the humour. Avoid getting involved in a detailed study or word-for-word translation at this stage; as a text, it has been written to be read for pleasure.

- Decide whether or not you want to use the recording. It will help your learners get a feel for natural sounding English, although some teachers may prefer not to use it, as the cartoon was originally written as a text to be read, not listened to.

Once you have dealt with the language in the **natural English** boxes, you could consider other activities:

- Some of the cartoons lend themselves well to reading aloud and acting out in pairs or small groups, e.g. units five and seven. This could either be done in a very controlled way, or learners could read the conversations a couple of times, then shut their books and improvise them.

- Some cartoons might stimulate discussion, depending on the teaching context, e.g. unit three: homework; unit five: giving presents to children.

- You may find other well-known cartoon strips in the local culture which you could take into class for learners to translate, or you could blank out the mother tongue dialogue and write an English version yourself, or ask your learners to write the dialogue.

how to ... use the jokes

You can use the lead-in speaking activity as with the Bretécher cartoons.

- The pictures are there essentially to help learners understand the joke by setting the scene. You can pre-teach key vocabulary, or give learners time to work out the story and use the glossary themselves. If anyone recognizes the joke, and knows the punchline, do your best to prevent them from revealing it – otherwise it will spoil the listening activity.

- Always read the joke yourself before the lesson in case there is anything culturally problematic. You can then decide, in advance, how to deal with it.

- The response bubbles (*That's a good joke. / I don't get it. / That's an old one.*) are important, and it should be no stigma if a learner doesn't get the joke; it often happens to native speakers too. You can use the second listening and the **listening booklet** to clear up any misunderstandings. By the end of the book, learners will have acquired quite a lot of ways of reacting to jokes. Even groans indicate involvement and recognition, and that is a common response to jokes. Don't be put off by them!

After dealing with the **natural English** box and the vocabulary activity, there are other possibilities:

– You can suggest that they learn the joke for homework. Jokes, like songs, are often very memorable, and they are excellent for building confidence.

– If your learners are adventurous, they could translate a joke from their mother tongue into English to tell other learners.

natural English boxes

Most of the **natural English** boxes consist of natural English phrases. They normally occur five or six times in each unit, with one or two boxes in each main section (excluding **wordbooster**) leading up to the extended speaking activity.

what do the natural English boxes contain?

These boxes focus on important aspects of everyday language, some of which fall outside the traditional grammatical / lexical syllabus. They include:

– familiar functional exponents, e.g. expressing preferences, making offers and requests (*Do you mind if I borrow your dictionary?*)

– communication strategies, e.g. inviting people to speak (*What about you, Henri?*), introducing a request (*There's something I wanted to ask you – do you …?*)

– common features of spoken English, e.g. *anyway, actually, and that sort of thing*

– lexical chunks, e.g. *have a (good / bad / lovely) time; is there / have you got any left?*

The language here is presented in chunks, with each box containing a limited number of phrases to avoid memory overload. The phrases are practised on the spot, and then learners have the opportunity to use them later in freer activities, e.g. in **it's your turn!** and the extended speaking activity at the end of each unit.

how to … use the natural English boxes

These boxes have been positioned at a point within each section where they are going to be of immediate value. Some of the phrases are recorded to provide a pronunciation model. There is almost always an instruction in each **natural English** box for controlled practice of the phrases, and in many cases it is followed by a personalized practice activity. In the classroom, you could vary the presentation of the language in the following ways:

– If the target phrases have been recorded, you could ask learners to listen to them first. They could do this with books shut and treat it as a dictation, then compare their answers with the **student's book**; or they could listen and follow in the **student's book** at the same time, and then repeat from the recording or the model that you give them yourself.

– You can read the phrases aloud for learners to repeat; alternatively, you can ask individual learners to read them out as a way of presenting them.

– You can ask learners to read the box silently, then answer any queries they have, before you get them to say the phrases.

– You could write the phrases on the board or OHP for everyone to focus on. Then ask learners about any problems they have with meaning and form before they practise the examples.

– You could sometimes elicit the phrases before learners read them. For instance, ask them how they could ask for repetition, or what they would say in formal / informal phone greetings. Write their suggestions on the board, and then let learners compare with the **natural English** box. In some cases learners will know some important phrases, but they may not be very accurate or be the most natural way to express these concepts.

– Once learners have practised the phrases, you could ask them to shut their **student's book** and write down the phrases they remember.

– If you have a weaker class, you might decide to focus on one or two of the phrases for productive practice; for a stronger group, you may want to add one or two phrases of your own.

– For revision, you could tell learners they are going to be tested on the **natural English** boxes of the last two units you have done; they should revise them for homework. The next day, you can test them in a number of ways:

  – give an error-spotting test

  – fill gaps in phrases

  – write four-line dialogues in pairs

  – give stimuli which learners respond to, for example:

agree with these statements:
I like Frank Zappa.   *I don't enjoy going to the opera.*
Me _____ .   *Me* _____ .

– The **workbook** provides a number of exercises offering consolidation and further practice of the **natural English** phrases (and, of course, other language presented in the **student's book**).

– Because the phrases are clearly very useful, you may want to put some of them on display in your classroom. You could also get learners to start a natural English and vocabulary notebook and record the phrases under headings as they learn them. You should decide together whether natural (rather than literal) translations would be a useful option for self-study.

wordbooster

Wordbooster is a section in each unit devoted to vocabulary development. It is divided into two parts, each one focusing on a different lexical area. One is often topic-based, the other may be based on the grammar of vocabulary, e.g. compound nouns or phrasal verbs.

why wordbooster?

Throughout the other sections in each unit, you will find vocabulary input which is practised within the section, and is often needed for the extended speaking activity. Some of the vocabulary in **wordbooster** is also useful for the extended speaking activity, but the main role of **wordbooster** is to provide essential vocabulary expansion for learners at this level that goes beyond the immediate requirements of the unit. In this way, learners cover a comprehensive vocabulary syllabus.

The **wordbooster** section is designed to have a different feel from the other more interactive sections in the course, and it provides a change of pace and activity type.

how to ... use wordbooster

Each **wordbooster** will take approximately 25 to 30 minutes to complete, and it can be used flexibly.

- In some units, you can do the **wordbooster** activities earlier or later than they appear in the unit. This will be highlighted in the teacher's notes.
- You don't need to do the whole **wordbooster** in one session. As it is divided into two sections, you can do one part in one lesson, and the other part in a later lesson. In other words, you can use this section to fit in with your own teaching timetable. For instance, if you have 15 minutes at the end of a lesson, you can do one of these sections.
- You can do some of it in class, and some of it can be done for homework.
- You can bring in a competitive or fun element by turning some of the exercises into team games or *against the clock* activities, e.g. unit two: hotel rooms or compound nouns. This approach is not suitable in all learning contexts, however. If you are new to your teaching environment, consult your colleagues for advice.
- Encourage learners to record the language learnt in these sections in their natural English and vocabulary notebooks.

test yourself!

Test yourself! is an end-of-unit test or revision activity enabling learners to assess their progress, and consider how they performed in the extended speaking activity. It is a short, easily-administered test covering lexis, natural English phrases, and grammar from the unit in a standardized format:

- producing items within categories
- transforming sentences
- correcting errors.

how to ... use test yourself!

You can use it either before the **extended speaking** activity for revision purposes, or afterwards, as an end-of-unit test. You may want to give learners time to prepare for it, e.g. read through the unit for homework, or make it a more casual and informal revision activity. Make it clear to learners that their answers in the test should only include new language from the unit, e.g. in unit one, learners have to write down six jobs. Don't accept *doctor* or *teacher* which they obviously learnt at elementary level.

The test can be used in different ways:

- A formal test; ask learners to complete it individually, and then collect in their answers to mark.
- An informal test; ask learners to complete it individually, then go through the answers with the whole class.
- A more interactive test; ask learners to complete it in pairs. Go through the answers with the class, or ask a pair to mark the answers of another pair.
- You could get learners to complete the test individually or in pairs, then they can check their answers by looking back through the unit. Asking learners to search for answers in this way may not give <u>you</u> as much feedback on their progress, but it may be more memorable for them as learners.
- You could give the test for homework. Learners can then use the unit material as they wish.

Refer learners back to the checklist of language input at the beginning of the unit. They can then tick the areas they now feel more confident in. This is an important way for you to discover which areas they feel they need to revise. You may still have **workbook** and **cover & check** exercises which you can use for this revision.

why ask learners to mark their performance?

Asking learners to give themselves a mark for their performance in the speaking activity may seem an unusual thing to do. In fact, the precise mark is irrelevant, but we have found it a useful way to encourage learners to reflect more generally on their ability to communicate, and their contribution to the activity, without getting too involved in minor errors, grammar mistakes, etc. It also gives you a chance to have a one-to-one chat with learners, and provide them with some positive feedback and encouragement. It may take several units before learners are able to do this effectively, so your support will be essential in the early stages.

listening booklet

The **listening booklet** is a separate booklet in the back cover pocket of the **student's book**. It provides:

- complete tapescripts for all of the **student's book** listening material
- tapescript based exercises
- optional listening and pronunciation activities
- the phonemic chart on the back cover, with example words for each sound.

The activities and exercises focus on:

- features of natural English
- pronunciation in context, including focuses on individual sounds, wordstress, sentence stress, and intonation
- development of listening sub-skills.

why a separate booklet?

Until recently, tapescripts have often been buried in the back of coursebooks and largely under-exploited. In **natural English**, listening is a very important part of the syllabus, with the majority of recorded material being improvised, unscripted, and delivered at natural speed. It is, therefore, an invaluable source of natural spoken English, so we have set out to exploit the material as much as possible, both for acquiring new language and developing listening sub-skills. Following the tapescript after one or two attempts at listening is a valuable way for learners to decode the parts they haven't understood; it is not only useful, but also a popular activity.

Learners should find the separate booklet very convenient, and it also allows them to make greater use of the listening material.

how to ... use the listening booklet

Use the **listening booklet** whenever you want to refer learners to the tapescript.

Within the main listening section of each unit in the **student's book**, there's a page reference to the **listening booklet** for the related tapescript(s) and accompanying exercise(s).

You may decide to do the **listening booklet** exercises in class. Alternatively, the learners can do them at home, using the **student's CD** and answer key.

You might also wish to devise your own activities around the listening material, along similar lines to those already provided in the **listening booklet**.

language reference and cover & check exercises

The **language reference** section contains more detailed explanations of the key grammar and lexical grammar in the units, plus a large bank of exercises (**cover & check**) for further practice and consolidation. **Cover & check** exercises have been included for two main reasons:

– they make the language reference much more engaging and interactive

– they provide practice and consolidation which teachers and learners can use flexibly within the lesson when the grammar is being taught, in a later lesson for revision purposes, or for self-study.

Most of the exercises are objective with a right-or-wrong answer which makes them easy for you to administer.

go to **language reference** p.151 to p.175

how to ... use language reference and cover & check exercises

– Use them when the need arises. If you always tell learners to read the **language reference** and do all the **cover & check** exercises within the lesson, you may have problems with pace or variety. Rather, use them at your discretion. If, for instance, you find that the learners need a little more practice than is provided in a grammar section, select the appropriate exercise, e.g. unit one, questions ending with prepositions: do exercise 1.4 in **cover & check**. Areas of grammar are not equally easy or difficult for all nationalities. **Cover & check** exercises provide additional practice on all areas; you can select the ones which are most relevant to your learners.

– The **cover & check** exercises are ideal for self-study. Learners can read the explanations on the left, then cover them while they do the exercises on the right. Finally, they can look again at the explanations if necessary. You can give them the answers to the **cover & check** exercises at the back of this **teacher's book** p.173 to p.175.

– If learners write the answers in pencil or in a notebook, they will be able to re-use the exercises for revision. Some learners also benefit from writing their own language examples under the ones given in the **language reference**. They can also annotate, translate, etc.

workbook

The **workbook** recycles and consolidates vocabulary, grammar, and natural English from the **student's book**. It also provides language extension sections called **expand your grammar** and **expand your vocabulary** for stronger or more confident learners. These present and practise new material that learners have not met in the **student's book**. Another important feature of the **workbook** is the **say it!** sections, which encourage learners to rehearse language through prompted oral responses. There are two other regular features: **think back!** (revision prompts) and **write it!** (prompts for writing tasks). You can use the workbook for extra practice in class or set exercises for learners to do out of class time. The **with key** version allows learners to use the **workbook** autonomously.

puzzle book

what's in the puzzle book?

The 32-page **puzzle book** features a wide range of word games, word lists, puzzles, jokes, cartoons, and anecdotes, and comes complete with an answer key. It includes the following topic-based pages:

– food and drink (*pp.4–5*)

– the body (*pp.6–9*)

– entertainment (*pp.12–13*)

– shopping and money (*pp.16–17*)

– relationships (*pp.20–21*)

– transport (*pp.24–25*)

how to ... use the puzzle book

The **puzzle book** is designed to expand learners' vocabulary, and to encourage reading for pleasure and learner independence. It's not directly linked to units in the **student's book** – rather, it is intended as a fun and motivating optional extra. You may wish to refer learners to particular pages for homework (the topic pages listed above, for example) or you might want all your learners to have the **puzzle book**, so that it can be used in class for warmers and fillers. Otherwise, the 'dip-in' nature of the **puzzle book** means you can just encourage learners to use it as and when they like.

teacher's book

This **teacher's book** is the product of our own teaching and teacher training experience combined with extensive research carried out by Oxford University Press into how teacher's books are used.

lesson plans

The teaching notes are presented as flexible lesson plans, which are easy to dip into and use at a glance. We talk you through each lesson, offering classroom management tips (**troubleshooting**), anticipating problems (**language point**), and suggesting alternative ways of using the material (**ideas plus**). In addition, each lesson plan provides you with the exercise keys, a summary of the lesson contents, and the estimated length of the lesson.

At the beginning of each **teacher's book** unit, there's a photocopiable list of **natural English** phrases and vocabulary items from the **student's book**. This is a useful reference for you, and a clear, concise record for the learners, which they can annotate with explanations, translation, pronunciation, etc. and use for their own revision.

teacher development chapters

You'll find the teacher development chapters after the lesson plans, starting on *p.136*. These practical chapters encourage reflection on teaching principles and techniques. At intermediate level the areas covered are **how to ... activate vocabulary**, **introduce new language**, **teach listening**, **monitor and give feedback**, **do free speaking**, and **teach phonemic script**.

The chapters are regularly cross-referenced from the lesson plans but you can read them at any time and in any order.

Each chapter contains the following features:

– **think!** tasks for the reader with accompanying answer keys (see *p.136*)

- **try it out** boxes offering practical classroom ideas related to the topic of the chapter (see *p.141*)
- **natural English student's book** extracts to illustrate specific points (see *p.140*)
- **follow up** sections at the end of each chapter providing a short bibliography for further reading on the topic (see *p.142*).

This **teacher's book** also contains a photocopiable key to the **student's book** language reference section (*pp.172–173*).

welcome

use *quantifiers* to say how many people learners know, e.g. *quite, a few, everyone, most*

listen to a conversation on the first night of an evening class

practise introducing themselves and others and respond, using **natural English** phrases

talk for thirty seconds about different topics

glossary

quantifiers adverbs or adverbial phrases expressing quantity

lexical phrase a fixed or semi-fixed phrase

feedback information given to learners following an activity

class drill repeating a word or phrase as a class

monitor listen to check an activity is progressing correctly and note examples of good or incorrect language use

intonation tone of voice expressing meaning and attitude

personalize use personal information to perform a task

lead-in

- If you are using this section as the opening lesson with a new group, we assume that you will first find out learners' names and perhaps what they do. If, however, you are teaching a group who know each other very well, you may wish to go straight to unit one.

- For **exercise 1**, show learners the speech bubbles and draw attention to the fact that there are fewer and fewer characters in each picture. Ask them to order the statements alone, then compare with a partner.

- In **exercise 2**, go over the answers, perhaps eliciting them onto the board, and check learners can pronounce the phrases correctly. Notice that there are some phonemic transcriptions for potentially difficult items; you will find these throughout the course. Go on to **exercise 3**, which you could demonstrate yourself first, e.g. *I know most people in the class*, and *I know quite a few people in the school*, etc.

Want to know more? Go to **how to ...** teach phonemic script *p.168*.

listen to this

- You could lead in by asking learners if they go to other classes, e.g. a hobby, language, or professional classes. Give them a few moments to talk to each other in small groups, then ask them to feed back to the group.

- Tell learners that they are going to listen to a short conversation in natural English, and that they may not understand every word. You could pre-teach the word *kid* = child. Reassure them that they only need to find out the answers to the two questions in **exercise 1**. After they have compared with a partner, ask all the pairs what the answers are before you confirm or correct any of them. Play it again only if a lot of learners had problems.

- Ask them to read the statements for **exercise 2** before they listen and answer the questions if they can. They can then use the listening to confirm their answers. Ask learners to compare after listening. You can go round and see how individuals have coped, and see whether they need to listen again. If necessary, they could listen with the tapescript in the **listening booklet** *p.2*.

- **Exercise 3** gives them a simple task for a different but parallel conversation.

- Direct learners to the questions at the bottom of the **natural English** box. Put them in pairs to discuss their answers, then do *feedback*. You can either practise the phrases as a *class drill*, or ask them to practise in threes. Alternatively, you could use the recording, pausing to allow learners time to repeat the phrases before they work together. Go round and *monitor* and correct while they are practising. Give learners a model of this tag question first, *We've met before, haven't we?* (see **language point** on the right).

- It is best if you demonstrate **exercise 5** with two learners using the phrases in the **natural English** box.

Want to know more? Go to the **introduction: natural English** boxes *p.6*.

it's your turn!

- The aim of **exercises 1**, **2**, and **3** is to give learners an opportunity to speak freely and get to know a bit about each other. For you, this is an opportunity (as it is the first lesson) to assess their oral ability, and also find out about the learners yourself. It sets the tone for the course: speaking is a very important component.

- For **exercise 1**, choose a topic yourself and demonstrate the activity by giving your talk and answering their questions. Then give learners time to choose their three topics, and plan what they might say. This thinking time is indicated throughout the course with the **Think!** symbol, and is a crucial stage in any speaking activity in enabling learners to achieve tasks more effectively and with greater confidence.

- During **exercise 2**, monitor to make sure they are doing the task correctly, and listen and make notes. In this first activity, you should aim to give learners very encouraging feedback. In feedback for **exercise 3**, ask one or two learners to tell the class something they learnt about other people. Give praise where possible.

Want to know more? Go to **how to ...** monitor and give feedback *p.156*.

exercise 1

I know practically everyone.
I know most people.
I know quite a few people.
I only know one or two people.
I don't know anyone at all.

language point lexical phrases

The phrases in **exercise 1** will not be difficult for learners to understand, but in our experience, they are not the phrases that the majority of intermediate learners would choose to express these meanings. They may say things which are inaccurate, e.g. ~~I know all people~~, ~~I know some persons~~, or not very natural, e.g. *I know nobody*, *I know many people*. This is the first time in the course that they will come across these natural **lexical phrases**, so point out that this is a feature of the course and that they are included throughout. It is important for learners to learn and record these as whole phrases, so encourage them to copy them out in their notebooks.

exercise 1

1 two speakers   2 Sophie and Brian

exercise 2

1 true   3 false (they met last year)
2 true   4 false (the man has a little girl)

exercise 3

three speakers; they all know each other

natural English

to introduce two people: *(Max), this is (Annie). Do you know (Annie)?*
when you meet someone for the first time: *Nice to meet you.*

exercise 4

conversation 1: *We've met before, haven't we? I'm really sorry, I don't remember your name.*
conversation 2: *Do you know ...? We already know each other. Nice to see you.*

language point introductions and responses

There are a number of pitfalls with introductions, the main one being that there are very specific conventions/ways of introducing and greeting people in different cultures, which do not often translate very directly. Learners tend to sound quite formal when they introduce/greet in English. Point out that these phrases are among the most common in natural English.

We already know each other is often expressed as ~~We already know us~~ by some nationalities.

Learners may also have a problem with the question tag in *We've met before, haven't we?* In the recording, the **intonation** falls, because the assumption is that it is true.

We've met before, haven't we?

You can point this out, or leave it until **unit one** where it is dealt with more thoroughly.

troubleshooting speaking activity

You may be worried that your learners will be daunted at the idea of extended speaking on topics. However, the topics chosen are **personalized** and simple, and intermediate learners should be capable of speaking for 30 seconds on at least three; *my family*, *my hobbies*, and *where I live* could even be tackled by elementary learners. In addition, they do not have to speak to a large group, only two or at most three other learners. If you know someone is particularly shy, put them with one (sympathetic) classmate who will encourage them. You will also be giving them time to think about what to say, which will make the task easier. Tell them at the beginning that the important thing is to communicate, and not to worry about making mistakes.

one

wordlist

natural English

making people listen
Listen, …
Right, …
Look, …
OK, …

inviting people to speak
How about you?
What about you?

conversation openers
Excuse me, is anyone sitting here?
Have you got the time, please?
I think we've met before, haven't we?
It's really hot, isn't it?
Are you going all the way to …?

responding with interest
Oh, really?
How exciting / interesting, etc.
That sounds great / interesting, etc.

hopes and plans
I'm going to …
I'm planning to …
I'm hoping to …
I'm thinking of -ing …

responding with sympathy
What a pity!
What a shame!
I am sorry.
How terrible!

glossaries

granny ⑥
blood
urgent
peel (v)
bother sb (v)
break the ice
carry on (doing sth)
kid ⑥

vocabulary

conversation topics
leisure activities
current affairs
the opposite sex
clothes and fashion
gossip
sporting events
pop music
TV programmes
famous people
work-related issues

wordbooster

jobs
spy
judge
politician
lawyer
accountant
mechanic
civil servant
surgeon
fashion model
nurse
composer
professional sportsman / woman

work
He / she is training to be a (doctor).
work freelance
I'm looking for (a job).
work for (+ company, e.g. Sony)
work in (+ an area, e.g. banking)
unemployed
retired
run (a business)
give up (a job / career)
involve -ing, e.g. my job involves travelling

life with Agrippine   30 mins

Want to know more about using life with Agrippine? Go to the **introduction** *p.5*.

- This section starts with personalization to motivate and relax the learners. If you feel that you can change the questions to make them more relevant to your group, e.g. talk about normal phones rather than mobile phones, then do so. It often helps if you talk about your own experience as a model for the learners.

Want to know more about live listening? Go to **how to** ... teach listening *p.153*.

- When you tell learners to read the cartoon, point out the highlighted words and the glossary on *p.9*. Glossaries have been provided to make it easier for learners to read quickly and therefore enjoy the humour of the cartoons.
- You'll see some words here (and throughout the book) with phonemic symbols.

Want to know more? Go to **how to** ... teach phonemic script *p.168*.

nE
Right, today we're going to look at the economic situation in Europe.
Look, I said no mobile phones in class!
Listen, Crystal, how many times do I have to tell you?

---

language point formal and informal language

Notice that in glossaries and **natural English** boxes, there is a ⑥ symbol to highlight informal language. You should point this out to the learners, and they might like to use it to record informal items in their notebooks.

Informal language in this course does not mean slang, which is very informal language that may cause offence to certain people. It indicates language which is more likely to occur in spoken English or more informal written English. As the **student's book** concentrates more on spoken than written English, you will meet this symbol regularly.

---

listening small talk

discuss what people talk about using vocabulary on conversation topics

invite people to speak using **natural English** phrases

listen to people describing conversations

practise maintaining a conversation with a **focus** on question forms and tags

vocabulary conversation topics

- Notice the **Think!** instruction. This appears throughout the **student's book**. The idea is to give learners time to collect their thoughts and possibly rehearse mentally what they are going to say in English. They may also want to make brief notes on language they are going to use. In our experience, learners perform with much greater confidence and fluency when they have had this preparation time. Even for quite short speaking activities, a minute or two to think can be very beneficial.

- When you go over the answers to **exercise 3**, you could give oral models of the phrases and encourage learners to practise saying them in pairs.

- Give learners a couple of minutes to think about **exercise 4**. Then use the recording in the **natural English** box to teach them how to include other people in a conversation. They can then practise this in **exercise 5** when they compare their answers.

listen to this

- Each unit has a listening section which includes the main listening activity. This consists of a number of stages:

  tune in The aim is to overcome the limitations of listening to recorded material by easing learners into the recording with a fairly guided task. The **tune in** extract is very short (in most cases, it is just the first part of a longer passage). This enables learners to get used to the voices and the context.

  listen carefully Here, the learners listen more intensively to the whole passage with a more demanding task, such as completing tables, answering more detailed comprehension questions, completing a summary, etc.

  listening challenge This is an opportunity for learners to test their understanding of a new and different listening passage which is parallel to the first listening on a similar topic or of a similar genre.

  listening booklet By referring to the booklet containing the tapescript, learners get an opportunity to analyse and learn from parts of the tapescript which contain a rich source of natural English. There are a number of exercises in the booklet focusing on pronunciation / vocabulary and listening strategies.

Want to know more? Go to **how to** ... teach listening *p.150*.

- In **tune in exercise 1**, explain that an A to Z is a book of London street maps.

- You could do the **listening challenge** in the next lesson if you feel learners have listened enough.

- You could get learners to react to the conversations. How do they feel about each one? Which do they think is the most interesting or amusing? Have they ever had a similar conversation?

grammar question forms and tags

- Most of this should be revision for intermediate level learners. The questions in **exercise 1** highlight some of the most common errors learners at this level make. If you find your learners are continuing to have problems with one particular area, there are explanations and reinforcement exercises (**cover & check**) in the **language reference** on *p.151* and *p.152* and in the **workbook** on *p.5* and *p.6*.

Want to know more? Go to the **introduction** *p.8*.

it's your turn!

- This heading, which is used throughout the book, generally indicates a longer, *personalized* speaking activity for learners to do in pairs or small groups (three or four learners).

- During the speaking activity, you should monitor unobtrusively. Avoid eye contact with the learners, or you may inhibit their speaking, but if they need to ask you something, be available. You need to check that all the groups are doing the task correctly, and you can also make notes on examples of language use which are particularly good, or where there are problems. It is best to conclude the activity before learners' motivation starts to wane. Give them some positive feedback on the activity, and see if they can correct some of the errors you have noted.

Want to know more? Go to **how to** ... monitor and give feedback *p.156*.

- Draw your learners' attention to the **extended speaking** box at the end of the section. Explain that this includes key language from the section that they will be able to use again in the **extended speaking** activity at the end of the unit.

exercise 3

1 leisure	5 gossip	9 famous
2 current	6 events	10 issues
3 opposite	7 music	
4 clothes	8 programmes	

ideas plus nE inviting people to speak

If you want to practise this language in a game, tell a learner to say what their favourite food / drink / hobby is. They must invite another learner to do the same, who then invites another person to speak.

example **Learner 1** *My favourite food is yoghurt. How about you, Ritta?*
Ritta *I love strawberries. What about you, Carmen?*
Carmen *I really like prawns. How about …*

You may want to use pictures on the board to demonstrate this interaction.

exercise 1

Marcella: a motorbike courier; find my way somewhere; look at his A to Z
Nigel: he's just got engaged; Malcolm from the Accounts Department; Angela, who's my supervisor

exercise 2

	Marcella	Nigel
Who did they speak to?	a motorbike courier	Malcolm, a colleague
Where?	in the street	at work
What about?	his life in England and Columbia	his horrible supervisor, Angela
How did they feel about it?	she thought it was a very interesting conversation	he was embarrassed because the colleague was engaged to the supervisor

exercise 3

The stranger was a bank robber. She was surprised he told her that.

question forms
exercise 1

1 Who did Marcella talk to?
2 Why did the doctor become a courier?
3 Who works in the Accounts Department?
4 How long did the man spend in prison?
5 What did the bank robber look like?
6 What did he go to prison for?

exercise 2

1 a motorbike courier
2 he had decided to change his life and try something different for a while
3 Malcolm, Nigel's colleague
4 ten years
5 young, with a shaved head
6 presumably for burgling a house

exercise 3

1 What do you do?
2 What are you learning English for?
3 Who do you look like in your family?
4 Where do you live, exactly?
5 How long have you lived in your present home?
6 Where are you going for your next holiday?
7 Which countries would you like to go to?
8 Who do you live with?

question tags
exercise 2

1 isn't he?	3 doesn't he?	5 isn't he?
2 wasn't she?	4 didn't she?	6 haven't they?

language point question tags

Highlight the falling intonation pattern in **exercise 1**. The intonation falls here because the speaker is pretty sure they know the answer, but just want the facts confirmed. Learners find *rising tags* quite easy, but falling tags require practice. You can isolate the tag and give a model to show them that the voice falls from the auxiliary to the pronoun, like this:

wasn't she?

Want to know more? Go to **Practical English Usage** by Michael Swan *pp.478–480.*

ideas plus question tags

Ask learners to write some tag questions of their own to ask different people in the class in order to find out or confirm information about them, e.g. *You're from Stockholm, aren't you?* Remind them to use rising or falling intonation depending on how sure they are of the answer to the question. Let them mingle to ask and answer their questions.

reading first meetings

60 – 70 mins

start up a conversation using the **natural English** conversation openers

read a newspaper human interest story

describe events in your life using the present perfect and past simple

lead-in

- In the **natural English** box, you have the opportunity to focus on the intonation of these questions, and to get learners to try to copy it. One way of doing this is to play one of the questions, and you then hum it to the group, keeping the same intonation. This helps them isolate the intonation from the words. You can also use hand movements to show the intonation pattern as you are speaking / humming.

- In feedback, elicit the learners' ideas about other phrases, and discuss whether they are appropriate with the class.

- In **exercise 5**, learners could a) write a dialogue together and practise it; b) make notes and use these to practise a dialogue; or c) improvise the conversation. You should decide which approach is best for your group and tell them at the beginning to decide how the conversation will develop.

read on

- Draw attention to the glossary. Alternatively, you could ask learners to cover it, and working in pairs, guess the meaning of the highlighted words from the context, then check their ideas against the glossary definitions. This should help to 'fix' any new vocabulary.

- In **exercise 3**, you could start this off as a class activity; show learners that they can make the story more natural by adding in connectors such as *and then, so, anyway, but.*

- In **exercise 4**, give learners a minute to think about the answers first. Remember to give listeners a task as they listen to each others' stories, e.g. to think of a follow-up question.

grammar present perfect and past simple (1)

- Our approach with language work in the course is not to do a long, detailed analysis of a language area in one go. Instead, we have selected the particular use or uses of the tense which learners need most in the **extended speaking** activity. You will see that other uses of the present perfect occur later in the **student's book** and in the upper-intermediate **student's book**.

- Ask learners to look at the conversations first. They can also practise by reading them aloud. In **exercise 1**, decide whether you want to ask learners to do this as a whole class activity, or to answer the questions together, or to work alone then compare answers.

- Look carefully at the **language point** on the right. Demonstrate briefly what to do in **exercise 2** with a learner. Look at the **cover & check** exercises on *p.152* and *p.153* of the **language reference** section if you think learners need more practice.

 wordbooster

25 – 30 mins

jobs

This **wordbooster** can be used at any point in the unit before the **extended speaking** activity. It fits most suitably before the **how to ...** section in terms of topic.

See **ideas plus** on the right for a way to practise the vocabulary in **exercise 1**.

talking about work

- Once learners have marked the stress, check their answers and get them to repeat the words for pronunciation practice.

exercise 1
photo 1: on a bus   photo 2: on a station platform

exercise 3
photo 1: *I think we've met before, haven't we? Are you going all the way to San Francisco? It's really hot, isn't it? Sorry, have you got the time, please?*
photo 2: *I think we've met before, haven't we? Sorry, have you got the time, please?*

exercise 4 possible answers
Sorry, have you got the time, please? Yes, it's ten past three. / No, I haven't got a watch.
I think we've met before, haven't we? Yes, we have. / No, I don't think so.
It's really hot, isn't it? Yes, it's terrible. (It would be quite rude to directly contradict this in this situation, but you might say something like *Yes, it's nice, though, isn't it?*)
Are you going all the way to San Francisco? Yes, I am, are you? / No, I'm getting off at …

ideas plus warmer

As a lead-in to the lesson, ask the learners if they know where and when their parents met. You could tell them where your own parents met, perhaps. Let them talk in small groups, then ask if anyone's story is particularly romantic or interesting. Get them to tell the class. It is a good idea to give learners a listening task in order to provide a focus as they listen, e.g. decide whose story is the most romantic or unusual, or find out whose story is the most similar / different from your story.

exercise 1
1   the couple in photo 2

exercise 2
1h   2c   3g   4b   5e   6a   7f   8d

troubleshooting telling anecdotes

In **exercise 4**, learners are asked to personalize. It is quite unusual for every learner to come up with an appropriate anecdote quickly, so don't expect everyone to have a story. Give them time to think, and then ask for a show of hands to see how many have a story. If half the class do, then put learners in pairs or threes so that at least one has a story to tell. In the meantime, the others may well think up a story; if they don't, it doesn't matter. It can help to trigger memories if you tell an anecdote first. You could also feed in useful phrases for responding, e.g. *Something similar happened to me.*

exercise 1
1   *Have you been; We've met … haven't we? Have you ever bought …?* They are all present perfect.
2   yes
3   no
4   answers are in the present perfect because she doesn't say when they happened
5   answers are in the past simple because the speaker is saying when things happened
6   – ever   – before   – just

exercise 3
1   I started learning English …
2   Have you ever forgotten …?
3   He has (He's) just got …
4   Have you been there before?
5   I've never had …
6   Did she see the film …?

language point present perfect and past simple

For many nationalities, this language area is problematic. In some languages, there is no equivalent of a perfect form, so learners have to learn both form and use. In other languages, a perfect form exists, but may or may not be used in a similar way to English.

examples   French *Je l'ai vu*: *I've seen him*; but *Je l'ai vu hier*: *I've seen him ~~yesterday~~*.

Most languages do not have a literal translation for *just*, as in *I've just done it.*

At intermediate level, learners will already have come across the present perfect simple to talk about indefinite time, e.g. *I've been to Poland. She's never had a cold.* Our experience is that most learners won't have internalized the use or be very fluent in the form, so some revision and extension is needed here.

You may need to clarify the difference between:

Have you ever eaten Chinese food? = in your life (and you aren't eating it, or about to eat it now)

Have you eaten Chinese food before? = before this occasion (in which the person has ordered Chinese food, is about to eat it, or is going to a Chinese restaurant)

Want to know more? Go to **Practical English Usage** by Michael Swan *pp.418–422.*

exercise 1
The three jobs which are in the wrong place are: politicians, mechanics, nurses.

These sentences should read: politicians are elected by the people; mechanics repair machines and cars; nurses look after people in hospital.

exercise 1
fr<u>ee</u>lance; multi<u>na</u>tional <u>com</u>pany; re<u>tired</u>; unempl<u>oy</u>ed; comp<u>u</u>ter <u>in</u>dustry; <u>bu</u>siness; inv<u>ol</u>ves

ideas plus vocabulary practice

This is a game you can get learners to play with a partner. Together, they choose any six jobs from **exercise 1**, and think of the name of someone famous – they could be from history, fiction, TV soap opera, drama, film, etc.

examples   spy – James Bond; composer – Beethoven; lawyer – Ally McBeal.

They then work with another pair, say the names and the others have to say the job.

how to ... keep a conversation going

60 – 75 mins

ask follow-up questions and respond with interest using **natural English** phrases

listen to a conversation between strangers at a party

talk about your hopes and plans using **natural English** phrases

glossary

controlled practice repetition of specific (target) language

mingling a whole class activity in which learners get up and speak to a given number/all of their classmates

ask follow-up questions

- In **exercise 2**, you need to allow learners time to plan the way their conversation might develop. Again, you should decide how much to guide them: writing the dialogue, working from notes, or improvising it. You may choose a different approach from the one you used in **reading exercise 5**, *p.13*.

- Other pairs' performances can be a useful source of additional listening in the classroom, and in **exercise 3**, it would be more interesting to listen to a different conversation. Don't worry if most learners have chosen to do the same conversation; the results will be different. You may wish to tell learners to give each other some praise or encouragement here so that any future activities like this will be approached positively.

- If you prefer, you could provide your own oral model of the phrases in the **natural English** box instead of using the recording.

- In **exercise 4**, check that learners in A/B pairs aren't looking at each other's prompts. Demonstrate the activity first with one learner.

party talk

- Draw attention to the photos of Emma and Clive to set the scene for **exercise 1**. Ask if learners think they're friends or strangers (they're strangers). You could lead in to the topic by asking learners if they like talking to strangers at parties, or if they prefer to keep to their friends.

- For the **natural English** box, you could either read the sentences aloud yourself, or ask learners to read them silently / aloud. If you go to **language reference** on *p.153* and *p.154*, you will see that the meaning of these phrases is spelled out. You could write the meanings on the board and ask learners to match them with the phrases, or you could ask them orally:

  examples   Which phrases mean 'it's a plan'?
  Which phrase means it is something you want to do, but aren't sure it will happen?
  Which phrase means it is something that you are thinking of as a future possibility?

- Alternatively, ask learners to go to **language reference**, let them read it, and ask if they have any problems. Use the **cover & check** exercises if necessary.

it's your turn!

- This **it's your turn!** brings together all the conversational strategies learners have worked on in this section. It would be fun to make it into a game where the listener has to try to keep the other person talking as long as possible by using follow-up questions and expressions to show interest. You can best demonstrate this before **exercise 2** by working with one learner in front of the group and asking them lots of questions, showing interest yourself. To provide variety, swap the pairs, or do it as a class *mingling* activity.

exercise 1 possible questions

conversation 1: *How about you? Whereabouts? Is this the first time you've done a course here? Really? What's it like? How long are you planning to stay?*

conversation 2: *How about you? Have you been there before? Is this the first time you've been to Singapore? Really? What's it like? Is this a business trip, or are you on holiday? How long are you planning to stay?*

language point keeping a conversation going

We noticed in our recordings of learners doing the **extended speaking** activity that they sometimes had problems keeping the conversation going. We therefore decided to focus on a series of conversational features which facilitate interaction, some of which have been taught earlier in the unit:

- follow-up questions: *Where are you from? Whereabouts? Really? What's it like?*
- showing that you are interested in or sorry about what the speaker has to say: *That sounds interesting. / What a pity!*
- inviting people to speak: *How about you, Pedro?*
- question forms and question tags: *We've met before, haven't we?*

It may be helpful to ask learners to think about how they keep conversations going in L1. Reminding learners that this is what they normally do in L1 may help them to do it in English.

It is important to stress that when learners are using these forms, they show through their intonation that they are interested and involved. When you are providing a **controlled practice** stage, use the recording or give a clear oral model which they can copy.

exercise 1

Yes, they sound very interested in each other. They say *Right, That sounds interesting, Oh right, Did you?* Their intonation also expresses interest.

exercise 2

1 Emma is at school.
2 She's studying physics and chemistry.
3 She's hoping to study medicine.
4 She's thinking of doing some of the course in America.
5 Clive studied in Australia.

ideas plus using the tapescript

You could ask learners to look at **listening booklet** *p.4* before they listen. Tell them to read and circle any ways in which Emma and Clive show interest in each other. Give or elicit an example first. Do feedback at the end, then tell them to shut their booklet and listen. Do the people sound interested or not? (They do!)

This isn't a very common way to use listening material, but it is a way of focusing on language in context, and it provides a different kind of approach for learners.

language point hopes and plans

Going to is often tackled as part of the grammar of talking about the future in English, but we have treated it differently in this unit. We wanted to provide learners with useful and high frequency phrases which they can easily activate. The future in English is analysed more grammatically in **unit eight** *p.95*, but here you may need to point out that when we talk about plans in English, we don't use *will*.

ideas plus talking competition

You could add a competitive element to the talking game. Set it up as a mingling activity and tell the learners you are going to time them to see which pair can keep their conversation going for the longest. When there is only one pair left talking, tell the other learners to listen carefully to the follow-up questions, to make sure they are well expressed and sensible. Stop the conversation if it is not natural or when you feel it has gone on long enough. Repeat this several times and congratulate the pairs who kept their conversations going for the longest.

extended speaking strangers on a train   60 – 70 mins

- It is important at the beginning of this activity to let learners read the left-hand column, or put it on the board, or tell them what they are going to do in the lesson. This will enable them to get the whole picture.
- It is also a good idea to tell them that the **extended speaking** section allows them to practise all the main language taught in the unit. You should give them time to look back at the blue **extended speaking** boxes which occur at the end of each section in this unit. This will enable them to see how language learnt can be used in the activity, and will refresh their memories. As this is the first **extended speaking** activity, it is important that they see how each section works towards the final activity.

collect ideas

- If appropriate, you could begin by asking learners to talk about any unusual train journeys they have made or interesting people they have met on trains.
- **Exercise 1** is important in helping learners to think about what it is appropriate to say to strangers on a train. (For instance, in Britain it would be very inappropriate to ask a stranger how much they earn or how old they are.)
- The aim of the listening activity in **exercise 3** is to provide a model for the type of role play learners are going to do themselves later. You could pre-teach *blind date* = a romantic meeting arranged between two strangers and *scared of* = afraid or frightened.

exercise 2

1 Lola	1 Andrew
2 Vienna, Austria	2 Glasgow, Scotland
3 an acrobat	3 a dentist
4 she's going on a blind date to meet another acrobat	4 he's going on holiday

create a new identity

- You should decide whether you would like learners to complete the profile individually or in pairs. If you think it is necessary, you could show them what you would write yourself in an invented profile. While they are completing it, monitor and help where necessary.
- **Exercise 6** is an important rehearsal stage which will give learners more confidence in the role play.

role play a conversation

- Reorganize the learners into groups of three, according to your knowledge of who will work best together. If the class isn't divisible by three, include a group or several groups of four.
- When learners are ready to act out their train conversations, you could get them to rearrange their chairs so that they are facing each other, as in a train.
- The role play should last for at least ten minutes. In many cases, it could continue for up to twenty minutes. Make it clear to learners that this is their opportunity to use their English freely and practise as much as possible. Equally, don't let the activity go on beyond the point where it is motivating and purposeful.
- The role play does not need to be done in the same lesson if you don't have time.
- This is a role play which you can easily re-use at a later stage for revision. You could also use it with higher level learners; you could do it as a conversation on a long distance flight or on a cruise ship.
- During **exercise 7**, it is important that you monitor unobtrusively. Check that learners are doing the task throughout, and judge when the activity has run its course. You may wish to collect examples of good language use and language problems for feedback at the end.

Want to know more? Go to **how to ...** monitor and give feedback *p.156.*

write an e-mail

- As an alternative writing activity, learners could work in pairs to write a postcard to a friend, describing the other people that they met on the journey.

feedback checklist

During the **extended speaking** activity, note down examples of …

- **good language use**

- **effective communication strategies**
  (turn-taking, interrupting, inviting others to speak, etc.)

- **learner errors**
  (vocabulary, grammar, pronunciation, etc.)

- **particular communication problems**

Make sure you allow time for feedback at the end of the lesson. You can use the notes you make above to <u>praise</u> effective language use and communication or, if necessary, to do some remedial work.

test yourself!

Encourage learners to use **test yourself!** to reflect on their progress as well as doing the test activities. Give them a few minutes to mark the line before they do the **test yourself!** activities and to go back to the unit contents and tick the language they can now use confidently. This should motivate learners and will help them to be analytical about their own learning.

Want to know more? Go to the **introduction** *p.7* for ways of using **test yourself!**

1 judge, politician, lawyer, accountant, mechanic, civil servant, surgeon, fashion model, nurse, composer, professional sportsmen and women
2 ever, just, before
3 current affairs, the opposite sex, leisure activities
4 planning to, hoping to, thinking of

1 Is anyone sitting here?
2 Does your job involve a lot of travel?
3 She's unemployed.
4 What a pity / shame about the party.

1 She's married, isn't she?
2 Who knows the answer?
3 I stayed in that hotel two years ago.
4 Who is she talking to?

two

wordlist

natural English

be / have got sth *left*
I haven't got any left.
I've got (three) left.
There's nothing left.

giving opinions, agreeing and disagreeing
I think we should ...   Yes, I agree.
(Personally,) I don't think we should ...   No, maybe not.
I think it would be better to ...   I'm not sure about that.

talking about priorities
I think the most important thing is ...
(Good weather) is a priority.
I think you have to have ...
You don't need ...

postcard language
greetings
Hi, Jim / Hello, Jim / Dear Jim
saying goodbye
See you soon / next week
Take care
All the best
Bye for now
common phrases
Lovely weather!
Delicious food!
Great beaches!
Having a great time!

offers and requests
I'll get someone to (have a look at it).
I'll ask (the electrician to have a look at it).
Could you get someone to (have a look at it)?

vocabulary

types of journey
trip
journey
flight
tour
excursion
to travel (v)

adjectives describing journeys
safe / dangerous
noisy / quiet
tiring
useful / useless
boring
smelly
bumpy
stressful / relaxing
exciting

(im)practical
romantic
enjoyable
(un)comfortable
frustrating
(in)convenient
luxurious
(un)reliable
(in)appropriate

everyday problems
I'm having problems with (the bathroom taps).
I'm having problems *-ing*
(The TV) isn't working properly.
out of order
leak (v)
There's something wrong with (the iron).

wordbooster

hotel rooms
mirror
curtains
sofa
cushions
taps
lift
coffee table
stool
washbasin
four-poster bed
table lamp
rug
wardrobe
fan
balcony

compound nouns
snack bar
swimming pool
beauty salon
tennis court
booking office
table tennis
air conditioning
room service
gift shop
travel agent

glossaries
camel
tie
damage (v)
item
shark
celebrity

in unit two ...

do you get it?
joke lost in the desert
vocabulary types of journey
natural English *be / have got* sth *left*

listening travelling can be fun
vocabulary adjectives describing journeys
listening stories about journeys
grammar comparatives and modifiers
natural English phrases giving opinions, agreeing and disagreeing

wordbooster
hotel rooms
compound nouns

reading what makes a great holiday?
natural English phrases talking about priorities
reading The most expensive hotel suite in the world
grammar superlatives
writing postcards
natural English postcard language

how to ... make a complaint
vocabulary everyday problems
grammar present simple and continuous
listening get someone to help
natural English offers and requests

extended speaking a holiday complex
collect ideas make decisions about a new holiday complex
prepare and give a presentation
role play explain a problem in their villa

test yourself!
revision and progress check

do you get it?   25 – 30 mins

listen for pleasure
vocabulary types of journey
nE *be / have got* sth *left*

Want to know more about using **do you get it?** Go to the **introduction** *p.5.*

- The first activity on *p.21* is personalized, so you could ask learners to look at the different types of holiday given and possibly include some others from their own experience.
- The **joke time** activity based around the pictures is important, as it will teach learners the key vocabulary needed for the joke, and it will help to make the joke much easier to follow. Point out the glossary, and let learners talk in English about the pictures for a few minutes. If anyone happens to know the joke, ask them not to reveal the punchline, or it will spoil the listening activity.
- We have provided some responses in speech bubbles on *p.20* so learners can respond naturally to the joke. You could go over these before they listen to the joke, so that each person can then respond instantly to a partner once they have heard it. It is very possible that one or two learners won't get the joke; this can even happen amongst native speakers. If possible, let other learners explain the joke to them, or explain it yourself.

nE *be / have got* sth *left*
1 You've only got three left.
2 There aren't many people left.
3 There isn't any bread left.
types of journey
1 trip   2 journey   3 flight   4 trip   5 tour   6 travel

---

language point types of journey

Learners often find these vocabulary items confusing in English.
travel = the general act of moving from one place to another. This is the most commonly misused word; learners often use it as a noun, where they should be using *trip* or *journey*. In English, *travel* is used more often as a verb, e.g. *I was travelling through Russia*, or as an uncountable noun, e.g. *Air travel is cheap these days. Travelling* is a common noun form, e.g. *Do you enjoy travelling?*
journey = the time and distance moving from A to B, often regularly, e.g. *The journey back from Prague was terrible. I have an easy journey to work.*
trip = a journey to a place and back, especially for a short visit, e.g. *He's away on a business trip. I'm going on a day trip to France.*
tour = a journey for pleasure to several different places
excursion = a short, organized journey to visit a place, usually for a group
voyage = a long sea or space journey. No longer common in English, but a false friend for speakers of romance languages, which is why it is included.

---

listening travelling can be fun
75 – 90 mins

listen to informal anecdotes about travelling experiences

describe and compare different forms of travel using comparatives and modifiers and adjectives describing journeys

give opinions, agreeing and disagreeing, using **natural English** phrases

glossary

peer teach learners teach each other, often in pairs or groups

test-teach the teacher gives material to learners, monitors their understanding and knowledge while they perform an activity, and subsequently teaches to fill the gaps in that knowledge

brainstorm a group discussion to solve a problem or generate ideas

lead-in

- **Exercise 1** is a 'Find someone who…' activity. Explain the procedure carefully. Make sure they can turn the prompts into question forms by eliciting the questions from the group, e.g. *Do you have an interesting journey to work? Do you travel in the rush hour?* At this stage, you can also explain any unknown words. During the mingling, monitor to ensure that they are doing the right thing and developing conversations where appropriate, i.e. giving more details, asking why, etc. It doesn't matter if you stop the activity before everyone has finished; it's best to stop while learners are still motivated. Keep the class feedback brief. If possible, get a learner to recount anything interesting you heard in the mingling. See **troubleshooting** on the right. Focus on the pronunciation of certain phrases, e.g *an interesting journey* /ən 'ɪntrəstɪŋ 'dʒɜːni/, *for work or pleasure* /fə 'wɜːk ɔː 'pleʒə/, *in the rush hour* /ɪn ðə 'rʌʃ aʊə/, *a world tour* /ə wɜːld 'tʊə/.

vocabulary adjectives describing journeys

There are different ways that you can deal with the meaning of any unknown vocabulary in **exercise 1** (and in similar activities throughout the book).

- If you feel there will be a lot of new vocabulary in **exercise 1**, you could go through the words together with the class, explaining the meanings yourself or eliciting them from the class. Be careful, though; learners can easily get bored if you go over words they already know. Alternatively, you could put learners into small groups to *peer teach* any new words, then do a brief check at the end as a class.
- If you feel there are a few unknown words, you could ask pairs to use dictionaries to check the meaning.
- If you feel there will only be one or two new words, you could use the whole of **exercises 1** and **2** as a *test-teach* activity, and just clarify meaning as you are going through the answers to exercise 2.

listen to this

- In **exercise 1**, learners will probably need help identifying the more unusual forms of transport. Ask if they would like to travel on these forms of transport. Focusing on the photos will help them understand the recordings.
- After learners have done **exercise 3**, you could highlight some of the vocabulary in **listen carefully**:
  whirl round = move round quickly in a circle, *splash* = what happens when water hits you, *sink* (v) = go under the water, *zigzag* = move forward, making sharp turns to the left then right, *masses of* = lots of.
- For **exercise 4**, emphasize that learners do not need to understand everything. The main things to say are that Juliet found the rickshaws sometimes comfortable, sometimes not; the ride can be bumpy and very hot, but it is a great way to see the city.

Want to know more? Go to **how to …** teach listening *p.150*.

grammar comparatives and modifiers

- In **exercise 1**, encourage learners to swap roles when they are half-way through the adjectives.
- **Exercise 4** can be done in different ways. You can *brainstorm* the examples together as a class, then learners work in pairs to make the comparisons in **exercise 5**. Alternatively, elicit a couple of examples, then the learners produce their own examples in pairs. They could then ask another pair to make comparisons based on their prompts to see if they come up with the same answers; this would make it more communicative.
- For extra practice of modifiers, go to **language reference** on *p.155*, and do **cover & check 2.4**.

it's your turn!

- Once learners have thought about **exercise 1**, go over the language in the **natural English** box. You could model the phrases and replies yourself and ask learners to repeat them, then practise the two-line dialogues across the class.
- When learners have done **exercises 1** and **2**, and you have given them some feedback, you could ask pairs to think up their own situations with two forms of transport. They can then try them out on other pairs.

troubleshooting Find someone who …

If you haven't done a 'Find someone who …' with your learners before, it will require careful setting up. Explain that learners circulate and ask others about their experiences, noting names and remembering relevant information. Make sure they understand that they will need to turn the prompts into question forms and check that they can do this. Show them that they can only write someone's name down if the answer is yes. You could get someone to ask you a question in front of the group, and give a positive answer, giving details, as a demonstration of what to do.

exercise 1
relaxing, dangerous, exciting, (im)practical, romantic, enjoyable
exercise 2
1 unreliable   5 frustrating
2 luxurious   6 stressful / frustrating
3 enjoyable   7 bumpy / stressful / uncomfortable
4 inconvenient 8 smelly

language point prefixes un-, in-, im-

The prefixes un-, in-, im- can be added to the beginning of some adjectives to give them a negative meaning. **un-** is the most common. **in-** is relatively common. **im-** is used before words beginning with m or p, e.g. immoral, impractical.
It is not easy to give rules of use, but often un- and in- occur with certain suffixes.

examples
un + -able uncomfort**able** unreli**able**   **in** + -ible inflex**ible** ined**ible**
un + -ic unromant**ic** undemocrat**ic**   **in** + -ent inconveni**ent** infrequ**ent**
un + -ful unsuccess**ful** unhelp**ful**   **in** + -ate inappropri**ate** inaccur**ate**

exercise 1
p.22 and p.23, from left to right: a steam train, a microlite, a rickshaw, a hot air balloon, an elephant, coracles, and a tandem.
exercise 2
Julia went to India; she went in a coracle.
Marcella went to Africa (Victoria Falls); she went in a microlite.
exercise 3
1 Julia's story   3 Julia's story   5 Marcella's story
2 Marcella's story 4 Marcella's story 6 Julia's story

language point comparatives and modifiers

The modifiers (a bit / slightly / much, etc. + comparative) are likely to be new, but learners will probably have covered some rules of comparative forms before. **Exercise 1** is therefore a revision activity, but, productively, learners tend to make mistakes with these forms, as we discovered through our data.

examples
It is more cheaper than hotel.
It's more useful that a beauty salon.
You will need to highlight these points:
• don't use more + adjective +er
• older than not that; it is pronounced / ðən /

Want to know more? Go to **Practical English Usage** by Michael Swan, *pp.119–126*.

exercise 1
+er: slow, fast, cheap, quiet   + r: safe, nice
+ ier: noisy, easy, smelly, bumpy
More / less + adjective: boring, stressful, tiring, useful, useless (quiet is possible, but less common); all adjectives with three or more syllables
exercise 2
a big difference: much cheaper; far more expensive; a lot cheaper;
a small difference: a bit cheaper; a little cheaper; slightly more expensive;
exercise 3
a lot and a bit are more informal

 wordbooster

In this case, the **wordbooster** is most appropriate before the reading section as preparation for the article.

hotel rooms

- **Exercise 1** gives you the opportunity to check that your learners are familiar with all the vocabulary. Clarify meaning and pronunciation where necessary.
- In **exercise 2**, learners will be able to use some, but not all, of the vocabulary from **exercise 1**.

compound nouns

- If you want to vary the focus in your lesson, put the words in **exercise 1** on flashcards (those in the left-hand column in one colour, and the right-hand column in a different colour). Ask learners to match them to form compounds. To make it more challenging for stronger learners, you could put them in groups with the twenty words on pieces of paper, not distinguished by colour, to form compounds.

reading what makes a great holiday?

60 – 75 mins

read a descriptive magazine article

describe and explain priorities using **natural English** phrases

describe the best and worst features of something using superlatives

write a postcard using appropriate phrases

glossary

warmer a brief activity to begin a class with, often called an 'icebreaker'

collocation two or more words often used together (see the examples in **ideas plus** on the right)

lead-in

- Monitor the learners during **exercise 1** so that you can ask one or two learners at the end to talk about a holiday of interest to most people.
- In the **natural English** box, learners could practise the phrases with a partner using the activity in the box. When they go on to **exercise 3**, put the learners into new groups so they can expand on the phrases by giving reasons.
- In **exercise 4**, learners are doing a prediction activity for the text to motivate them to read with interest. It doesn't really matter if what they write is different from the content of the article, as long as they have the right idea in general. This could be done with a partner. The **wordbooster** should provide them with any vocabulary they need (see **wordbooster** above).

Want to know more? Go to **how to ...** activate vocabulary *p.136*.

read on

- Here and elsewhere in the **student's book** you will notice that learners have to read and complete the glossary. The aim of this in the reading section is to encourage learners to use the context to guess meaning. We find that this is best done 'little-and-often'. The glossary is an additional source of receptive vocabulary input. You may decide to have occasional revision activities. For example, ask learners to study the glossaries from different sections for homework, then test them quickly in the following lesson.
- You could ask learners to try to answer the questions in **exercise 2** before they read the article again. In that way they would be reading to confirm their guesses and find the answers they don't know.

grammar superlatives

- For extra practice if necessary, use **cover & check 2.3** in **language reference** on *p.155*, which tests comparatives, superlatives, and modifiers. Remind learners that they always need *the* with the superlative form. This is especially important for nationalities that don't use articles, e.g. Russian and Polish speakers.

exercise 2 items in the photo

1 mirror /ˈmɪrə/, curtains /ˈkɜːtənz/, sofa, cushions /ˈkʊʃənz/, coffee table, four-poster bed, table lamp

---

ideas plus revising vocabulary

You could easily devise revision **warmers** for other lexical sets by using pictures or, e.g. omitting the first letter of each word. You could also make it a team game where learners make up lists of words themselves within a category to test each other.

---

exercise 1

snack bar; swimming pool; beauty salon; tennis court; booking office; table tennis; air conditioning; room service; gift shop; travel agent

exercise 3 possible answers

tennis: racket, ball, match

swimming: trunks, costume, cap

shoe, duty-free, corner: **shop**

sitting / living, dining, bed, waiting: **room**

---

language point compound nouns

Compound nouns are made up of two or sometimes three words, but they may be written as single words, hyphenated, or as separate words. As a general rule:

* short, common compounds are often written as one word, e.g. *postman*, *bedroom*.
* a few compounds are hyphenated – usually those with a letter, e.g. *T-shirt*, *x-ray*; or with a preposition, e.g. *cover-up*, *brother-in-law*. Sometimes you will see different forms in different dictionaries, e.g. *baby-sitter* and *babysitter*.
* the majority are written as separate words, e.g. *traffic lights*, *bus stop*.

Certain nationalities have a problem with compound nouns which would be expressed in their own language by the construction *noun + preposition + noun*, e.g. ~~agent of travel~~; ~~shop of gifts~~.

---

ideas plus sorting and ranking

Sorting and ranking activities like the one in **exercise 2** are a very good way to teach and provide meaningful, personalized practice of vocabulary and **collocation**. You can use this technique in a range of contexts (and at different levels).

examples

Choose the most important aspects of a new job:

job security; a good salary; pleasant working conditions; job satisfaction; opportunities for travel; good promotion prospects; flexible working hours, etc.

Choose the most important qualities in a partner:

good-looking; good sense of humour; reliable and honest; intelligent; having common interests; similar outlook on life; good family background, etc.

---

glossary

shark; celebrity

exercise 2

1 false	4 true
(the suite has 18 rooms)	5 false (from every room)
2 true	6 false (outside)
3 true	

---

ideas plus learning glossary words

There are new vocabulary items in the glossaries for the cartoons and jokes, and the reading texts. You could gradually build up a set of cards of these with the word and a definition / pronunciation / style. Keep them in a box in the classroom, and every now and again, distribute them to learners in small groups. They take turns to define a word and see if the others can guess it.

---

exercise 1

1 the most interesting	4 the most incredible
2 the best	5 the silliest
3 the worst	6 the most attractive

---

language point superlatives

Learners will have studied superlatives before, but will still make mistakes. Examples from our data include: *The ~~more important~~ is a mini-supermarket. Disco is ~~first important~~.* The first example is also incomplete. It should be *The most important* **thing** *is ... .* Notice that this is dealt with in the **natural English** box on *p.25*.

Want to know more? Go to **Practical English Usage** by Michael Swan, *pp.119–126*.

how to ... make a complaint   50 – 60 mins

describe everyday problems using lexical phrases and a present tense

request and offer help using **natural English** phrases

listen to people explaining typical problems and getting help

vocabulary everyday problems

- Learners could look at the pictures at the top of the page first: What can they see? What problems might someone have with these objects in a holiday home? This would allow you to pre-teach the items they aren't sure about first, e.g. *tap, fan, leak, drip*.

- **Test your partner** is an activity used throughout the **student's book**. It is a way of giving learners very controlled pair practice, with the opportunity to try out the pronunciation of target language and memorize items. You can set it up by demonstrating one or two exchanges with a learner in front of the class before asking them to do the rest of the exercise in pairs. One learner in each pair has their book open to test their partner, so he / she can correct them. When they have run through the exercise once, they swap.

- In **exercise 3**, there are a number of possible answers. Accept any sentences which are logical, e.g. *the roof is leaking and water is coming through the ceiling; the air conditioning isn't working properly, so it's very hot in the villa.*

grammar present simple and continuous

- This is a revision activity for most learners at this level, but for some nationalities these tenses are a common problem, especially if they do not use a continuous form in the same way. A simple way to help learners see the general difference is to describe activities as being more *permanent* or more *temporary*, i.e. for a long / short time.

get someone to help

- See **ideas plus** before you begin the listening activity.
- For **exercise 3**, if necessary replay the tape with pauses, allowing time for learners to make corrections.
- In the **natural English** box, the phrase *have a look at sth* is very common. It can mean:
  – to look at and read sth, e.g. *Can I have a look at your paper?*
  – to examine sth because there is a problem, e.g. *The doctor had a look at my knee.*
  The electrician had a look at the light switches.

  It is also worth practising the whole phrase as a class and showing how the words link together.
  I'll get someone to have a look at it.

- The practice activity in **exercise 4** is quite controlled as there is a more extended role play of a similar type on *p.30*. However, you can build it up a little and make it more natural by looking at typical ways in which someone would introduce a problem.
  examples
  Good morning, hello, etc.
  I'm sorry to bother you, but I'm having problems …
  I'm staying in Villa 27, and I'm afraid there's something wrong with …

- It is a good idea to monitor learners during **exercise 4** and give brief feedback before they change roles. This will give them a chance to improve their performance the second time. Keep the feedback short and focused in preparation for the longer role play which follows.

exercise 1

1b 2e 3a 4g 5c 6d 7f

language point *out of order, it isn't working*

out of order = used when a <u>public</u> machine or piece of equipment is not working, e.g. public telephone, drinks machine, office photocopier.
My washing machine is ~~out of order~~. My washing machine isn't working.
it isn't working = used when a machine or piece of equipment is broken; can be used about a public or domestic machine.
My TV isn't working at the moment.
My front door ~~isn't working~~. There's something wrong with the door. (A door isn't a machine or piece of equipment.)
it isn't working <u>properly</u> = it's working, but not very well.

exercise 1

In each pair of sentences, the use of the present continuous means that the problem is happening around now and is temporary. The use of the present simple means that the problem is long-term or recurrent.

exercise 2

1 pick up   4 usually comes
2 're building   5 are having
3 are sitting

ideas plus permanent and temporary habits

For groups studying outside their own country you can practise the use of the present simple and continuous by focusing on the difference between their habits at home and in the country they are studying in. Get learners to ask each other questions about leisure time, e.g. reading habits, TV, going out, food and drink, etc.

examples

What do you normally read at home? What are you reading at the moment?

What TV programmes do you watch in your country? What are you watching here?

exercise 1

The first guest has a problem with the washing machine. The second guest has a problem with his front door lock.

exercise 3

1 10 minutes (not seconds); one more week (not two weeks); the manager offers to get someone to look at it (not to look at it himself)
2 The key goes in the lock (the lock is broken, not the key); the kitchen tap has been fixed.

natural English

I'll get someone ... to have a look at it.
Could you get someone to have a look at it?

ideas plus personalized discussion

People make complaints about goods or services differently from culture to culture, and even within a single culture. You could introduce the listening with a small group discussion on complaining, using these questions as stimuli:

When did you last complain about goods or services?

What were you complaining about, and where did it happen?

What was the result?

Do you find it easy or difficult to complain?

What is the best way to complain: be gentle and polite, or quite aggressive?

You could ask the learners to translate a complaint directly from L1, especially with a multilingual class; this often illustrates the cultural differences between countries and generates discussion in itself.

extended speaking a holiday complex

70 – 85 mins

make decisions about a new holiday complex

prepare and give a presentation

decide on the best complex

role play a service encounter at the complex

- Remember to outline what will happen in the lesson before you begin by telling learners, putting it on the board, or referring them to the left-hand column on *p.30*. Give them time to look back at the blue **extended speaking** boxes in the earlier parts of this unit.

collect ideas

- Before you begin the activity, organize the learners into small groups and rearrange the seating so that they can all see each other and communicate clearly. Avoid having groups larger than four so no learners will be excluded, and everyone gets an opportunity to speak. Look at **ideas plus** for an additional warmer activity.
- Give them a few minutes to discuss their ideas in **exercise 1**. Don't worry if they decide quickly; this is not the main speaking activity.
- Give the class instructions for **exercise 2** and tell them to study the map carefully. Let them concentrate alone for a few minutes to gather ideas before discussing in groups. As you monitor, make sure that they are discussing reasons. At the end of these two exercises, quickly go round and check what each group has decided, but don't do class feedback, or you will spoil the later presentations.
- If you like, you could give the groups two minutes at the end of **exercise 2** to write notes on what they have decided so far. This will help with the presentations later.
- In **exercise 3**, get the learners to look at the facilities information, and ask if there is any vocabulary they don't understand. (Point out that *bureau de change* / bjʊərəʊ də ˈʃɒnʒ / is a term borrowed from French, and we keep an approximate French pronunciation in English. If you think it is necessary, give them the spelling of the plural, i.e. *bureaux*.) Then give them a few minutes alone to think about their answers.
- If they are having problems thinking of attractions and services, give them an example, such as a fancy dress disco, or a water-skiing competition.
- **Exercise 4** is the main speaking activity, so allow at least ten minutes for this activity. If it takes longer, and all the learners are engaged, so much the better. Make sure you monitor the activity and make notes on the language used.

prepare a presentation

- It is important that learners use the information in the checklist. In our original piloting of this activity, we found that they had difficulty structuring their presentations and being aware of what their listeners needed to know. They also didn't know how to start the presentation, which is why we have included a couple of introductory phrases.
- Rehearsal in their group is very important in terms of the organization of the material and the fluency with which it is presented. Learners will be much more confident if they have rehearsed their part.

present your ideas

- If you have a small class, each group could do their presentation to the whole class. Do encourage questions and comments from other learners; this will validate the work done by the presenters and make the whole activity more rounded.
- At the end, give the class some feedback on the way they handled the presentations and language points you noted earlier; be as encouraging and positive as possible. This may be the first time intermediate learners have done a presentation, so you need to be particularly supportive.

role play

- If you are short of time, you could leave this activity until the next lesson.
- Outline the context of the role play before you divide the class into pairs, and tell them where to find their role cards. Give them a couple of minutes to think about what they will say.
- Monitor the role plays and give feedback at the end.

feedback checklist

During the **extended speaking** activity, note down examples of …

- **good language use**

- **effective communication strategies**
  (turn-taking, interrupting, inviting others to speak, etc.)

- **learner errors**
  (vocabulary, grammar, pronunciation, etc.)

- **particular communication problems**

Make sure you allow time for feedback at the end of the lesson. You can use the notes you make above to <u>praise</u> effective language use and communication or, if necessary, to do some remedial work.

---

ideas plus personalized discussion

You could begin by asking learners whether they've ever stayed in a holiday villa or apartment block, and get them to share their experience of them: where they were, what they were like, etc.

You could also talk about such places in their own country which may be visited by (foreign) tourists. What do they think of them? Are they good for the town? Are they good for the country?

---

troubleshooting managing time

In **extended speaking** activities you are likely to find groups working at a different pace. Some will 'finish' an activity while others are still clearly engaged in discussion.

In this activity, you could give learners a time limit of ten minutes for **exercise 4**. This allows you to bring it to a conclusion if most groups have finished and perhaps one is a little slow: give this group a two-minute warning. If, however, all of the groups are engaged and still doing the task after ten minutes, be prepared to be flexible and let it run on. Most learners expect the teacher to decide when an activity should end, so use your judgement.

If one group finishes early, and you are satisfied they have done the activity effectively, you may need an additional activity up your sleeve to keep them occupied. In this particular case, you could ask them to think up more possible facilities.

Want to know more? Go to **how to …** monitor and give feedback *p.156*.

test yourself!

Want to know more? Go to the **introduction** *p.7* for ways of using **test yourself!**

1 noisier, more boring, more dangerous, more useful
2 wardrobe, curtains / cushions, lamp, mirror, rug
3 snack bar, travel agent, tennis court, coffee table, air conditioning

1 Lisbon is much cheaper than Monaco. / Lisbon is much less expensive than Monaco.
2 I've only got £10 left.
3 There's something wrong with the phone.
4 We should stay here.

1 It's a bit cheaper.
2 The children are still playing, so we can't leave yet.
3 The most incredible thing …
4 It's a long journey to the airport.

---

three

wordlist

natural English

me too / me neither

I like this one.   Me too.
I don't like this.   Me neither.
I like this one.   Really? I don't.
I don't like this.   Really? I do.

on my own

on my own
by myself
alone
lonely

like, such as, and that sort of thing

I love music such as / like (jazz and samba).
I like (jazz, rock) and that sort of thing.

imprecise periods of time

for a couple of years
for several years
for quite a while
for ages

fun (n) / funny (adj)

great fun
good fun
It's very funny.
It's making a funny noise.

talking about memories

I remember -ing ...
I can just remember -ing ...
I can't remember -ing ... at all.

never used to

We never used to (go there).
(I like it now, but) I never used to.

vocabulary

music

lead singer
songwriter
composer
solo artist
drummer
group / band
choir
orchestra
soloist
keyboard player
violinist
base guitarist
conductor

lyrics
record (a song)
release (a CD)
a hit

stages in your life

When I was ...
a teenager / a child / younger / in my twenties
at primary school / at secondary school
out of work
When I ...
left school / first got married / retired

wordbooster

likes and dislikes

I really love / like it.
I don't mind ...
I'm not too keen on ...
I'm not mad about ...
I don't like this at all.
I hate / can't stand it.
It's great.
It's not bad.
It's awful.

verb + noun collocation

make a mistake
join a club
play a game / a musical instrument
give up sth
practise your English
take up a hobby

glossaries

glad
shut up! ©
stink (v) ©
delighted
charity
funeral

art forms

in unit three ...

life with Agrippine
cartoon perfect day
natural English *me too / me neither*

reading a perfect day
natural English *on my / your own, by myself / yourself, alone, lonely*
listening song: *Perfect Day*
vocabulary music
reading Lives of the great songs
natural English *like, such as, and that sort of thing*

listening what's happened to you?
grammar present perfect and past simple with *for* and *since*
natural English imprecise periods of time
listening actors talk about their work
natural English *fun* (n), *funny* (adj)

wordbooster
likes and dislikes
verb + noun collocation

how to ... talk about your past
natural English phrases for talking about memories
grammar past simple and *used to* + verb
vocabulary stages in your life
natural English *never used to*

extended speaking musical tastes
collect ideas read about music in someone's life
prepare for an interview create a questionnaire
interview talk to a partner
writing write a music profile

test yourself!
revision and progress check

life with Agrippine   25 – 30 mins

nE *me too / me neither*
Want to know more about using life with Agrippine? Go to the **introduction** *p.5.*

- Before starting the personalization activity at the beginning of *p.33*, you could teach these lexical items which might be useful in the activity:
  to sing out loud   to sing something in your head
  to hum a tune   to whistle a tune   to sing out of tune
- You could teach these by writing the phrases on the board, then demonstrate each action randomly and ask learners to say which one you are doing. Focus on the pronunciation of *loud* /laʊd/, *whistle* /'wɪsəl/, *tune* /tʃuːn/, and *hum* /hʌm/.
- The song Byron is singing is called *Perfect Day,* and the recording is in the next section.

language point *me too / me neither*
We have focused on *me too / me neither* as they are very common in spoken English. However, you may want to take this opportunity to feed in and practise *so do I / neither do I* where the opinion of both speakers is the same. If you do this, you will also need to point out that the auxiliary changes according to the stimulus:
example
A *I **can't** swim very well.* B *Neither **can** I.*

33

reading a perfect day

---

describe a perfect day spent alone, using **natural English** phrases

listen to the words of a song

read a magazine article about great songs

talk about music using vocabulary and **natural English** phrases

glossary

chunks phrases of varying length where the words naturally appear together, e.g. in her mid twenties

---

lead-in

- This a good example of a warmer activity which would benefit from a model by you. Tell them briefly what your perfect day would be like, using the framework in **exercise 1**. This will give learners a clear idea of what you expect them to do.
- Before you do **exercise 4**, find out what learners know about Lou Reed and his song *Perfect Day*, which has already appeared briefly in **life with Agrippine**. Before you listen to the song, you could explain the last line of the song: *You're going to reap what you sow* = what you get from life depends on what you put into it. (Lou Reed is an American singer / songwriter who first came to fame in the late 1960s as a member of the rock band *Velvet Underground*, before becoming a solo artist in the early 70s. He is an unconventional figure, and many of his songs have non-conformist lyrics. Possibly his most famous song is *Walk on the Wild Side*.)

---

vocabulary music

- As a lead-in to **exercise 1**, you could have a brainstorming competition in small groups. How many words related to music can learners think of in two minutes? See which group has the highest number, then ask them to read out the list. Explain any items other groups don't know or ask learners to explain unknown words.
- **Exercise 1** can be done alone or in pairs; be sure to check learners' pronunciation of the words and phrases.
- If you like, you could turn **exercises 3** and **4** into a team competition.

---

read on

- With a strong class, you could put **exercises 1** and **2** together. With a weaker group, you may want them to read the article to get an overview, complete the glossary, and go over the answers before going on to exercise 2.
- If you want to exploit the text for more discussion, you could ask learners to think and talk about songs in their own culture which are / have been used for TV advertisements, national / sporting events, political / election campaigns, charity events, etc. What do learners think about these songs?

exercise 4

Just a perfect day, drink <u>lemonade</u> in the park.
And then later when it gets dark, we go home.
Just a perfect day, <u>feed</u> animals in the zoo.
Then later <u>a movie too</u>, and then home.

(chorus)
Oh! it's such a perfect day.
I'm <u>glad</u> I spent it with you.
Oh! such a perfect day.
You <u>just</u> keep me hanging on.

Just a perfect day, problems <u>all left alone</u>.
Weekenders on our own, it's <u>such</u> fun.
Just a perfect day, you made me forget <u>myself</u>.
I thought I was someone else, someone good.

exercise 1
rock and pop
lead singer, songwriter, solo artist, drummer, group /
band, keyboard player, bass guitarist
(The words *group* and *band* are more or less
synonymous.)
classical music and opera
composer, choir, orchestra, soloist, violinist,
conductor
(We generally use the word *composer* for people who
write serious music which is respected or considered
classic of its type. For example, it is now possible to
describe Paul McCartney as a composer, but when he
wrote pop music in the 1960s, he would have been
called a songwriter.)
exercise 2 possible order
1 write the music   4 record the song
2 write the lyrics   5 release the song
3 choose a recording artist 6 the song becomes a
                             hit

glossary
1c   2d   3b   4a
exercise 2
1 *Perfect Day* was used in the film *Trainspotting*, by
  the BBC as an advertisement for themselves, and
  then released as a record for charity.
2 *Candle in the Wind* was rewritten, used at Princess
  Diana's funeral, and released as a record.
3 *Nessun Dorma* was used as the theme tune for the
  1990 football World Cup in Italy.
natural English
line 10: **such as** David Bowie, etc. *line 32*: the works of
classical composers **like** Beethoven and Vivaldi ...

ideas plus using songs

Songs are often hugely popular as learning activities with people of all ages.

The Internet is a wonderful source of lyrics. You could use this website as a source:
http://music.yahoo.com/launch/lyrics.html

Two particularly useful books on songs are:
Heinemann ELT Hits by Karen Ludlow and Patricia Reilly. This includes a cassette of
songs with a booklet of photocopiable worksheets.

Music and song by Tim Murphey, OUP Resource Books for Teachers, 1992

Here is one simple idea from this book for using songs *(p.73)*:

Choose a suitable song for the level, and give each learner a piece of paper with a
word, expression, or line of the song to listen for. Ask the group to stand up. When
you play the song, learners have to listen for their bit and arrange themselves
physically (in a line across the class) in the order in which they hear their word,
expression, etc.

ideas plus sequencing activities

Sets of phrases (as in **exercise 2**) form part of a chronological sequence of events
which are familiar to learners. If you jumble the order of phrases, you have a ready-
made vocabulary comprehension activity, and you are also teaching useful *chunks* of
language. After putting them in a logical order, learners can write down the phrases
and memorize them. See also the sequencing activity in unit six **wordbooster** on
p.73. Here are other sequences for intermediate level learners. Make up your own
scripts to suit your class.

examples
• cooking or preparing a dish   • applying for and getting a job
• buying something to wear   • going to / staying at a hotel
• planning and giving a party   • early morning routine from waking up to
                                         leaving the house

In many cases, there is no definitive correct order, but differences can promote more
interesting language practice. You can ask learners to order the phrases alone, then
compare with a partner. Don't number the phrases, otherwise learners will say the
numbers rather than use the phrases.

Want to know more? Go to **how to ...** activate vocabulary *p.140*.

language point vague language

In communication, speakers sometimes find they don't have the exact words they
want, or there is no need for them to be exact or precise. For these reasons, a
common characteristic of spoken language is the use of 'vague language'. A good
example of this is the last phrase in the **natural English** box: *and that sort of thing*.
Similar examples would be *and that kind of thing, and that kind of stuff, and
things / stuff like that*.

You will find another example of vague language in the **natural English** box on *p.37*:
imprecise periods of time, e.g. *for a couple of years / several years / quite a while /
ages*.

listening what's happened to you?

80 – 90 mins

describe life experiences using
– present perfect and past simple
– *for* and *since*
– **natural English** phrases of imprecise time

listen to actors talking about their life experience

talk about the life and work of a famous actor

lead-in

- **Exercise 1** will work best if you can demonstrate this yourself by giving learners three sentences about your own life. If you like, let them ask questions about the three experiences to try and catch you out. This will make the activity interactive.

grammar present perfect and past simple (2)

- Make sure that learners take time to look at the pictures of Paul at different stages in his life; this will help them with **exercise 1**. You could encourage learners to work together, or work alone and compare answers.
- As there is quite a lot of grammar practice on *p.36* to *p.37*, we would recommend that you ask learners to do the **cover & check** exercises in the **language reference** on *p.157* at home. Only use them in class if your learners are having a particular problem with a concept.
- **Exercise 6** could be done in pairs, and learners could then find a new partner for **exercise 7** to ask the questions. Before you begin exercise 7, demonstrate with one question and answer exchange in front of the class.

Want to know more? Go to **how to** ... introduce new language *p.143*.

listen to this

- If learners don't understand the first part of the recording in **exercise 1**, i.e. in **tune in**, don't go on to **listen carefully**. Replay the recording to give them another chance, then if necessary, let them listen with the tapescript. (See **troubleshooting** on the right).
- Make sure learners read the table first to familiarize themselves with the vocabulary. After the listening you could also highlight *slot-machine* = a machine you put money into and if particular pictures appear together on the screen, you win more money back, *stunt driver* = a person who takes the place of an actor to do dangerous things while driving a car.
- In **exercises 2** and **3**, the actors mention certain names / plays / films, etc. which are generally well-known, but if they are not familiar to learners in your teaching context, don't worry.

▁▄▆█▄▆ wordbooster

25 – 30 mins

This wordbooster is best done before the **how to...** section because the vocabulary selected here will be useful, particularly in the grammar section, as well as in the **extended speaking** activity.

likes and dislikes

- For **exercise 1**, you could bring in postcards of works of art and give them to small groups of learners to react to. If you circulate the pictures every few minutes, learners can get a lot of personalized practice.
- **Exercise 3** could be done as a mingling activity for variety. (The painting on the left is a Rothko, the top right-hand corner one is a Goya, and the one below that is a Picasso.)

verb + noun collocation

- To speak and write naturally, learners need to focus on collocations like these. Suggest that your learners keep a record of words that often go together in their notebooks.
- In **exercise 2**, highlight the question form *Would you prefer to* + verb? and elicit *I'd prefer to* + verb. It would be a good idea to practise the pronunciation with the group before learners work in pairs.

troubleshooting revision

Notice that the examples given in **exercise 1** include both the present perfect and past simple. This activity is intended as a brief revision of the use of the difference between these tenses as illustrated in unit one, i.e. general experience versus events at a specific time in the past. Monitor the learners' tense use, and provide feedback at the end of **exercise 2** if necessary.

exercise 1

1 studied   2 hasn't played   3 took up   4 studied   5 was
6 became   7 has worked   8 joined   9 has been

exercise 2

past simple: sentences 1, 3, 4, 5, 6, and 8
present perfect: sentences 7 and 9
negative sentence: 2
for is used with a period of time; *since* to say when something started

exercise 3 possible answers

He joined the choir three years ago.
He's played the guitar for 20 years / since he was 15.
He's had his present job for 12 years / since he was 23.
He hasn't been out of work for 12 years / since he was 23.
He has been in a band for 8 years / since he was 27.

exercise 4 nE

1d   2a   3b   4c

exercise 5

How long did he study ...? We use the past simple because the period of studying the piano is finished.
How long has he sung ...? We use the present perfect because he started singing in the past, and still sings now.

language point *He's worked /*
hasn't worked there for ...

For many learners, this use of the present perfect (unfinished past) is translated in their own language by the present simple tense, and the concept therefore may be difficult to grasp, particularly in the negative form, i.e. the idea that something has continued not to happen.

He hasn't worked at the bank for two years.

This means *It's two years since he worked at the bank.*

This paraphrase (along with a timeline) can make the concept more accessible.

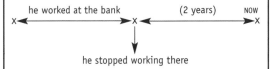

You can put the timelines in **language reference** on the board to clarify concepts.

troubleshooting tune in

Tune in is there to help learners connect with the context, so that they find **listen carefully** easier. But it is also useful diagnostically; if learners are struggling at this stage, you will see whether you need to give them more help, e.g. by clarifying the context, or helping them with a specific stumbling block such as a phrase or name.

Want to know more? Go to **how to ...** teach listening *p.151.*

exercise 1

1 They are both actors.
2 Lorelei: 20 years; Chris: 12 years
3 Lorelei mentions radio, Chris mentions (short) films

exercise 2

Lorelei: acting on TV and film, radio, voice-overs
Chris: acting on film and in the theatre, writing plays, writing for TV, commercials

exercise 3

Julia has worked in radio, TV, theatre, films, and advertising. She's met Alan Rickman (a British actor, famous for his roles as the Sheriff of Nottingham in *Robin Hood*, Hans Grüber in *Die Hard*, and Severus Snape in *Harry Potter*) and Bob Hoskins.

exercise 1

1 really love; great   3 don't mind; not bad   5 at all; awful
2 nice   4 keen on; mad   6 can't stand; hate

exercise 1

join a university; play skiing; give up breathing; practise sport; take up chocolate

how to ... talk about your past

60 – 70 mins

do you remember?

- For an alternative lead-in to the lesson, see **ideas plus** on the right.

- Once learners have filled the gaps in the phrases in the **natural English** box, point out the following: firstly, that here, *remember* is followed by *-ing*; that *just* here means 'only a little', i.e. it is a vague memory; and the **natural English** phrase *I can't remember ... at all*. Check that learners are using the forms accurately in the practice stage.

- At the end of **exercise 2**, you could ask learners to think about other things they can remember learning to do in the past, e.g. read, write, rollerskate, ski, etc. Give them a minute to think, then tell their partner or the class.

- If you want to develop the conversations in **exercise 2**, learners could talk about when and where they learnt the skill, who taught them, whether they found it easy, boring, fun, etc.

vocabulary stages in your life

- This vocabulary brings together useful lexical chunks describing life stages. Deal with the meaning of any unfamiliar items, and highlight the pattern in the 'ages & stages' table using the board:

in	my	early	teens
	your	mid	twenties
	his / her	late	thirties

- If necessary, do controlled practice of these. See **ideas plus** on the right.

- If there are other items that need checking, e.g. *out of work*, *retired*, do so before learners tick the phrases relevant to themselves. You could demonstrate the ticking activity by showing them some things you would tick for yourself. If you want to double-check after the ticking exercise, ask one learner that the others know well to read out the ones they ticked, and ask if they think it is correct; then ask other learners to tell you anything else they ticked.

grammar past simple and *used to* + verb

- We have used a diagnostic approach to this grammar point as we feel it will be familiar for some learners at this level. If you think none of your learners will know this construction, you could do **exercises 1** and **2**, and then use the sentences to explain the concept to your class. You could pause the recording between the sentences in exercise 1 if you think the learners will find it too fast. You may also want to make more extensive use of the **cover & check** exercises in the **language reference** on *p.158*, and / or the exercises in the **workbook** on *p.21*.

- **In exercise 4**, give learners time to think up sentences. You may wish to ask them to write them down so that you can monitor and correct as necessary before they compare their answers in small groups.

it's your turn!

- You could begin by telling learners how <u>your</u> tastes have changed and relate it to the table of interests. This activity is a useful preparation for the **extended speaking** activity. If you like, you could change some of the ideas in the list of interests to make it particularly relevant to your class, but avoid the topic of music, or learners will simply be repeating themselves when they do the extended speaking.

- Make sure learners write something for each of the six interests. While you are monitoring, check that learners are not using *used to* + verb for present interests (see **language point**).

Want to know more? Go to **how to ...** monitor and give feedback *p.156*.

nE

I can remember learning to swim very clearly.
I can <u>just</u> remember learning to ride a bike.
I can't remember learning to tie my shoelaces at all.

ideas plus memory game

This is a game which links with the theme of memory and practises vocabulary. Bring in about 15 common items, e.g. ruler, stapler, sellotape, biro etc. Put these on a tray or table where they can be seen by everyone, and let learners ask you any words they don't know. Then give the learners one minute to study and memorize the items. Cover them up and either alone or in pairs, they have to write down as many as they can remember. Alternatively, you could ask learners to study and memorize things in a picture from earlier in the book (e.g. the hotel room in unit two, on *p.26,* or the photos of forms of transport on *p.22* to *p.24*). This would serve both as vocabulary revision and an introduction to the topic of memory. From this, you can lead in to the questions in **exercise 1**.

ideas plus ages and stages

Learners could use the phrases to describe members of their families. Alternatively, learners could put the phrases in a logical order, highlighting the ones which could be placed in different positions.

exercise 2
See **listening booklet** *p.12*.
exercise 3
1 The speakers say *used to* to describe past habits and states which are now finished. You can't use *used to* with a specific past time or period of time (see **language point** on the right for examples).
2 In sentence 3 *used to* is not possible, because the speaker is talking about single actions in the past. In sentence 4 *I used to draw* is possible. In sentence 5 *used to* is not possible, because the period of time is stated (for six months).
3 /ˈjuːstə/

language point *used to* + verb

In some languages there is no literal equivalent for *used to* + verb, and there are a number of typical problems with this structure. It is important to clarify that *used to* is only used to describe **past** habits which have changed or are discontinued. It cannot be used to describe how long or how many times something happened.

~~I used to live in California for three years.~~
~~My sister used to go to the hospital three times.~~

1 Learners need to be clear that this form cannot be used to talk about the present, e.g. *These days, ~~we use to~~ go everywhere by car.*
Instead, they should use *usually* + present simple.
2 A common form error is to use *be used to* + verb. Normally, learners don't encounter *be used to* +*ing* until later, and the error is more likely to be one of form than of meaning. You should highlight and correct these errors in the lesson.
3 Pronunciation: *I used to go* /aɪ ˈjuːst ə ˌgəʊ/: Notice the weak form *to* /tə/ and the pronunciation of *used* /juːst/. Learners may confuse this with *used* /juːzd/ meaning *make use of*, e.g. I used a knife to open it.

Want to know more? Go to **Practical English Usage** by Michael Swan, *pp.604–605.*

extended speaking musical tastes

read about music in someone's life

create a questionnaire

interview a partner

write a music profile of oneself or a partner

- It is important at the beginning of this activity to let learners read the left-hand column or tell them what they are going to do in the lesson, or put it on the board. This will enable them to get the whole picture. You should also give them time to look back at the blue **extended speaking** boxes which occur at the end of each section in the unit.

collect ideas

- The text is there for two reasons: it serves as a model for the later speaking and writing activities, but it also contextualizes some useful time phrases which learners will be able to use in the activity to structure their discourse. You could, if you wish, prepare a parallel text of your own musical profile, in which you could include factors which are culturally relevant to your teaching context. It could be a written or an informal spoken model.

collect ideas

1   paragraph 1: childhood
    paragraph 2: growing up and late teens
    paragraph 3: nowadays

2   First she liked pop music, then pop and rock music, and then classical music and opera. Now she listens to everything but isn't very keen on noisy rock music.

prepare for an interview

- During the early stages of piloting this activity, we found that learners were quite effective in talking about music in their lives, but less effective at asking a wide range of questions to elicit interesting information from their partner. We therefore decided to structure the interview and give learners time to prepare questions. The first three questions in **exercise 2** are provided to ensure that learners talk about past and present, but the prompts for the other questions give them choice and enable them to generate their own ideas.

- Equally important is the need for learners to plan what they intend to say in **exercise 3**. Our experience with these activities is that learners really do want and benefit from time to think, so don't be nervous of silence. They may want to take the opportunity to consult you or ask for help.

interview

- These interviews will take varying amounts of time; some learners will have more to say than others. Monitor the pairs, and if one pair has finished early (and you are happy that they have fulfilled the brief), you could split them up and ask them to listen in on another pair who are still talking.

- Bring the activity to a close when <u>most</u> pairs have finished. If you wait for everyone to finish, you may find that some learners have nothing to do. If you like, give the class a two-minute warning before they have to bring the activity to an end.

- Give learners feedback on the activity, using any notes you made while monitoring.

write a music profile

- Learners may need to use the **natural English** phrases on *p.37* on imprecise periods of time when writing their profiles, and of course, **how to ... talk about your past** on *p.40* contains very useful language for the writing activity.

feedback checklist

During the **extended speaking** activity, note down examples of …

- **good language use**

- **effective communication strategies**
  (turn-taking, interrupting, inviting others to speak, etc.)

- **learner errors**
  (vocabulary, grammar, pronunciation, etc.)

- **particular communication problems**

Make sure you allow time for feedback at the end of the lesson. You can use the notes you make above to praise effective language use and communication or, if necessary, to do some remedial work.

---

troubleshooting responding to individual learners

All the extended speaking activities have been designed to appeal to a wide range of learners. In this case, for example, everyone has exposure to music throughout their lives, and for most people it is a pleasure and interest to a greater or lesser extent. However, no activity can hope to work equally well for every individual. If you have one or two learners who don't particularly like music, focus them on the more factual side of the activity, e.g. their exposure to music as a child / at school / in their daily lives.

A very important element of this activity is expressing likes and dislikes. You shouldn't, however, let the interviews degenerate into a 'shopping list' in which learners just exchange names of performers they like or don't like. Make sure that they are talking about their past influences, interests, and general experiences, as this will all be more 'language rich'.

test yourself!

Want to know more? Go to the **introduction** on *p. 7* for ways of using **test yourself!**

possible answers
1 a band, an orchestra, a choir
2 join a band, a club, a choir; play a game, a CD, a musical instrument; take up the guitar, riding, acting; practise your English, the violin, your tennis serve
3 when I was in my teens / in my early / mid / late twenties, etc. when I was a child / at primary / secondary school, when I got married, when I retired

1 I can't stand this record.
2 I'm not too keen on opera.
3 I haven't seen him for two years.
4 I was in my mid twenties at the time.

1 He did his homework on his own / by himself.
2 She used to play the guitar when she was a child.
3 How long have you studied English?
4 I can just remember learning to tie my shoelaces.

four

wordlist

natural English

expressing a preference
I'd prefer to ...
I'd rather + verb

asking for repetition
Pardon?
Sorry, I didn't quite catch that.
Sorry? I missed that.

expressing interest
I'm really / quite interested in ...
I'm not interested in ...

saying how much you know
I know (quite) a lot about ...
I know a bit about ...
I don't know very much about ...
I don't know anything about ...

phone greetings
Is that (Bruno)?
Is that you, (Bruno)?
Could I speak to (Bruno), please?
Yes, speaking.
It's / this is (Elena).
My name's (Elena Ponti).

vocabulary

facial actions
grin (at sb)
yawn
laugh (at sb / sth)
whistle
cry
wink (at sb)

food and drink
well done / rare steak
still / sparkling water
shrimps
prawns
sugar / sweetener
green salad / mixed salad
lettuce
cabbage
melon

TV programmes
documentary
quiz show
comedy
sports programme
news and current affairs
drama series
chat show
soap opera

wordbooster

phrases expressing your opinion
It's a bit boring.
It's quite interesting.
It's very dull.
It's a waste of time.
It's absolutely fascinating.
It's intriguing.
It's great fun.
It doesn't interest me.
I get fed up with it. ☺
It doesn't appeal to me.

synonyms
chance / opportunity
examine / look at
view / opinion
extract / clip
talk / lecture
topic / subject

glossaries

vinaigrette
decaff
flick through sth

choices

do you get it? 20 – 30 mins

listen for pleasure
vocabulary facial actions
nE phrases expressing a preference

- Learners could brainstorm what kind of things people do in parks, or you could give them two minutes in pairs to write as many down as possible.
- You could start the storytelling (**joke time**) using the pictures as a class activity. Elicit the content of the first two pictures together, then learners can do the rest in pairs.
- In **facial actions**, once learners have matched the words and pictures, check that they can pronounce the words written in phonemic script.

---

language point nE expressing a preference

Intermediate learners should know *prefer*, but are unlikely to know *would ('d) rather* despite its high frequency in spoken English. Notice that the examples in the **natural English** box are both hypothetical, i.e. *would prefer / would rather* <u>on this specific occasion</u>. Compare:

A *Do you like tea?*	A *Would you like a glass of orange?*
(in general)	(on this occasion)
B *I prefer coffee.*	B *I'd prefer water, actually.*

Notice the form in these examples:

*I **prefer to work** / **working** at home.*

*I'd **prefer to work** at home.*   NOT *I'd prefer ~~working~~ at home.*

*I'd **rather work** at home.*   NOT *I'd rather ~~to~~ work at home.*

Prefer to do / prefer doing have the same meaning.

Although *prefer* and *would rather* are often practised in whole sentences comparing two things, e.g. *I'd prefer to go to the cinema than the theatre*, it is more common and natural in English to express a preference like this:

A *Would you like to come for a swim?*

B *No, I think I'd rather stay here.*

---

reading difficult choices

60 – 80 mins

expand vocabulary on the topic of food and drink

read an article about choosing items from a menu and tell a partner about it

ask for repetition using **natural English** phrases

develop a role play conversation based on the texts

lead-in

- We start with a focus on *choose* (v) / *choice* (n) because learners often have problems with form and pronunciation.

vocabulary food and drink

- Tell learners to cover the words, look at the pictures with a partner and see how many they can label. They can then look at the word list for more ideas and more precise answers.

- Practise the pronunciation of the difficult items, i.e. the ones written in phonemic script. Learners can then test each other in the **test your partner** activity.

- In **exercise 2**, look at number 1 together (about steak), and ask the class to define the difference between *well-done* and *rare*. When they have given a satisfactory definition, ask them to continue in pairs. At the end, have a class feedback on the answers.

read on

- See **troubleshooting** on the right on setting up the jigsaw reading activity.

- Tell everyone to read the questions in **exercise 2** before they read their article. They should <u>only</u> answer those questions and not go into detail. Monitor the pairs to check they have the right answers.

- In **exercise 3**, learners have time to take in the detail. If you think the class need a lot of support, they could practise this stage orally with a partner who read the same article.

- For **exercise 4**, match up A and B pairs from each side of the class to tell each other about their article. They should not use their books at this stage. Be sure to give them an opportunity to react to the texts at the end.

- Now look at the **natural English** box. For the practice activity, illustrate it yourself by saying something very quietly to elicit the phrases before they work in pairs.

it's your turn!

Illustrate this activity with the whole class, using a different prompt, e.g. apple tart (or something from the local culture). This should be a light-hearted activity, and it would be fun if their options are a bit silly, e.g. would you like a round pizza or a square one?

 wordbooster

20 – 25 mins

This **wordbooster** is best used at this point as the phrases will be useful in the listening section.

phrases expressing your opinion

In **exercise 1** focus on the pronunciation of the phrases, particularly word stress and intonation:
It's <u>absolutely</u> <u>fascinating</u>. It's a <u>waste</u> of <u>time</u>.

synonyms

These items will be very useful in the **extended speaking** activity. You should check that they can pronounce words like *lecture*, *subject*, and *views* before they do the **test your partner** activity.

exercise 1

1 choose   2 chosen   3 chose   4 choice

---

exercise 1

The pictures illustrate: sparkling water, rare steak, prawns and shrimps (the prawns are bigger), watermelon, sweeteners, mixed salad, red cabbage, and a baked potato.

exercise 2

1 *Well-done* means cooked for a long time, *rare* means cooked for a very short time.
2 *Sparkling* and *still* both describe water but *sparkling water* has air bubbles in it.
3 *Prawns* are bigger than *shrimps*. (In American English, they only use the word *shrimp*.)
4 *Sweetener* is artificial, *sugar* is natural.
5 A *green salad* is usually only lettuce; a *mixed salad* has lettuce and other things, e.g. tomatoes, onion, cucumber.
6 *French fries* are fried (in oil); *a baked potato* is cooked in the oven.
7 *Lettuce* isn't usually cooked, and is eaten in salad; *cabbage* is usually cooked.
8 *Watermelon* is red inside and larger than a melon; *melon* is yellow or orange.

troubleshooting paraphrasing exercises

What's the difference between ...? exercises are very useful for helping learners to paraphrase, but need to be devised with caution. It is important that learners have the necessary language to define the differences between the selected items. For instance, *strawberry* and *raspberry* are similar types of fruit, but many at this level would find it difficult to define the differences adequately; visuals would be much clearer.

Want to know more? Go to **how to** ... activate vocabulary *p.136*.

---

exercise 2

text A

1 a waitress called Jo
2 The waitress gives him several choices for everything he orders.
3 impatient

text B

1 the person from Room Service
2 He orders a cup of tea and is offered several choices for types of tea, milk, sugar, etc.
3 impatient

nE

Pardon? I didn't quite catch (the last part of your request).

troubleshooting jigsaw reading

It is very important with jigsaw reading activities to make the procedure clear to the class. Explain to the group at the beginning that half of them will read one text and the other half will read a different one, and that they will have to explain what they read about to a partner who read a different text.

In this case, it is easiest if you divide the class so that the half on the left read text A and the half on the right read text B. This will help you when you go round the pairs and monitor their answers in **exercise 2** without giving the game away to the other half of the class. If you have an odd number, form a group of three for **exercise 4**, with two learners who read the same article working together for the retelling stage. In this case, it can be useful to put two weak learners together to help each other.

---

exercise 1

positive: it's quite interesting; it's absolutely fascinating; it's intriguing; it's great fun
negative: it's a bit boring; it's very dull; it's a waste of time; it doesn't interest me; I get fed up with it; it doesn't appeal to me

ideas plus using learners' ideas

Instead of using the prompts given in **exercise 2**, you could ask your learners to shout out things they find interesting, boring, a waste of time. They should not say what their attitude is at this stage. Write their topics / suggestions on the board. Learners can then use these to practise the phrases in **exercise 1**.

---

exercise 1

1 chance   2 examine   3 views   4 extracts
5 talk   6 topic

language point synonyms

Teaching synonyms helps learners to expand their vocabulary and to store words in written form. Remember, however, that words may be synonymous in one context but not another. For instance, we talk about a topic of conversation, not ~~a subject of conversation~~, subjects you study at school, not ~~topics you study at school~~.

listening TV tastes

talk about TV programmes using
– vocabulary
– **natural English** phrases expressing interest

say how much you know about topics using **natural English** phrases

listen to TV executives discussing ideas for TV documentaries

focus on modal verbs, and use them to talk about the programmes mentioned earlier

discuss TV programming in their country

vocabulary TV programmes

- Learners could compare their answers to **exercise 1** in small groups. Multilingual groups can often discuss American imports or TV in the country they're studying in.

- In the **natural English** box, once learners have completed the phrases, you can focus on them. See **language point** on the right.

- In **exercise 2**, before learners think about their answers, check that they are familiar with all the TV programme types. Explain or give your own examples. Check that they can pronounce the words in phonemic script. Give them a minute or two to think about their answers before they work in groups for **exercise 3**.

- Learners should be able to do **exercise 4** with a partner through simple deduction. You may also need to check they understand and can pronounce certain words such as *psychologists* /saɪˈkɒlədʒɪsts/, *hypnosis* /hɪpˈnəʊsɪs/, *survive* /səˈvaɪv/, as they will need to use these in **exercise 5**.

listen to this

- To set the scene for the listening activity, refer learners to the picture of the TV executives and explain the situation, i.e. that these people are choosing subjects for the documentaries which are to be made for a TV channel. Tell them to look back at the possible subjects in **vocabulary**, **exercise 4** and discuss in pairs which would appeal to different groups. (*Appeal to sb* was taught in **wordbooster** on *p.48*; check that they remember it.)

- In **exercise 2**, give learners a moment to focus on the table. They can complete the first part about the programmes Mike chooses. Make it clear that they will only need to write very short notes; not more than five or six words. Before you listen in **exercise 3** you could pre-teach: *wildlife* = animals and birds living in natural conditions. Afterwards, highlight: *struggle* (n) = something which is hard or difficult to do, *drop* = (in this case) to leave / forget about something.

- At the end of the recording, give learners a chance to compare with a partner. This will give you time to monitor and see what they wrote. If they found it difficult, go back and replay the recording.

Want to know more? Go to **how to ...** teach listening *p.154*.

grammar modal verbs *would, could / might*

- Ask learners to look at the pairs of sentences and try to answer the questions with a partner. Monitor to see how they are coping, then suggest that they check their answers in the **language reference** on *p.159*. At the end, go over the answers as a class and clear up any problems. You'll need to check that they know the form and pronunciation of these modal verbs.

- If you feel this is too demanding for your class, you could write each pair of sentences on the board, and talk about the possible differences together. You can also refer them to the **language reference** and use the supplementary **cover & check** exercises on *p.159* for further practice.

- Give learners a minute or two to think about their reasons in **exercise 2** before discussing the programmes with their groups.

- In **exercise 4**, learners have the opportunity to personalize and talk about TV programming generally. At the end of their group discussion, have a general class feedback to compare opinions.

Want to know more? Go to **how to ...** introduce new language *p.143*.

nE expressing interest
really; not very; definitely not

exercise 4
left-hand column pictures:
Choosing your next car, How to survive alone in the Amazon rainforest, Getting started as a fashion model

right-hand column pictures:
Training to be an Olympic athlete, Animal psychologists – what can they do for your pet?, Hypnosis – does it really work?

---

language point *be interested in*

Learners may make a number of errors with this form. *I'm ~~interesting~~ in ...; I'm interested ~~by ... / about ... / on ... / for ...~~; I'm interested ~~to study~~ ...*

They would probably not use the emphatic *I'm definitely not interested in* ... and would rarely express degrees of interest with modifiers, e.g. *really*, so it's worth activating these.

Another pitfall is the pronunciation of *interested* /ˈɪntrəstɪd/, which usually has three syllables, not four, and is stressed on the first syllable.

Want to know more about the difference between +ed / +ing?
Go to the **workbook, unit four** *p.24.*

---

exercises 2 and 3

	programmes	reason(s)
Mike	1 choosing your next car	it affects everyone
	2 surviving in the Amazon rainforest	a) it would appeal to all age groups
		b) it would cost very little to make
Eric	1 getting started as a fashion model	a) young women would like it because they may want to become models
		b) men would like it because they like looking at pretty girls
	2 surviving in the Amazon rainforest	interesting; beautiful pictures; stories of survival are always popular
Mary	1 hypnosis – does it really work?	it could help people to give up smoking or lose weight
	2 animal psychologists	

exercise 4
They choose the survival programme and the hypnosis programme.

---

exercise 1

1 *Might* means it is possible; *would* means you are more sure. In both cases it is the speaker's opinion.
2 There isn't a significant difference in meaning here.
3 Sentence **e** is correct. Sentence **f** is not possible, because you haven't seen the documentary so you can't use the present simple. You can only imagine it would be interesting.

---

ideas plus using local information

To give learners in their own country more concrete information to support their opinions in **exercise 3**, you could bring some copies of the TV listings for their country or region to class. Allow them time to look through the listings and make some notes about the scheduling. You can also prompt them by asking them if they think there are too many soap operas or not enough news programmes, or too many programmes for young people, etc.

how to ... make a phone call   60 – 80 mins

learn appropriate language for telephone greetings

practise introducing yourself and giving your reason for calling

listen to someone invite a speaker to give a talk and make arrangements

focus on *will* and practise making offers and promises

glossary

discourse structure the way in which people organize their ideas and convey them in speech or writing

colligation the grammatical company a word keeps, e.g. to bear, as in *be born*, is nearly always used in the passive; *enjoy* can only be followed by a noun or *-ing* form, not the infinitive

answer the phone

- You could introduce the section by putting a few questions on the board for groups to discuss.
  – How many people have you spoken to on the phone today or in the last two days?
  – Who were they, and how many calls were social?
  – How often (if ever) do you make calls in English? Do you find it easy / difficult? Why?
  – What can help you make better calls in English?
- You could look at the first conversation in **exercise 1** together, then ask pairs to continue.
- In **exercise 2**, you could pre-teach: *colleague* = somebody you work with professionally, *slot* = (in this case) a period of time in a programme or timetable, *have sth in mind* = be thinking of, *the nitty-gritty* = the most important details, *confirm* = say that something is definite. After listening to check, you could elicit the answers and put them on the board so that learners can check their spelling. The practice stage is important; either use the recording to drill the dialogues, or provide the model yourself. You could encourage pairs to memorize the conversations.
- When they have finished, refer learners to the **natural English** box. As there are so many likely errors, it may be very useful to focus on the differences between L1 and L2, as suggested in the **natural English** box.

give the reason for your call

- In our data we found that learners were very poor at introducing themselves on the phone and explaining the reason for their call. This focus on *discourse structure* should encourage learners to prepare what they need to say before starting a telephone conversation, and will give them more confidence. (See **troubleshooting** on the right.)
- Set the scene for this section clearly so that learners understand who they are calling and why.
- Monitor during **exercise 2** while learners are writing, and help where necessary.
- In **exercise 3**, learners can practise their introduction with a partner, and then they can go back and practise the initial phone greetings and introduction together. Remember that learners will do a complete role play in context as the final part of the **extended speaking** activity.

invite and make arrangements

- Direct learners to the photo of Chris Jackson on the phone to set the scene for the conversation. Play the recording and check that they have understood this part before going on to **exercise 2**.
- Give learners time to read the e-mail in **exercise 2**. Explain that it was sent after the phone conversation (to confirm the arrangements). They can then listen to the whole conversation and fill in the gaps. Pause the recording at appropriate moments so that learners have time to write and replay sections on request.
- Learners could use the transcript in the **listening booklet** on *p.16* to check their answers in pairs. Don't get involved in detailed language analysis, however, as this is dealt with in the next activity.

grammar uses of *will*

- You don't need to play the whole of **part 2**, if learners are becoming tired. Start from *We can offer you a fee of £300*.
- You could do the example in **exercise 2** orally and elicit a number of different possible responses so that learners get the idea of the exercise before they work in pairs.
- Check that learners understand that *be going to* is not acceptable in **exercise 2**. *Will* is needed because these are spontaneous, not pre-planned, decisions.
- Go over their suggestions as a group before they practise the dialogues in **exercise 3**.

exercise 1

1 A Hello?
  B Oh, hello. Could I speak to David Stone, please?
  A Yes, **speaking.**
  A Oh, good morning. **My name's** Angela Green
     and ...
2 A Hello?
  B Oh, good afternoon. Is that Mrs Carter?
  A Yes, **it is.**
  B Oh, hello. My name's Chris Jackson, and ...
3 A Hello?
  B Oh, hi, Jim, **it's** Carrie.
  A Oh, hi, Carrie. How are you?

language point telephone greetings

There are a number of pitfalls for learners with telephone greetings in English.

1 The person who receives the call is the first to speak; this is not the case in every culture. At home, people usually say *Hello?* In more formal business situations, they will answer the phone with the company's name (especially the switchboard operator) or their own name if they are on an extension, e.g. *Jane Swift (speaking)*.

2 The caller will usually reply with a greeting, e.g. *Oh, hello / good morning / hi* (informal) before either announcing themselves or asking to speak to someone.

3 Identifying yourself to the other speaker calls for the use of **It's** *(David Brown) /* **This is** *(Chris) /* **Is that** *Mrs Slocum?* Learners find these phrases particularly tricky. *This is ...* is a little more formal than *It's ... .*

exercise 1

The second introduction is better because the speaker
– gives her <u>full</u> name.
– explains her status / who she is.
– uses a phrase to introduce the reason for the call
   (*I'm ringing to invite you ...*).
– gives a simple clear description of what she wants.
The first caller doesn't give her name or status; the listener doesn't know who or what *we, school,* or *students* refers to.

troubleshooting structuring discourse

There are a number of situations where there is a recognizable way of organizing your ideas, e.g. meeting strangers on holiday: predictable introductory questions such as *How long have you been here? Is this the first time you've been to ...?*

Focusing on predictable discourse structures can help learners to plan and memorize certain routines. Of course, these ways of organizing ideas may not be the same in their own culture, so you may need to look at the differences between L1 and L2. You can give learners a typical situation (as in the example above) and ask them to predict what happens in that context. This gives a framework around which learners can plan what to say.

exercise 1

He wants her to talk about interviewing techniques.

exercise 2

1 interviewing   2 2nd   3 10.00   4 11.30
5 one hour   6 30   7 Park Hotel   8 £300

exercise 1

I'll give you my e-mail address.
I'll get an e-mail off to you.

language point *colligation*

We use *will* when we make a decision to do something at the moment of speaking. This often involves making offers and promises, and the following verbs and phrases occur quite frequently in this context with *will*. These can be learnt as phrases.

I'll write to you.   *I'll send you an e-mail / a memo.*   *I'll fax it to you.*

I'll ring / call / phone you.   *I'll give you a ring.*   *I'll contact you (tomorrow).*

I'll let you know (on Monday).   *I'll be in touch (next week).*   *I'll get back to you.*

Try eliciting these phrases from the learners. They can record them as a lexical set and use them in the **extended speaking** activity.

Want to know more? Go to **how to ...** activate vocabulary (colligation) *p.137.*

extended speaking a weekend English course   60 – 90 mins

choose speakers for a conference

decide on an extra talk and
write a description

role play a phone call inviting a speaker and making arrangements

• It is important at the beginning of this activity to let learners read the menu in the left-hand column, tell them what they are going to do in the lesson, or write it up on the board. This will enable them to get the whole picture. You should also give them time to look back at the blue extended speaking boxes which occur at the end of each section in the unit.

collect ideas

• Set the scene by telling the class to imagine that they are going to attend a free weekend of English (perhaps in a luxury hotel). Direct them to the programme on *p.53* and give them time to decide which parts they would enjoy most, and compare ideas with a partner. They could also discuss where they would like the weekend to take place.

• Point out **Talk 1** and **Talk 2** in the weekend programme (Saturday and Sunday 2.00 p.m.) and explain that they are going to have a choice of speakers and topics for these talks.

• **Exercise 2** is important as a model for the discussion that they will have in **choose your speakers**. We found that when we prompted learners with ideas and ways of reacting to the talks, they had more to say and the discussion was sustained longer. After exercise 2, you could ask the class for their opinions on this talk.

choose your speakers

• Give learners plenty of time to read and think about the six speakers, and remind them that they have to say what they specially like or dislike about the talk (as in the speech bubbles in **exercise 2**). You could suggest that learners make a few notes on their ideas for each talk if you think that would help your group. They should not have many problems understanding the texts, but if necessary, deal quickly with any words they don't know. Try not to get too involved in vocabulary here, though; the aim is to proceed to the speaking activity as soon as they are ready. Do not worry if there is silence during this phase: learners will need time to concentrate.

• Deal quickly with the **language reminder**, then put the learners in small groups of three if possible (not more than four). Timing for this activity will vary, but allow ten to fifteen minutes. Monitor and make notes on language use, and bring the activity to a close when they are running out of things to say.

Want to know more? Go to **how to ...** monitor and give feedback *p.156*.

decide on a new talk

• This is the learners' opportunity to create their own talk / imaginary speaker. If the groups are working well together, don't change them. Alternatively, you could let the whole class brainstorm topics for talks, then they get together in small groups to develop their preferred talk and write the paragraph. Monitor and correct their writing as necessary.

• You could keep to simple, handwritten descriptions which learners pass to each other; alternatively, you could ask learners to produce a poster for their talk. If you have access to computers, learners could work together on their talks, then compile them into one handout or 'brochure' for the whole class to read in the next lesson.

• The learners' own choice of topics will be interesting for you in terms of lesson planning, and you may find that their talks could spark off a mini-project, where learners prepare the talks and make presentations to the class.

role play

• This role play could be done in the next lesson. Begin by giving learners a few minutes to look back at the **how to ... make a phone call** section on *p.51* and revise their telephone greetings and introductions.

• Reorganize the learners into pairs for the role play. It is important that you allow time for them to plan what they are going to say. Make sure that they are either writing / planning their questions or, in the case of the student of English, completing the information.

• Change the seating arrangements if possible (see **ideas plus**), then make a ringing noise and tell the guest speaker to pick up the phone and speak, otherwise learners may take a while to get going.

• Monitor the activity. If you can see a common problem that is impeding their performance, e.g. they aren't being clear enough about the dates / times, give them some quick feedback after the first role play so that they can improve when they swap roles and do it again. Remember to allow time for them to prepare their new role cards.

feedback checklist

During the **extended speaking** activity, note down examples of …

- **good language use**

- **effective communication strategies**
  (turn-taking, interrupting, inviting others to speak, etc.)

- **learner errors**
  (vocabulary, grammar, pronunciation, etc.)

- **particular communication problems**

Make sure you allow time for feedback at the end of the lesson. You can use the notes you make above to <u>praise</u> effective language use and communication or, if necessary, to do some remedial work.

---

ideas plus phone call role plays

When learners are going to role play phone conversations, it is more realistic if they rearrange their chairs so that they are sitting back-to-back, and can't see each other. Alternatively, seat them so that one person is speaking over the other's shoulder; this is a quieter option.

In this particular context, especially if the classroom is noisy, learners may need to ask for clarification and repetition. Notice whether they are using appropriate language. If necessary, feed it in after the first attempt at the role play.

Most learners enjoy phone call role plays. They can liven up an everyday conversation, provide a bit of challenge, and also revise phone greetings.You could, for instance, do a warmer at the beginning of a lesson where pairs sit back to back and ring each other to find out how they are, what they did last night and what they are doing at the weekend.

Want to know more? Go to **how to ...** do free speaking (role play issues) *p.166*.

test yourself!

Want to know more? Go to the **introduction** *p.7* for ways of using **test yourself!**

1 documentaries, quiz shows, news and current affairs, drama series, chat shows, soap operas, comedies
2 sparkling, mixed, rare, sweetener, fries
3 boring, talk, views, subject, Sorry?

1 I'd rather go out tonight.
2 Sorry, I didn't quite catch that.
3 It doesn't appeal to me.
4 It's great fun.

1 Hello is that Claudio? Yes, **it is**.
2 I'm not very interest**ed** in music.
3 OK, I**'ll** go.
4 I'm sure that programme **would** be fascinating.

five

wordlist

natural English

thanking and replying
Thanks a lot / very much.
Thank you (very much indeed).
That was / 's very kind of you.

No problem.
That's OK.
Don't mention it.

suggestions and responses
Why don't you ... ?
Have you thought about ... ?
You could ...

That's a good idea.
I'm not sure about that.
That sounds sensible.

intensifying adverbs
extremely (uncomfortable)
unbelievably (lazy)
incredibly (easy)

it depends
It depends who / what kind of / why / how / if / whether ...
It depends on ...

generalizations (1)
Generally, I think most people ...
People tend to ...
It's not very common for people to ...

giving instructions
The most important thing is to ...
The first thing is to ...
Don't forget to ...
Make sure ...

vocabulary

clothes and dressing
suit
tracksuit
trainers
tie
shorts
jewellery
T-shirt
top
evening dress
sandals
casually / smartly-dressed
trendy
elegant
scruffy ◉

supermarkets
till
trolley
cashier
carrier bag
shelves
basket
checkout
wheels
goods

wordbooster

shopping
pack your (goods / shopping)
attract / get sb's attention
serve customers
do the shopping
stand / wait in a queue
push in
order (goods / shopping)
go shopping

uses of *get*
1 = buy / obtain
2 = receive
3 = arrive / reach

glossaries
well-behaved
thrilled
quid ◉
mean (adj)
can't afford
chauffeur
solve a problem
stare (v)
upset (adj)

behave yourself!

life with Agrippine   20 – 25 mins

read for pleasure
nE phrases for thanking and replying

- You could start by telling the class about a present you received recently: Who gave it to you? Why? How did you feel?

- Make sure that learners understand the adjectives in **cartoon time** before they read, i.e. *well-behaved*, *generous*, etc.

- For the **natural English** box, start by drilling different combinations of the thanks and replies round the class to check learners are saying them appropriately. Before they discuss the situations in the **natural English** box, you could give the class the information from **language point** below. They could compare this with responses in their own culture.

cartoon time
Agrippine: badly-behaved and rude
Byron: rude
Auntie Mo: kind and generous

---

language point thanking and replying

We can respond to *thank you* in various ways in English (*that's OK*, *no problem*, *don't mention it*, etc.) but unlike some languages, these replies are not compulsory. It is only necessary to respond verbally to thanks for 'big' things, e.g. when someone thanks you for a present you gave them. On other occasions, a smile, nod of the head, or wave of the hand is sufficient, e.g. in service encounters such as shops and bars.

---

reading those difficult situations ...

make and respond to suggestions using **natural English** phrases

read and discuss a joke problem page

talk about themselves using **natural English** intensifying adverbs

focus on adjectives and adverbs and use them to talk about themselves

lead-in

- Give learners a minute to think about **exercise 1**, then have a class feedback at the end.

- For the language in the **natural English** box, encourage learners to copy the stress and intonation on the recording. You can ask them to memorize the dialogues and say them without the book or recording.

- In **exercise 2**, divide the class into pairs and tell them who is A or B. Remember that learners will need to look at each other's problems and decide what suggestions to make. After **exercise 3**, put each pair with another pair so that they can act out their conversations and compare their ideas.

read on

- Before they read, you can ask learners if they ever read problem pages in newspapers or magazines. If so, what kind of problems do people write about? Do they get good advice? This will lead in to the reading activity.

- Learners should read the text then complete the glossary. The aim of this is to encourage learners to guess meaning from context. In this instance, you may find it easy enough to incorporate **exercise 2** at the same time.

- In **exercise 3**, the first question is important. If learners mistakenly think this is a serious text, it is important to make clear that it isn't! The answers are clearly either silly or implausible.

- The meaning of the intensifying adverbs in the **natural English** box should be clear from the explanations. It was obvious from our data that adverbs such as these are rarely part of an intermediate learner's productive vocabulary. Do encourage your learners to try and use them, and not rely just on *very* to emphasize a gradable adjective. Check that the learners are pronouncing and stressing the adverbs as on the recording.

- While learners are doing **exercise 5**, monitor their use of the adverbs in the **natural English** box and correct any problems with stress and intonation.

grammar adjectives and adverbs

- If you prefer to avoid starting with an analytical approach to adjectives and adverbs as in **exercise 1**, you could introduce the grammar in different ways (see **troubleshooting** on the right). Learners can work together to do the exercise or compare afterwards.

Want to know more? Go to **how to ...** introduce new language *p.144*.

- Before the lesson, look at the **cover & check** exercises in the **language reference** on *p.160* so that you can decide whether there are particular exercises you may need to use with your group in the lesson.

ideas plus problems and suggestions

As an alternative to **exercise 2** you could ask the class to brainstorm problems relevant to their own lives. Put a list on the board, then ask learners to each choose a problem. They can then continue as in **exercise 2**, i.e. show their partner the problem, so they can decide what suggestions to make.

exercise 1 glossary
money; driver; solution; look

exercise 2
1 Sleeping Beauty   2 Please save our marriage!   3 Red faces in public

ideas plus problem page

Before they read the text, ask learners in pairs to decide what they might write about to a problem page. It could be something light hearted (as in **Best Behaviour**), or it could be something more serious. Then follow the rest of the lesson in the **student's book**. At the end, go back to the learners' ideas. They should work together to write a short letter to a problem page, if possible incorporating one or two adjective / adverb constructions from the lesson. In the next lesson, they swap letters with another pair. Now they have to write a reply to the letter they received, offering advice, and send it back. During the planning and writing stages, monitor and give feedback as necessary.

exercise 1
1 adjectives   2 adverbs   3 adjectives   4 adverbs   5 adverbs, adjectives

exercise 2

reacts angrily: rule 2	*extremely uncomfortable*: rule 5
play it loudly: rule 2	*lovely man*: rule 1
artificial way: rule 1	*extremely kind*: rule 5
incredibly unpleasant: rule 5	*feel embarrassed*: rule 3
drives fast and dangerously: rule 2	*badly-behaved*: rule 4

exercise 3
1 loud   2 angry   3 smartly, casually   4 fast
5 carefully   6 incredibly   7 good   8 slowly

troubleshooting appproaches to grammar

1 Give learners sentences to complete (based on grammar rules 1 to 5), e.g. *I'm wearing _____ shoes today. My teacher speaks English _____. It feels _____ outside today.* Learners complete the sentences and you go over their answers, correcting where appropriate, and build up the rules on the board. Then do **exercises 2** and **3**.

2 You could use another diagnostic approach and start with **exercise 3**. Learners could compare and justify their answers in pairs; then, in feedback, you can go through the exercise and put the rules on the board, or get them to complete **exercise 1**. Finally, do **exercise 4**.

listening getting dressed up

talk about what to wear on special occasions using **natural English** phrases

revise and expand vocabulary on clothes and dressing

listen to anecdotes about wearing the wrong clothes

talk about their experiences

talk about appropriate clothes for different occasions using **natural English** phrases

lead-in

- The best starting point here is for you to model **exercise 1** yourself by telling the class about a recent experience you have had. When learners are telling their own stories, monitor for any particularly interesting or amusing stories which you can ask those learners to tell the class at the end.

- When you have been through the answers to the **natural English** box, you may need to focus on word order (see **language point**).

- Give an oral model of the sentences in the **natural English** box, so that learners can copy your stress and intonation before practising the sentences with a partner.

Want to know more? Go to **how to ...** teach listening (teacher talk) *p.153.*

vocabulary clothes and dressing

- Some of the vocabulary items in **exercise 1** will be known, but you can ask learners to look at the pictures and see if there are any items they don't know. Refer them to the vocabulary box to see if they can identify the correct word, and clarify any further difficulties. Then give them 30 seconds to memorize the words and pictures.

- Learners are more likely to say *A man is wearing …* than the more natural *There's a man wearing …* so you may need to highlight this before they begin the pair activity.

- **Exercise 3** is a quick revision activity. You could make it a competitive game. Give pairs a time limit, say, of 60 to 90 seconds in which they have to write down at least ten more items. In feedback, one pair reads out their ten items of clothing while other pairs cross off any which they mention; for every item the others have left, they get two points. The winner is the pair with the highest score. Remember too that learners' dictionaries often have visuals of clothing; these are useful for learners to know about.

- Tell learners to circle the verbs in the sentences in **exercise 4**, and quickly check that they understand them, particularly: *get dressed up* = put on smart clothes, usually for a special occasion, *get changed* = change the clothes you are wearing.

  Some nationalities confuse *wear* and *carry*: *wear* = have clothes / jewellery / glasses on your body, *carry* = have / take something in your hands or arms, e.g. *carry an umbrella*.

- Monitor the group work and listen for language to give feedback on afterwards (see **troubleshooting**).

listen to this

- If you have your own story about wearing the wrong clothes for an occasion, tell it as a warmer.

- To set the scene for the listening activity, learners should look at the pictures of Major and Mrs Wise, and say how they look: are they friendly? formal? serious? rich? Let them do the prediction activity (which will tune them in to the story) in small groups. Don't correct their ideas at this stage; play the first part, then let them compare. You may need to remind them about the meaning of *fancy dress* = special clothes that make you look like somebody famous or unusual. After the listening, highlight: *outrageous* = very unusual, funny, or shocking, and *scream* = cry out very loudly.

- For **exercise 2**, learners don't need a word-perfect answer, simply the gist of the story, as in the answer key. Replay **part 1** if they haven't understood it, but don't worry about detail.

- Before you listen in **exercise 4**, you could pre-teach: *silk* = a fine, smooth, usually expensive fabric, *in shirtsleeves* = just wearing a shirt, not a jacket, *casual* = not formal, relaxed. Trude speaks very clearly.

- Give learners a minute to think about **exercise 5**. If necessary, prompt them with some ideas, e.g. weddings, parties, interviews, sporting activities, going on a date. If only a few people can think of a story put each of them in a small group. Stories may occur to other learners during the activity.

- Make it clear that you are moving on to a language focus in the **natural English** box on generalizations. When learners have matched the phrases with the situations in **exercise 6**, drill the sentences.

nE *it depends ...*

1b   2d   3a   4e   5f   6c

exercise 3 possible answers

It depends how much money you have.

It depends what time of year it is.

It depends who is going to pay
for the clothes.

It depends how well you know
the person / people.

It depends what kind of wedding it is.

It depends what other people will be
wearing.

It depends whether there's a party
afterwards or not.

It depends whose wedding it is.

---

language point *it depends ...*

There are a number of pitfalls with this verb.

1 Learners often use the wrong preposition, e.g. *it
depends ~~of~~ the weather*.

2 They confuse the form and produce ~~*it's depend*~~.

3 When *it depends* is followed by a *wh-* clause, they
sometimes use interrogative word order, e.g. *it
depends ~~where are you going~~*.

Be prepared to highlight these errors if they arise.

---

exercise 1 from left to right:

There's a girl wearing shorts, a T-shirt, and sandals.

There's a man wearing a suit and a tie.

There's a woman wearing an evening dress and jewellery.

There's a girl wearing jeans and a top.

There's a boy wearing a tracksuit and trainers.

exercise 2 from left to right:

scruffy, smartly dressed, elegant, trendy, casually dressed

---

troubleshooting personalized activities

The majority of learners enjoy and benefit from
personalized activities; they are accessible and can be
very memorable. Occasionally, however, they can be
too personal, and it is not always obvious when
someone is likely to be sensitive to a topic. If you
think a personalized activity is potentially very
sensitive for the class, then you should adapt the
exercise or avoid it. We would urge you to take a few
risks, though; otherwise your learners will be
restricted to fairly bland forms of practice. If you are
slightly worried about an activity, you can always tell
learners that they can refuse to answer certain
questions. It's a good idea to teach them these very
useful phrases: *I'm sorry, I'd prefer not to answer that*,
or *I'd rather not say*, or even *That's none of your
business!* This allows them to edit the conversation as
they would do in real life.

---

exercise 2

Tom's father rang Major and Mrs Wise (a very formal
couple) to invite them to another neighbour's drinks
party. He told them it was a fancy dress party.

exercise 3

suits; dresses; Tarzan and Jane; Me Tarzan; spoke to
us again.

exercise 4

Trude wore elegant clothes to a wedding. Everyone
else was wearing jeans, and she felt like an idiot.

exercise 6

1   *People tend to ...*

2   *It's not very common ...*

3   *Generally, I think ...*

---

troubleshooting adapting tasks for listening

It would be extremely difficult to provide listening tasks to suit intermediate
learners in every teaching situation around the world. Learners in an English-
speaking country often find listening easier than those studying in their own
country, simply because they have more exposure and therefore more practice. We
feel the recordings themselves are appropriate and achievable for intermediate
learners (indeed, they need this kind of exposure to natural English), but you can
adapt the exercises in **tune in**, **listen carefully**, and **listening challenge** to make
them easier or more challenging. For instance, in **exercise 3**, you can make the task
more challenging by giving learners sentences to complete, e.g. *At the party, the
men_____. The women _____. Major and Mrs
Wise_____*, etc. Or make Trude's story in the **listening challenge** easier by
giving them a little background, e.g. *Trude went to a wedding. How do you think she
was dressed? What was everyone else wearing?* (Tell learners to bear in mind that the
recordings are about people wearing the wrong clothes.)

Want to know more? Go to **how to ...** teach listening (live listening) *p.153.*

 ## wordbooster

shopping

This **wordbooster** is best used before the **how to ...** section as the shopping vocabulary will be useful.

- **Exercise 1** is a collocation exercise. You will need to point out the difference between: *do the shopping* = buy food, or things that you need regularly and *go shopping* = go to the shops, often for pleasure, e.g. to buy clothes, etc. The plural noun, *goods*, is used to refer to things produced to be sold, e.g. sports goods, expensive goods.

uses of *get*

- Spray diagrams like the one for *get* are quite an attractive way for learners to store key words. You could revise meanings of verbs like *take* and *give* in this way. One approach would be to put the skeleton spray diagram on the board, and ask the learners to put the examples in **exercise 1** in the appropriate place.

Want to know more? Go to **how to...** activate vocabulary *p.136*.

how to ... explain what to do

learn supermarket vocabulary

focus on modal verbs of obligation and permission and use them to **talk** about supermarket behaviour

listen to someone give instructions for looking after a shop

role play giving instructions

vocabulary supermarkets

- Tell learners to look at the vocabulary box and point to the items in the picture so that you can check they understand the words. Drill any items which are difficult to pronounce, i.e. the ones in phonemic script. Elicit from the class a sentence describing the picture, then tell them in pairs to continue, using all the words in the vocabulary box.

grammar obligation and permission

- Play the recording for **exercise 1**, then elicit the answers and put them on the board so that learners can check their spelling and you can highlight forms, e.g. *mustn't ~~to~~*, *don't have <u>to</u>*, *aren't allow<u>ed</u> to*, etc. Then let learners practise the contractions in whole sentences.

- Modal verbs are potentially quite difficult for learners, and you may find it useful to refer to the **language reference** on *p.160* and *p.161* for guidance before you teach this lesson, and to see if there are **cover & check** exercises you want to use. However, most of the language in **exercise 2** will be revision; the form that they are least likely to know is *be allowed to*, and the form that they will most misuse or confuse is *don't have to*. There is also a considerable degree of overlap between *shouldn't* and *mustn't*.

- As a lead-in to **exercise 3**, ask learners about local supermarkets. Which do they use? How often do they go there? What do they think of supermarket shopping? Direct them to the supermarket 'rules' and discuss the first example together, correcting it appropriately in terms of meaning. (The forms are all correct.)

- For **exercise 4**, if you have a multilingual class, make up the groups with learners of different nationalities, as differences in supermarket 'rules' in different countries should generate discussion and more language practice.

look after a shop

- Use **exercises 1** and **2** to set the scene and make the listening activity more accessible. You could elicit the group's ideas for exercise 2 and write them on the board, which will help with the feedback for **exercise 3**. Before you listen in exercise 3, you could pre-teach: *bear in mind* = remember, *sneak* (v) = steal something small, *change* (n) = the money you get back if you pay more than something costs, *stocktaking* = keeping a list of all the goods in a shop. If there are other instructions in the listening which aren't on the board, play the tape again for learners to identify them.

exercise 1

1 serving
2 go
3 do
4 push in
5 get, attract
6 order
7 pack, put
8 stand, wait

exercise 1

1A 2B 3A 4A 5C 6B 7C 8A

exercise 2 possible answers

1 me some aspirin
2 home last night
3 a letter from my girlfriend
4 those shoes
5 two messages
6 something to eat

language point *get*

Get is the most common verb in spoken English, but is rarely used in formal written English where it is considered too informal. The reason for its frequency in spoken English is its versatility. It has many different meanings and grammatical forms, e.g. *have got, have got to,* and it combines with different particles to form many common phrasal verbs, e.g. *get on, get by,* etc.

Want to know more? Go to **unit seven**, *p.84* and **unit ten**, *p.117.*

exercise 1

The *checkout* is the whole area shown by the arrow in the picture. The *cashier*'s left hand is on the *till*. The *carrier bags* are hanging at the end of the conveyor belt and the *baskets* are on the floor next to them. The *trolley* is in the foreground and you can see three of its *wheels*. The *goods* are on the *shelves* in the background.

exercise 1

1 should leave
2 aren't allowed to take
3 mustn't push in
4 don't have to make
5 shouldn't leave

exercise 2

1b 2e 3a 4f 5g 6c 7d

exercise 3

These answers are based on Britain. Answers will depend on the country / group.
1 false (except for guide dogs for the blind) - *you aren't allowed to*
2 false - *you should*
3 it depends - most of the time you have to, but in some places you get help
4 false - you don't have to buy a minimum of five things
5 true
6 true
7 false - you don't have to pay by credit card
8 false - it is very common to put small children in a special seat in the trolley
9 false - you don't have to; you can take a basket or just carry things in your hands
10 true

ideas plus further practice

For further practice or in place of **exercise 4**, you could give learners in pairs a topic, e.g. travelling on a train or bus, being a pedestrian, or being a learner in a language class. Ask them to write down six sentences using the target language from **exercise 3**. Their sentences should contain some 'dos and don'ts' which are false, as in the supermarket list. They then pass their list to another pair, who have to make all the sentences true. You may even decide to adapt the material in exercise 3 and produce a set of 'rules' on a different topic as the basis of your presentation.

exercise 3

make sure people don't steal things; check people's money and their change; you mustn't sell cigarettes to children; ask for identity if you think they are under 16 and want to buy cigarettes.

exercise 4

The first thing is to ...
Make sure ...

extended speaking bar etiquette

60 – 70 mins

read about how people behave in bars in Britain and California

discuss how bars are different in the learners' country

produce an information sheet

- It is important at the beginning of this activity to let learners read the left-hand column or tell them what they are going to do in the lesson, or put it on the board. This will enable them to get the whole picture. You should also give them time to look back at the blue **extended speaking** boxes which occur at the end of each section in the unit.

collect ideas

- You could set the scene by getting learners to talk about which bars or cafés they go to regularly in their town, which they like / don't like, and why. Alternatively, direct them to the photos of bars in Britain and California. Which are most like bars in their country and why? Do they like the look of these bars? Why / why not?

- In **exercises 1** and **2**, you may feel your group needs extra support. If so, divide the class in half, and let learners who read the same text work together. Once they have read their text, they can discuss the most important points and practise giving the information so that they can do it without looking. It is important that they <u>don't</u> talk about bars in their own country at this stage. Then regroup the learners into A / B pairs for **exercises 2** and **3**. Monitor this activity to see how well they are communicating. You may notice problems with modal verbs; you should decide if you want to intervene at this stage so that they can be more accurate in the next discussion, or wait until the end to avoid interrupting the flow of the activity.

focus on your country

- The way you manage this part of the activity will depend whether you are working with monolingual or multilingual groups. In either case, impress upon learners the importance of adding their own opinions about bars.

  – If you have a monolingual group, follow the procedure in **exercises 4** and **5**. You will find that even within one nationality group, there will be different perceptions about bars and cafés. This will provoke discussion and provide realistic speaking practice.

  – If you have a multilingual group, put learners in small groups of different nationalities. They should tell each other about bars in their country, and discuss the differences between them. They should then write their information sheet at home in their own time, and show it to a partner in the next lesson. If you have several people of the same nationality, they could work together on the writing task or at least compare their final information sheets.

produce an information sheet

- Go over the checklist with the class so that they are clear what to do. You may want to do the third point as a class, i.e. looking for useful words and phrases.

- You should decide whether each member of the group should write a sheet or whether one person should do it. If you want learners to compare with a new partner in **exercise 7**, you will either need to make photocopies for each person, or each member will have to write out the sheet. Alternatively, you could put their sheets up on the walls and tell learners to walk round discussing differences with a partner. Afterwards, you may wish to display their sheets on a wall poster.

- When they have finished **exercise 7**, you should give the group some feedback on what they have achieved, and on their language use.

Want to know more? Go to **how to ...** monitor and give feedback *p.156.*

feedback checklist

During the **extended speaking** activity, note down examples of …

- **good language use**

- **effective communication strategies**
  (turn-taking, interrupting, inviting others to speak, etc.)

- **learner errors**
  (vocabulary, grammar, pronunciation, etc.)

- **particular communication problems**

Make sure you allow time for feedback at the end of the lesson. You can use the notes you make above to <u>praise</u> effective language use and communication or, if necessary, to do some remedial work.

test yourself!

Want to know more? Go to the **introduction** *p.7* for ways of using **test yourself!**

1 no problem, that's OK, don't mention it
2 till, shelves, trolley, basket, carrier bag, checkout
3 get / attract, stand / wait, do, go

1 You don't have to do that.
2 Are you allowed to sit on the grass in this park?
3 Make sure you shut the windows.
4 Do you drive fast?

1 You don't have to do it now.
2 It depends how you are travelling.
3 Have you thought about giving up smoking?
4 We all wear casual clothes here.

six

wordlist

natural English

giving and responding to exciting news
You'll never guess (what's happened)!
You won't believe (who is outside)!
What? You're joking!
No, really?

attitude adverbs
fortunately
hopefully
surprisingly

I don't think (that) ...
I don't think that's (a good idea).
I don't think (he should take the job).

advantages and disadvantages
The main advantage of (working abroad) is ...
Another advantage is ...
The disadvantage of (this job) is ...

sort / kind / type
What
sort of
kind of business are you in?
type of

ending a phone conversation
OK. I think that's everything I need.
OK. I think I've got all the details I need.
Thanks. You've been very helpful.
Thanks very much for your help.
Bye bye / Goodbye

vocabulary

jobs in a company
managing director
IT technician
financial controller
personnel manager
factory supervisor
management consultant

education
go to school / university
do a degree / a course
turn down an offer / a place at college
take a year off / an exam
leave school / home / university
get a grant / qualification

agreeing and disagreeing
I (don't) agree with that.
You're absolutely right.
I'm not sure I agree.
I'm not so sure about that.
I don't agree with that at all.

course enquiries
enrol (v)
brochure
application form
pay a deposit
fees
qualification
entry requirements
certificate

wordbooster

stages in a career
do a degree
apply for a job
get (a bit / a lot of) experience
work for a company
take a risk
borrow money
set up a company / business
give up (a job)

phrases in sequences
find a job
get married
settle down
start a family
have a baby
carry on (doing sth)
go back to work
look after (a baby / child)
take (six months / a year) off

glossaries
salesman
sales manager
colleague
eventually
'A' level exam
instead of

in unit six ...

do you get it?
joke a bad memory
vocabulary jobs in a company
natural English phrases giving and responding to exciting news

reading filling a gap
vocabulary education
grammar *if*, *when*, *unless*
reading Where do we go from here?
natural English *fortunately*, *hopefully*, *surprisingly*

wordbooster
stages in a career
learning phrases in sequences

listening for and against
vocabulary agreeing and disagreeing
natural English *I don't think* (*that*) ...
listening advantages and disadvantages
natural English phrases for talking about advantages and disadvantages
grammar *-ing* form

how to ... enquire about a course
vocabulary course enquiries
listening phone for information
natural English *sort, kind, type*
natural English phrases ending a phone conversation

extended speaking decisions, decisions
collect ideas read a case study about a couple who have to make an important decision
reach a decision discuss the advantages and disadvantages of the situation and decide on the best course of action
listen find out the couple's decision

test yourself!
revision and progress check

do you get it?   20 – 25 mins

> **listen** for pleasure
> **nE** phrases giving and responding to exciting news
> **vocabulary** jobs in a company

- To start learners off you could give a few examples of things to do with memory, e.g. remembering people's faces but not their names, having to write down dates and appointments in a diary, learning facts for tests and exams, etc.
- Before they talk in pairs about the pictures in **joke time**, get the class to point out the people highlighted in the glossary. Check the pronunciation of *colleague* /'kɒliːɡ/.
- When you go to the **natural English** box, see if learners can remember which phrase was in the joke, so that they make the link between the input and the joke. (It was the first phrase.) Check they can pronounce *guess* /ɡes/.
- Drill the vocabulary when you go over the answers to **jobs in a company**, checking pronunciation and word stress.

> **jobs in a company**
> 1 financial controller   4 IT technician
> 2 managing director   5 management consultant
> 3 personnel manager   6 factory supervisor

> **language point** giving and responding to exciting news
>
> If learners ask you about the use of *will* and the present perfect in the **natural English** box examples, you will need to explain that *will* is used here to express certainty or confidence about a present (or future) situation. Otherwise, we would advise you not to draw attention to this. We think that *you'll never guess ...* and *you won't believe ...* are best learnt as lexical phrases.
>
> The present perfect has already been looked at in unit one *p.14*, to talk about something that happened a short time ago and is important now.

reading filling a gap

learn education vocabulary and use it to talk about themselves

focus on *if*, *when*, and *unless* in zero and first conditional sentences

read and discuss an article about school leavers

focus on **natural English** adverbs showing feelings and opinions

talk about how to spend a gap year

vocabulary education

- The vocabulary in **exercise 1** will be useful for the speaking activity in **exercise 2**. Many of these items are useful verb + noun collocations which learners often don't know, e.g. *take a year off, do a degree*. Learners can do the exercise, then compare with a partner. When you go over the answers, it is worth pointing out what the correct collocation would be in the examples, i.e. *go to a language school*, **have / follow a career**, *do / take an exam, do research, do a course*.

- For **exercise 2**, you can either keep **A**s and **B**s separate or mix them in small groups. Monitor, and get one or two learners to share their experiences with the class at the end.

grammar sentences with *if*, *when*, and *unless*

- While learners are reading the text in **exercise 1** and thinking about the questions, you could write the sentences numbered 1 to 4 from the text on the board or show them on an overhead projector (OHP). You will find it easier to highlight the verb forms and the conjunctions. If you think it is appropriate with your class, you could compare the structures in L1 and L2 to highlight any differences.

- You can do the pronunciation practice in **exercise 2** as a class before learners work in pairs. You will need to highlight contractions, *won't* /wəʊnt/, and stress and intonation.

example

If she gets a job and lives at home, she'll be able to save money.

- Learners can work alone or in pairs for **exercise 3**. If they work alone, give them time to compare in pairs before going over the answers together.

- **Exercise 4** can be done orally, or learners can note down sentences together.

Want to know more? Go to **how to ...** introduce new language *p.143*.

read on

- Look at **ideas plus** on the right for a way of beginning the lesson.

- Learners have already talked about what to do when leaving school, so you can lead in to the text quickly. This introductory paragraph sets the scene for the two case studies.

- For the jigsaw reading activity in **exercises 2** and **3**, follow the procedure suggested in **troubleshooting** unit four *p.45*. **Exercise 3** gives learners a chance to discuss freely what they think of the two situations. Make sure they have time to do this, as it will increase the variety in the lesson. If necessary, learners can explain the glossary words to each other. You have the option of asking learners to read each others' texts at the end if they wish.

- The adverbs in the **natural English** box are extremely common, but intermediate learners rarely use them. Learners can do **exercise 4** together or alone; you can ask them to call out their sentence endings in class feedback and correct them as appropriate.

it's your turn!

- Learners are asked to give reasons why they would / wouldn't like to do the activities so that they will come to the discussion with more to say, and be able to develop it. If your learners need a lot of help, you could let them prepare their answers in pairs, then reorganize them into different groups for **exercise 2**. If there are particular activities that would work well in your teaching context and would generate a lot of discussion, you should adapt the activity. While they are talking, monitor and do feedback at the end, both on the content and the language used.

exercise 1

do a career, turn down an exam, take research, get a course; (*leave school / home / university* are all possible)

exercise 1

a present simple and *will* + verb. She's not sure she will get a job, but it's possible.

b *will* + verb and present simple. She's sure she'll go to university.

c *won't* + verb and present simple. *Unless she does it now* means *if she <u>doesn't</u> do it now*, so *unless* means *if* + *not*.

d because she is talking about something which is always true whenever something happens.

e 1: no; *if* is necessary because the sentence is hypothetical. 4: yes, because this is always true.

exercise 3

1 when   2 If   3 unless   4 unless   5 If
6 offer; I'll   7 I'll; don't   8 don't; won't

language point *if*, *when*, and *unless*

If and *when* are sometimes confused because of L1 transfer, e.g. *wenn* in German means *if*. Many nationalities tend to put a future form in *if* / *when* sentences in English through mother tongue transfer, e.g. *I'll phone you when ~~I will get home~~.*

Unless can often be used in place of *if not*. However, there are times we don't usually use *unless*, for instance, in unreal situations where something isn't true, especially those involving emotions, e.g.
I would be angry if he didn't come. / I would be angry ~~unless he came~~.
I'd be astonished if Maurice Green didn't win the gold medal. / I'd be astonished ~~unless Maurice Green won~~ the gold medal.
It is also worth remembering that *unless* is stronger than *if not*, e.g. *She won't take the job unless she gets a company car = She will <u>only</u> take the job if she gets a company car.*

exercise 1

The three things are: stay in Britain and work; go abroad and work; find a permanent job and study in the company's time.

nE

A *line 15: Fortunately, they speak English there ...*

B *line 26: ... but, surprisingly perhaps, she turned it down.*

B *line 40: Hopefully, I won't regret it.*

ideas plus discussing the topic

Before learners read the texts about school leavers, you could give them a short talk on a different education system that you know well, e.g. British, American, Australian, etc. If you are a non-native speaker teacher you will find some useful information about the school / university system in *The Longman Essential Activator* (*Education Word Bank*). You could give them a table to complete with children's ages down the left-hand column and spaces to complete on the right. Learners can then compare the differences between their own and another education system.

ideas plus vocabulary search

Throughout this lesson, there is a lot of useful vocabulary to do with education. In the next lesson, you could start by asking learners in pairs to go through the material on *pp.70–73* and their notes again and make a list of all the words and phrases relating to education. They should then try to organize them into categories of their choosing, e.g. words and phrases in a chronological sequence (*nursery school, primary school,* etc.); opposites (*pass / fail an exam*); collocations (*leave school, do a degree*); types of qualifications, etc. This is a useful revision activity, and provides a clear record for their vocabulary notebooks. In addition, it will lead into the **wordbooster** section which includes the idea of using chronology to aid vocabulary storage and retrieval.

Want to know more? Go to **how to ...** activate vocabulary *p.136*.

 wordbooster

> This **wordbooster** can be used at any point in the unit.

stages in a career

- Notice that there are two meanings of *get* in the exercise: *get experience* = obtain, and *get married* = become. Learners could add these to the word spray diagram they produced in **wordbooster** *p.63*.

- When learners are going to begin putting the stages in order, elicit the first couple of stages from the group to check they understand the exercise. If they have dictionaries, they can use them during the activity or they can consult a partner or you as a final resort to check words they don't know. In feedback, elicit the logical order and highlight / check any new vocabulary, e.g. *set up a business, carry on, settle down*. Learners have difficulties with accuracy in these phrases, so you should also get them to highlight prepositions that go with the verbs / nouns, e.g. *work for, apply for, a degree in*. When they test each other in **exercise 2**, encourage them to correct accuracy errors.

learning phrases in sequences

- The aim of this is to give learners a framework for lexical storage to which they can add new vocabulary as they encounter it.

listening for and against

> **talk** about who they agree / disagree with
>
> **talk** about issues using vocabulary and **natural English** phrases
>
> **listen** to people talking about work situations
>
> **talk** about advantages and disadvantages relating to work using **natural English** phrases
>
> **focus** on *-ing* form and agree / disagree with statements

vocabulary agreeing and disagreeing

- A good way to introduce the warmer in **exercise 1** is to give some examples of your own.

- Once learners have put the phrases in the speech bubbles in order, focus on pronunciation in **exercise 4**. Give models yourself with contractions, and encourage learners to copy your intonation. If you like, give them quick prompts to agree / disagree with, e.g. teenagers are better with computers than adults; children should start school at four, etc. The **natural English** box highlights a very common problem, so draw your learners' attention to it.

- In **exercise 5**, you may wish to provide other statements for discussion which are particularly relevant to your learners and would generate discussion. Make sure that learners are practising some of the phrases they have learnt.

listen to this

- Thinking about the advantages and disadvantages listed in **exercise 1** will help learners to tune in to the topic and make the listening more accessible. (The ideas are not expressed in exactly the same words on the recording, of course.) Learners will also be familiar with the phrases before they do the task in **exercise 3**. Be prepared to explain any words they don't know in sentences **a** to **g**, and replay the **tune in** section if they haven't grasped the answer. After **exercise 3**, you could highlight: *consequently* = as a result, *look forward to* = feel positive about a future event, *on the whole* = in general.

- In **exercise 4**, learners will find the recording easier to follow if they do this prediction exercise, perhaps in pairs. If you like, you could elicit their ideas and write them on the board. Don't say if they are correct at this stage.

- The **natural English** phrases will be very useful later in the **extended speaking** activity. At this point you should also highlight the *-ing* form in the phrase *the main advantage of working* … , and practise the phrases orally with the class.

grammar *-ing* form

- **Exercise 1** is designed to encourage learners to notice the very simple rule of use from a number of examples, i.e. preposition + *-ing*.

- In **exercise 2**, once you have demonstrated the pauses with the first couple of examples, tell learners in pairs to decide where the other pauses are. This is an exercise in identifying sense groups and to some extent a test of understanding. You will probably need to model a couple of sentences orally before they read in pairs in **exercise 3**.

exercise 1 logical answers

A you do a degree in business studies / you apply for a job / you work for a company for a few years / you get a lot of experience in the area / you decide to take a risk / you give up your job / you borrow money from the bank / you set up your own business

B you find a job in the computer industry / you get married / you settle down and decide to start a family / you carry on working for a few months / you take six months off work / you have a baby / you look after the baby / you go back to work

ideas plus sequencing activities

A useful warmer activity is to think of stages in other sequences, e.g. buying something to wear / going to a restaurant / starting a new relationship. You can choose the theme of the sequence to revise or introduce a topic. See **learning phrases in sequences** in the following activity.

Want to know more? Go to **how to ...** activate vocabulary (sequences) *p.140*.

exercise 1 possible phrases
you see a job you like / you apply for the job / they invite you to go for an interview / you have an interview / they offer you the job / you accept / you sign a contract

exercise 3
I agree with that.
You're absolutely right.
I'm not so sure about that.
I'm not sure I agree.
I don't agree with that.
I don't think that's true at all.

language point agreeing and disagreeing

There are a number of pitfalls with agreeing and disagreeing in English.

• A very common error is that learners use the verb *be* with *agree* through L1 transfer, e.g. *I am agree / disagree*.

• There are also cultural issues: many British speakers tend not to be very direct when disagreeing, and they will often use phrases of partial agreement, especially with people they do not know well. Phrases such as *I completely disagree / I disagree with you* can sound rude, particularly to strangers or acquaintances. Using *that* in place of *you* softens the phrase slightly, as does *I think / I don't think* used at the beginning of the phrase.

exercise 1
advantages: a, d, e   disadvantages: b, c, f, g

exercise 2
Chris mentions point d (job security).

exercise 3
Chris mentions points a, e, c, and f. He's generally happy; he says, *On the whole, I love it.*

exercise 1
a preposition

exercise 2
2 ... job **||** before ...   5 ... jobs **||** immediately ...
3 ... family **||** instead of ... 6 ... company **||** is that ...
4 ... business **||** without ...

ideas plus sentence search

As an alternative to **exercise 1** you could cut sentences 1 to 6 in half (or write them out on pieces of paper), jumble them up and hand out a half sentence to everyone in the class. Learners think of possible endings / beginnings (in pairs, so you can monitor as they discuss their ideas), then they mingle to find the rest of their sentence. Point out the *-ing* rule and focus on the pause as in **exercises 1** and **2**.

how to ... enquire about a course

70 – 80 mins

vocabulary course enquiries

- You could start this lesson by getting learners to talk about other courses they do / have done: professional courses or hobby courses; where they did them and why, what they learnt, what they thought of them. Start this speaking activity by highlighting the collocation *do a course* on the board.

- For **exercise 1**, learners could use dictionaries and shared knowledge to work out the meanings. You could draw a table with three columns on the board and elicit the answers to the exercise. Learners can then copy these into their vocabulary notebooks. Clarify any problems in feedback, and check pronunciation.

- The questionnaire includes some questions of fact and some of opinion, so that learners will have some different things to say in **exercise 4**. You can conduct the activity like an interview. A shuts their book and B reads out the questions for A to answer. Encourage learners to expand on their answers.

phone for information

- Tell learners to look at the picture of Matt and the advertisement. Look at **exercise 2**, and refer them to the questionnaire and the **natural English** box on *p.76* so that they can add more questions that Matt might ask. Complete the first couple of questions as a class and tell them to do the rest with a partner. If you elicit their questions and put them on the board, the class can concentrate on these for **exercise 3**, which will make it easier for you to manage.

- As they will have listened once already, they should find **exercise 4** a straightforward, fact-spotting exercise.

- Learners often find it difficult to know how to bring a phone conversation to an end in English, and sometimes there are cultural differences, so this **natural English** box (on *p.77*) should be useful input.

it's your turn!

Allow learners plenty of time to work on their role cards, either making up their information or thinking up questions. As we have suggested before, you can give learners more support if needed by putting them in pairs to work on the same role card together, i.e. the As together, and the Bs together. Then pair up As and Bs. Learners have had a clear model from the listening activity, so they should have plenty of ideas for the role play. If you want to make it more realistic as a phone call, sit As and Bs back-to-back, or with one learner speaking over their partner's shoulder (see **ideas plus** phone call role plays *p.51*). Monitor and make notes on the activity. Once they have discussed **exercise 2**, they can reverse roles and do the activity again using new prompts.

complete an application form

Give learners a couple of minutes to work alone and complete what they can of the form for their partner. The language used in application forms is formulaic and usually quite formal, e.g. *date of birth, occupation*, etc. You may wish to practise a few simple questions before doing **exercise 2** (see **language point** on the right).

exercise 1

money: pay a deposit, fees
starting a course: enrol, brochure, application form, entry requirements
the end of a course: qualification, certificate

language point words with overlapping meanings

Certain words in this topic area are confusing for learners at this level.

fees = money you pay doctors, schools, lawyers, etc. for professional services, e.g. school fees

price = money you need to buy a particular object, e.g. jacket, CD, book

cost (n) = money you are charged for services, activities, and goods in general, e.g. the cost of heating, a holiday, food, living

fare = the price of a train / bus / plane ticket, or for a taxi journey

certificate = a piece of paper proving you have passed an exam or done a course

qualification = a degree, diploma, or other form of recognition that you have passed (an) exam/s, completed a course successfully, or reached a certain standard within a field, e.g. a teaching qualification

brochure = a small book, often with pictures, giving information or advertising something, e.g. a holiday, a hotel, a school

leaflet = a sheet / a few sheets of paper giving information or advertising something

exercise 2 possible answers

What kind of courses do you run?
How long is the course?
Do I have to pay a deposit?
Do I have to take a test?
What are the entry requirements?

How do I enrol?
What are the fees?
Is it full-time or part-time?
What sort of certificate do you get at the end?
Do you get a qualification at the end?

exercise 4

length: 1) September to June
        2) January to December
starting date: September 12th
hours per week: 15
fees: £1,500

deposit: yes, £300
class size: 12 to 15
how to enrol: fill in application form and include deposit

nE

I think that's everything I need.   *Thanks very much for your help.*   *Bye bye.*

troubleshooting discussing the role play

It can be very helpful for learners to stand back and reflect on how they did in a role play or speaking activity, but it is not always easy the first time they do it. In order to check how successfully they conveyed the information, **A** should look at **B**'s completed role card to see if they understood correctly. A little reflection at this point may help them to do the reverse role play in **exercise 3** more successfully. For you as the teacher, it can be a useful way of assessing how aware learners are of their strengths and weaknesses.

Want to know more? Go to **how to ...** monitor and give feedback *p.156*.

language point the language of form filling

You could ask learners in pairs to think how they would express the language used in application forms in spoken English, e.g.

application form	spoken English
complete	fill in
delete	cross out
present address	Where are you living at the moment?
nationality	Where are you from? Where do you come from?
date of birth	When were you born?
occupation	What do you do? / What's your job?
mother tongue	What's your first language?

extended speaking decisions, decisions

60 – 70 mins

- It is important at the beginning of this activity to let learners read the left-hand column, or put it on the board, or tell them what they are going to do in the lesson. This will enable them to get the whole picture. You should also give them time to look back at the blue **extended speaking** boxes which occur at the end of each section in the unit.

collect ideas

- For **exercise 1**, you may need to adapt the situations slightly to suit your group, e.g. change *end a relationship* to *buy a new car* or *choose a holiday destination*. Once pairs have discussed their ideas, match them with another pair to see if people had similar or different strategies.

- Tell learners that Andrew and Rowena are a real couple (they are), and this is a true case study. It will add to the authenticity of the lesson. You could tell them to read the first paragraph (without the four choices), shut their books and tell a partner what they remember. Then go back and read the choices. This will check whether they have understood the basic situation and give them a little speaking practice. Before you go on to **exercise 3**, ask them if there is anything they are not clear about.

- For **exercise 3**, ask learners to note down one advantage and disadvantage for the first situation, go round and monitor to see if they are on the right lines, then give them time to complete the table. Impress on the learners that it is notes you are looking for, not complete sentences. You could ask them to copy the table into their notebooks so that they have space to make notes.

reach a decision

- Tell the groups when they start that they need to work through the situations systematically, discussing the advantages and disadvantages for each one. As a guideline, each choice should take a few minutes to talk through. It is perfectly acceptable for learners to talk about their own experience and what they would do, or to talk about people they know in similar circumstances.

- Give them a warning near the end that they have two minutes to finish the discussion, then they have to vote. Quickly reorganize learners so that they are working with a new partner to compare their final answers.

listen

- Learners will be so familiar with the information that they should be able to cope with the natural speed and delivery of the recording. You could pre-teach: *carry on* = continue doing something, *retrain* = learn a new type of work / skill, *grant* (n) = money given by the government to students for their education. In **exercise 8**, you will probably need to pause the recording at certain points to give learners time to write their answers.

exercise 7
They choose option 3: retraining in business management

exercise 8
photography business: too risky, doesn't know how to run a business, hasn't got the experience
Rowena returning to work: Andrew wants to continue working, Rowena wants to look after the baby
moving house: they don't want to move away because all their family and friends are in the area
retraining in business management: Andrew won't have much money for a while

feedback checklist

During the **extended speaking** activity, note down examples of …

- **good language use**

- **effective communication strategies**
  (turn-taking, interrupting, inviting others to speak, etc.)

- **learner errors**
  (vocabulary, grammar, pronunciation, etc.)

- **particular communication problems**

Make sure you allow time for feedback at the end of the lesson. You can use the notes you make above to <u>praise</u> effective language use and communication or, if necessary, to do some remedial work.

test yourself!

Want to know more? Go to the **introduction** *p.7* for ways of using **test yourself!**

1 after, up, down, on, for, up, of, of
2 possible answers: Smith, British, 5.7.80, teacher, English
3 enr<u>o</u>l, dep<u>o</u>sit, br<u>o</u>chure, cert<u>i</u>ficate, qualific<u>a</u>tion

1 We'll be late unless we leave / go now.
2 Thanks. You've been very helpful.
3 I don't think it's a good idea.
4 I took today off work.

1 If they move to another area, they will be unhappy.
2 I always feel better after going to the gym.
3 The main advantage of working there is the salary.
4 I don't agree with you.

seven

wordlist

natural English

have a good time
We had a great time last night.
I'm having a dreadful time at the moment.
Have a good time next week!

suggesting a change of topic
Shall we go on to the next one?
Let's move on to number 3.

do / did **for emphasis**
I <u>do</u> feel sorry for him.
I <u>did</u> enjoy the film.

anyway, so anyway
Anyway, when we got there ...
So anyway, after we left ...

time phrases in narrative
One day ...
A bit later ...
After that, ...
In the end / eventually ...
At the end of the film / story, ...

commenting on a book or film
It was very (silly / exciting, etc).
It made me (cry / laugh, etc).
I found it very (depressing / sentimental, etc).

vocabulary

reporting verbs
advise (sb to do sth)
warn (sb (not) to do sth) / (sb that ...)
persuade (sb to do sth)
refuse (to do sth)
offer (to do sth)
suggest (that ...)

relationships
have an argument / a row
feel guilty
bump into (each other)
split up
serious relationship

wordbooster

people in your life
relatives / relations
classmate / flatmate
colleague
neighbour
ex-boyfriend / girlfriend
current boyfriend / girlfriend
best / closest friend

phrases with *go* and *get*
get a job
get to know sb
get on well / badly with sb
get engaged / married / divorced
get into trouble
get angry / upset, etc
get ready
go abroad
go on a date with sb
go out for a drink / meal
go bankrupt
go wrong
go out with sb
go on holiday

glossaries
bum ⊚
gorgeous ⊚
dreadful
fall in love with sb
gossip (n)
tactless
outfit (n)
a mess ⊚
set off (on a journey)
it turned out to be ...
it cost a fortune

relationships

in unit seven ...

life with Agrippine
cartoon love
natural English *have a great / dreadful / good time*

listening handling relationships
vocabulary reporting verbs
natural English phrases suggesting a change of topic
grammar verb patterns
listening overhearing conversations

wordbooster
people in your life
phrases with *go* and *get*

reading going on a date
reading We went halves
natural English *do / did* for emphasis
natural English *anyway, so anyway*

how to ... tell the story of a book or film
vocabulary relationships
listening film stories
grammar present tenses in narrative
natural English time phrases in narrative
natural English phrases for commenting on a book
or film

extended speaking one couple's story
collect ideas learners use a sequence of pictures
to develop a story about a relationship
develop the story
tell the story
write the story

test yourself!
revision and progress check

life with Agrippine   20 – 25 mins

read for pleasure
nE *have a great / dreadful / good time*

- If you think the topic of the warmer, i.e. talking about first boyfriend / girlfriend is too personal for your group, tell learners to talk about their ideal partner, e.g. Which famous person would be your ideal partner, and why? Either warmer should work well if you start it off yourself with an example.
- Draw learners' attention to the glossary before they read the cartoon.

cartoon time
1 She thinks he's fantastic, maybe a little fat now, but he'll be gorgeous when he's older. She also thinks he's clever.
2 Her friend thinks he is awful; he's got a big bottom, and he wears dreadful clothes.

---

language point the part of the body you sit on ...

We feel we should clear up which items are neutral, informal, slang, or impolite / taboo in British English. We don't suggest you set out to teach these items; this is simply for information.
buttocks: this is neutral, but not very widely used in British English.
backside and *bottom*: these are informal but widely used, and not considered vulgar. (= *butt* in American English)
bum: this is also informal, but humorous, and slightly 'naughty'.
arse: this is slang, and impolite. Learners should avoid using this as it could cause offence. (= *ass* in American English)

---

listening handling relationships

focus on reporting verbs and the vocabulary and grammatical patterns used with them

practise them in a questionnaire

listen to two conversations in a restaurant

act out a situation from the questionnaire

vocabulary reporting verbs

- It is important in **exercise 1** that learners don't spend too much time thinking of what to say in situations 1 to 5. The aim is just to check that they understand the reporting verbs. It would be best to write the example situation on the board, i.e. advise a friend to look for a new job, and elicit what you would say. One good answer will be enough. Learners can then work in pairs on the others.

- The pronunciation in **exercise 2** is necessary; most of these items are not easy for learners to pronounce.

lead-in

- Introduce the questionnaire about attitudes to telling the truth in different situations. Get the class to read the situations quickly to get the gist. In **exercise 1**, look at the first question together and elicit the answers from the class. At this stage, the activity has only a linguistic aim, i.e. selecting the verb which fits in terms of meaning and form, so make sure learners don't start adding their own ideas, or discussing the questionnaire. Go over the answers.

- For information on how to make the most of questionnaires, see **troubleshooting** on the right.

grammar verb patterns

- Learners can complete most of the table in **exercise 1** simply by transferring patterns from the questionnaire. You could ask learners to copy it into their notebooks to complete. You could tell them to try to complete the table from their own knowledge with a partner, then use the questionnaire to check as many as possible. Alternatively, tell them to use the phrases in the questionnaire from the start to help them fill in the table. *Explain, realize,* and *ask* are not included in the questionnaire, but *explain* is given as an example in the table.

- After feedback on the answers, give learners a couple of minutes in silence to study the table. Then they can do the **test your partner** activity.

- Look at the **language reference** on *p.163*, before selecting additional **cover & check** exercises learners may need for consolidation.

Want to know more? Go to **how to ...** introduce new language *p.143*.

listen to this

- The prediction activity in **exercise 1** will help learners to tune in to the correct situations. After the listening, highlight: *train of thought* = series of connected thoughts, *on your mind* = something which is worrying you, *have sth in common with sb* = have similar interests, *over* = finished.

- The exercise in the **listening booklet** on *p.25* targets the language used when introducing a problem. If you focus on it, learners will find it useful in **it's your turn!** below.

it's your turn!

- You could use this activity as a warmer in the following lesson if you prefer. This would give learners a chance to look again at the verb patterns in the questionnaire.

- Learners can play safe and choose one of the situations from the listening, and just adapt it slightly, or take more risks and choose one of the other two situations. Look at **troubleshooting** on the right for more ideas.

exercise 1 possible answers
I don't think you should go to that nightclub
– it's dangerous.
Please come on holiday – it'll be great fun.
No, I'm sorry, I can't – I've got a bad back.
Can I carry that bag for you?
Why don't we go and see a film this evening?

exercise 1
1 a tell; b try; c decide
2 a explain; b advise; c warn
3 a offer; b persuade; c refuse (or *offer*)
4 a tell; b speak; c suggest
5 a tell; b phone; c write

troubleshooting questionnaires

When learners discuss questionnaires, they have a tendency to say *I would choose 'a'* or *I would choose 'c'*, rather than *I would tell her that I'm upset*, i.e. the phrase in the multiple choice answers. Your aim in **exercise 1** is to encourage practice of the patterns, so tell them not to refer to *a*, *b*, or *c*, but to use the phrases.
Learners also tend just to give the answer, rather than discussing the point or giving reasons. To exploit the questionnaire more fully, e.g. in **exercises 2** and **3**, writing in their own ideas and thinking about their reasons will give them a lot more to say, and make the discussion about the questionnaire come to life.
Finally, make it clear to learners that this is a speaking activity, not a 'compare your answers' activity.

exercise 1
verb + *that*: suggest, realize
verb + *to do* sth: try, offer
verb + sb *that*: advise, tell, persuade
verb + sb *(not) to do* sth: advise, persuade, ask, warn

exercise 2 possible answers
1 She told
2 My brother asked me
3 My father warned
4 her to go to the disco.
5 him to stay in bed.
6 to help me.

language point verb patterns

Learners of all nationalities have difficulty with accuracy in verb patterns. There are two clear problems: firstly, the pattern in L1 may be different from English; secondly, many verbs take more than one pattern. We have included several verbs which illustrate this, e.g. *tell sb that ...*, *tell sb to do sth*, but we have only done this for very common patterns, and we have not included less common ones, e.g. *advise sb of sth*. It is important to teach and recycle them, and learners need to keep a record of them. There are two other strategies for you and your learners:

- learners' dictionaries: show them how verb patterns are highlighted (and examples given) in their dictionaries, to make them more independent.
- the mother tongue: contrast verb patterns in English with those in L1, and encourage learners to concentrate on (and record) the ones that cause error, e.g. in Spanish, *say* can take a direct object, but it can't in English.

exercise 1
situations 4 and 5

exercise 2
1 they have nothing in common; their friends are very different
2 no
3 he suggests that he can change

exercise 5
1 it relates to situation 3
2 the listener is happy to help

troubleshooting it's your turn!

You may feel there are other situations which might be more interesting and relevant to your class; if so, go ahead and use them.
The stage where they talk **about** the situation before the role play is essential; this will help them to give the role play a framework and a direction. When they do the role play for the first time, they could decide whether it has worked well or needs improving, and they can rehearse it a couple of times before trying it in front of another pair in **exercise 2**. If you decide not to do **exercise 2**, you will need to monitor and provide feedback at the end.

 wordbooster

This **wordbooster** is best used at this point as some of the phrases with *go* and *get* come up in the reading section.

people in your life

- You will need to focus on the pronunciation of the words in phonemic script. See **language point** on the right for some common errors.
- You could do **exercises 2** and **3** as a model with some of the people in your life on the board.

phrases with *go* and *get*

- Remember that in unit five **wordbooster** *p.63*, learners looked at some uses of *get*; they could add these to the spray diagram they did before. For a change of focus, you could write the words and phrases, e.g. *a job, on a date with someone*, on separate flashcards, divide the board into *GO* and *GET*, and ask learners to stick the cards in the appropriate place on the board. When they all agree that the words are in the right place, they can copy them down.
- Instead of **exercise 2**, you could ask learners to make up a short story using as many of the phrases as possible, e.g. Jim **got to know** Betty when they met at a wedding. A few weeks later, they **went on a date**, and … .

reading going on a date

60 – 75 mins

describe an evening out, and discuss who pays in different circumstances

read an article about going on a date from the woman's point of view

listen to a man's version of going on a date

focus on *do / did* for emphasis and *anyway, so anyway* in storytelling

give their opinions

lead-in

- For **exercise 1**, make it clear to learners that they don't need to say exactly how much things cost. Walk round and monitor the activity and ask one or two people to talk about their experience in feedback.
- In **exercise 2**, check that learners are clear on the meaning of *share the bill* (= you pay your part of the bill) and *take it in turns* (= you pay one time and the other person pays next time) before they start thinking about their answers. *Share* has already come up in **wordbooster** *p.84* (i.e. a flatmate = someone you share an apartment with). At the end, do group feedback to see if there are different points of view.

read on

- **Exercise 1** is a revision activity for the present continuous, and it also helps to establish the context of the article. While you monitor, notice whether there are any useful items of vocabulary that you can feed in or highlight at the end. When you do **exercise 3**, don't tell them the answers as the learners have to read the text to find out. Go over the answers after they have finished reading.
- Until now, learners have generally learnt that *do / does / did* are only used in interrogative and negative forms in the simple tenses, so you could remind them of this and in addition, point out this new and very specific use highlighted in the **natural English** box. It is more for receptive than productive purposes at this level, although it is quite a common feature.
- Notice that in the true / false sentences in **exercise 7**, the causative *have* construction is used (*He had his hair cut.*). If necessary, you can explain that this means that he didn't cut it himself, but went to the hairdresser's, i.e. he paid for a service to be done. You might even wish to teach and practise other examples of this structure, e.g. *have sth repaired / painted; have your hair done / coloured*, etc. Before you listen, you could also pre-teach: *roughly* = approximately, *I'm not bothered about* = it's not important to me, *reasonable* = not expensive, good value.

exercise 1

1b 2d 3h 4g 5a 6c 7f 8e

language point some common errors

Certain errors are very common with these items:

Current: most learners want to say *actual* here, which is a false friend.

Relatives / relations: many speakers of European languages want to say *parents* here and will actually avoid using *relations* as it is a false friend.

A colleague = someone you work with, usually in a professional job, e.g. office, school, administration.

A workmate = someone you work with, in any kind of job (used more informally).

exercise 1

go: on a date with sb, out for a drink / meal, bankrupt, wrong, out with sb, on holiday

get: to know sb, on well / badly with sb, engaged / married / divorced, into trouble, angry / upset / excited / depressed, ready

language point *go / get* + adjective

Both verbs are followed by different adjectives to describe a change in state.

go red = become embarrassed

get upset = become upset

With the verb *go*, the change in state is usually negative in some way, e.g. *He went bald / mad / grey / bankrupt / deaf.*

This is not so often the case with *get*.

exercise 2

£103.64 for her and £46.32 for him.

exercise 4

Before the evening, Sally made phone calls, had a haircut, and bought clothes. During the evening, she took a taxi to the wine bar, put on make-up, and paid for her dinner. She didn't pay for the drinks after dinner; we don't know who paid for the drinks before dinner.

Joe bought drinks, gave the waiter a tip, and paid for his dinner.

nE

*My preparations **do** seem quite extensive. Joe **did** offer to pay.*

exercise 5

1 the meal	3 her clothes	5 her hair
2 her clothes	4 her hair	6 the meal

exercise 7

1 true	4 true
2 false: he took a taxi	5 false: it cost about £25
3 false: he wasn't worried about how he looked	6 true

nE

Anyway, erm, we arranged to meet for a drink.
So anyway, we, erm, we went to the restaurant.

ideas plus reading texts

If you are selecting your own reading materials it can be difficult to find texts of an appropriate length for intermediate learners, who can be overwhelmed by long texts. If you find an interesting and suitable text, but you feel it is too long, one solution is to do as we have done here: use part of it as a written text, and the rest as a spoken text. You could either record the second part yourself, or do it as a 'live listening', i.e. where you describe how the text continues in your own words. Alternatively, you could split it into two or three sections, and do a jigsaw reading (see unit four, **troubleshooting** p.45).

Want to know more? Go to **how to ...** teach listening (try it out) p.153.

how to ... tell the story of a book or film

70 – 80 mins

learn vocabulary about relationships

listen to two stories of films and analyse the structure

tell one of the stories using **natural English** time phrases and present tenses

focus on more **natural English** phrases for commenting on a book / film

tell their own stories using the **natural English** phrases

vocabulary relationships

- Give learners a minute or two to think about **exercise 1**, then start by giving a model yourself; if possible, a film about a relationship between two or more people. It is important that learners don't describe the story of the film, as they will probably tell the story later.

- **Exercise 2** contains examples of lexical cohesion,
  e.g. *Did they have **an argument**? Yes, they had an **awful row**.*

two film stories

- In this section, we are focusing on a predictable plotline of many films, books, and stories. The scene is set in which we meet the main characters, their relationship develops, a problem emerges and builds to a climax before a final resolution, which may be happy, tragic, comic, or inconclusive. This is a useful framework for learners, and will help them to produce a well-told story. In **exercise 1**, they predict the beginning of a story, individually or in pairs. If their predictions are not what actually happens, it doesn't matter; the aim is to provide a focus for listening.

- Before learners listen in **exercise 2**, you could pre-teach *moving* = makes you feel strong emotions, especially sadness.

- In **exercise 3**, they can complete the first part of story 1 before they listen and complete the rest after listening. Before you listen to story 2, you could pre-teach: *cute* (US) = attractive, *guy* = man.

grammar present tenses in narrative

- Some learners have a tendency to tell stories in the present tense, even when the past would be more appropriate. They do this because it happens in their mother tongue, or as a reduction strategy, i.e. learners are using a tense they are familiar with, which conveys their ideas well enough. Sometimes the present tenses are correct, as is the case here.

- You could introduce the **natural English** time phrases by telling a simple story. Ask learners to listen and look at the phrases in the box as you use them. Don't try to use them all – you may end up with something contrived. Focus on the meaning of *in the end / eventually*, as they are the most likely ones to be new to learners (see **language point** on the right). They can then retell the stories using the narrative tenses and the time phrases.

- This is a good point to deal with the language in the second **natural English** box on commenting on a book or film. This will allow them to do the **it's your turn!** activity uninterrupted.

it's your turn!

- The phrases in the **natural English** box can be used at the beginning of the story, e.g. *I saw a lovely film last week; it made me cry. It was called ...* , or at the end. Point this out before learners work in groups.

- In **exercise 2**, refer the learners to the table at the top of *p.89* which provides them with a structure for their story. However, you should warn them that the film / book they are going to talk about may not fit the structure perfectly, and that this is not a problem.

- Learners could practise their story with a partner first, then move to a new group to tell it. During **exercise 3**, monitor and make notes for feedback at the end.

exercise 2

1e 2c 3a 4b 5d

---

language point *argument* and *row*

Argument and *row* can both be used to talk about an angry disagreement between friends or family members. *Row* is slightly more informal; *argument* can be used in a wider range of contexts, and it is also a false friend in some European languages (it means the plot of a book in Spanish, for example). You will also need to distinguish between the pronunciation of *row* /raʊ/, and *row* /rəʊ/ meaning a line of things, people, etc.

Learners tend not to use the collocation *have a row / have an argument*, so point it out. It may also be worth mentioning that *discussion* means talking something over (not have an argument) as this is also a false friend in some European languages, meaning an argument.

---

exercise 3

They first meet in a railway restaurant.
They realize that they are falling in love.
The problem is that they are both married and she has children.
The most important point is when she's late home, her children are ill, and she feels guilty.
At the end of the film the relationship ends and he goes to Africa.

exercise 4

They first meet in his bookshop.
They realize that they are falling in love.
The problem is that she's famous and they live in different worlds.
The most important point is when he interrupts a press conference to tell her he loves her.
At the end of the film they get married and have a baby.

exercise 5

The films are *Brief Encounter* and *Notting Hill*.

---

ideas plus book and film genres

You could brainstorm book and film genres as an extra vocabulary activity, e.g.

book genres: romantic novel, thriller / mystery / crime, science fiction, biography, autobiography, adventure, contemporary fiction, travel, historical novel

film genres: romantic comedy, classic comedy, thriller, war film, western, horror and suspense, crime / mystery, science fiction / fantasy, costume / period drama, road movie, chick flick, martial arts, animation

This may help them in **exercise 5** and later when they are discussing films.

---

grammar present tenses in narrative

1 the present simple and continuous
2 no, but this is a summary of a film
3 the present makes it more immediate and exciting
4 it depends on your language

---

language point time phrases in narrative

Eventually emphasizes that something happened after a long time, often after a lot of problems or delays. It is a false friend in many languages, where it can mean *possible*. *Eventually* is similar to *finally* or *in the end* in a narrative.

At last is not interchangeable with *eventually*, and is often misused by learners. It means that something happened after you had been hoping for it for a long time. *I've passed my driving test at last.* **A** *Look, David has arrived.* **B** *At last!*

Don't introduce this next language point, but if it comes up, you will need to explain it briefly. Our advice is not to get too involved with the distinction at this level.

in the end = finally, after delays

at the end = in the last part of something, e.g. a book, a story, a sentence.

---

nE

It was very silly.
It made me laugh.
I found it very moving.

---

troubleshooting getting ideas

It may be asking a lot of certain learners to explain the plot of a film, book, or TV drama on the spur of the moment. These are options you could consider.

– Tell them a day or lesson in advance so that they have time to think of one. If you do this, tell them it should be about a relationship.

– They may be able to describe the film they mentioned in **vocabulary** exercise 1 *p.88*.

– Give learners plenty of time at the start of the activity. Identify those who are having problems and go round and prompt them with ideas, e.g. a TV programme, or part of a soap opera would be fine, if these are popular.

– If all else fails, they could tell the story of the film from the listening activity which they haven't yet described.

extended speaking one couple's story   60 – 70 mins

think about the characters in the story

decide how the central relationship develops

tell their story to another group

write their story

- It is important at the beginning of this activity to let learners read the left-hand column, or tell them what they are going to do in the lesson, or put it on the board. This will enable them to get the whole picture. You should also give them time to look back at the blue **extended speaking** boxes which occur at the end of each section in the unit.

collect ideas

- For **exercise 1**, you could elicit and build up information about Sally and Joe on the board in two spray diagrams. Ask learners to shout out what they can remember, and then give them a minute in pairs to imagine their characters. Elicit these suggestions and put them on the board too. This will provide a source of ideas for learners who feel they are not very creative.

- There are no correct answers to **exercise 2**. When we trialled this material with groups of learners, they came up with quite different stories. This meant that in the later stages when they told their stories, there was a reason to listen.

- The **language reminder** (use of the apostrophe) is there because it was an extremely common problem for the majority of learners in our data, and it is likely to occur quite frequently in the stories.

- For **exercise 3**, choose small groups that will work well together. Groups of three are probably best; for an irregular number, have a pair or a group of four, but avoid anything larger, as some learners will have little chance to contribute.

develop the story

- When they have read the continuation of the story and identified the tense, you should point out that while the main part of the story can be told using present tenses, there may be occasions where they need to use the present perfect or past simple as well.

- **Exercise 5** may take a while to get going, so allow plenty of time. At this stage just prompt or offer help where you think it is needed. It is important that the learners arrive at a story they both agree on. It would probably help to give them a time limit at the beginning, e.g. ten to fifteen minutes, and a time warning of two to three minutes before the end, so that the slower pairs catch up and all pairs are ready to proceed to the next stage. It is inevitable that there will be different rates of progress, however.

exercise 4
the present simple

tell your story

- This activity is structured to give learners rehearsal time to build their confidence and fluency. The final point in the checklist is very important; impress upon them the need to make their story very clear. Monitor at this stage and make notes for feedback later.

- For **exercise 7**, tell learners that it is important that they understand the story they are being told. You could teach them phrases for checking and seeking clarification, e.g. *I didn't understand the bit about … Could you explain the bit about … again? I don't understand why / who / what …*

- As you monitor the pairs, try to choose one or two stories that could quickly be retold at the end to the class. Finally, give learners feedback on language.

write the story

- Learners could start the stories in class, depending on how much time you have available in your lesson. Take them in at the end of the following lesson so that you can give them feedback on their written work. Give learners feedback on the language and the content of their stories, praising their efforts where possible.

feedback checklist

During the **extended speaking** activity, note down examples of …

- **good language use**

- **effective communication strategies**
  (turn-taking, interrupting, inviting others to speak, etc.)

- **learner errors**
  (vocabulary, grammar, pronunciation, etc.)

- **particular communication problems**

Make sure you allow time for feedback at the end of the lesson. You can use the notes you make above to <u>praise</u> effective language use and communication or, if necessary, to do some remedial work.

test yourself!

Want to know more? Go to the **introduction** *p.7* for ways of using **test yourself!**

1 refuse to do sth; tell sb that … / tell sb (not) to do sth; offer to do sth; advise sb that … / advise sb (not) to do sth; persuade sb (not) to do sth / persuade sb that…
2 get to know sb; get on well with sb; go on a date; get into trouble; go bankrupt; go wrong
3 awful; a row; eventually; relations; very attractive

1 We had a great time.
2 Shall we go on to question 5?
3 He's my ex-boyfriend.
4 They've split up.

1 He's Mr Uchida's boss.
2 The story made me laugh.
3 In this photo, a man is talking to a girl.
4 He says he's in love. / He tells me he's in love.

eight

wordlist

natural English

asking for help
Could you do me a favour? — Of course.
Could you give me a hand? — Sure.
Could you do something for me? — It depends what it is.

expressing difficulty
I'd find it difficult / hard to ...
I would have a problem *-ing* ...
I might have a problem (with that).

prepositions at the end of *Wh-* questions
How long are you going for?
Who are you working with?
What are you so angry about?

exclamations
Ah! Great!
Ooh! Wow!
What? Oh!
Ow! Ouch!
Oh no!
Oh dear!

permissions and requests
Could I ... ?
Do you mind if I ... ?
Do you think I could ... ?
Would you mind if I ... ?

introducing a question
I was going to ask you ... do you ... ?
I wanted to ask you ... can I ... ?
There's something I want to ask you ... . Is there ... ?

vocabulary

getting people's attention
tap sb on the shoulder
call out sb's name
wave at sb
touch sb
catch sb's eye
whistle at sb

everyday accidents
trip over sth
spill sth
fall off sth
crash into sth
bump into sth / sb
step on sth / sb's foot
drop sth
knock sth over

wordbooster

everyday events in the home
make a phone call
invite sb over
pay the rent
borrow the iron
hang a picture on the wall
send / receive e-mail messages
video a programme
use the washing machine
move the furniture round
cook a meal

uncountable nouns
weather
advice
accommodation
information
homework
luggage
traffic
news

glossaries
client
blind
cutlery
hug

life changes

do you get it?   20 – 25 mins

listen for pleasure
vocabulary getting people's attention
nE phrases asking for help

- Before learners work with a partner in the first activity, you could choose one of the photos together and think of questions to ask, e.g. *Bill Gates, what are you going to do with all your money?* Then, after pair work, elicit the questions from the class. Make the link between the photo of Bill Gates and the pictures of him in the joke. Highlight in particular *tap sb on the shoulder* in the glossary.

- After learners have listened and reacted to the joke, you can ask some of them to do the actions in **getting people's attention** in front of the class to check understanding. These have to be done in the context of getting someone's attention, e.g. wave at somebody so that they notice you, rather than waving goodbye to someone. Check that learners can pronounce the words. They can then do the activity in pairs.

- The activity at the end of the **natural English** box can be done in pairs or as a mingling activity. This is more fun (and realistic) if you emphasize that the requests should be achievable so that learners can actually do what they are asked to do by their partners. If they can't, they should refuse politely, giving a reason if possible.

> **language point** cultural issues related to lexis
>
> You may find it useful and interesting to discuss some of these issues with your class.
>
> – Tapping someone on the shoulder or touching their arm is quite an intimate gesture in British culture, and would normally only be done to people you know.
>
> – Whistling at someone is acceptable amongst boys and young men to their friends, but can be disrespectful in other circumstances; it is often associated with calling a dog.
>
> – If you need to attract the attention of a stranger who is not looking at you, you should call out *excuse me*, not ~~*Mister / Madam*~~, etc. It is not polite to call someone by their job title, e.g. ~~*teacher! waiter! barman!*~~ Again, use *excuse me*, or the person's name if you know it. In restaurants and bars, you normally attract the waiter / bar person's attention by catching their eye or raising your hand or saying *excuse me*.
>
> You could provide questions for learners to discuss about their own culture, e.g. When is it OK / not OK to ... tap someone on the shoulder, call them by their first name / title, whistle at them, etc. Whether you compare it with another culture, e.g. British, or not is up to you.

listening adapting to a new lifestyle

75 – 90 mins

lead-in

- Highlight the grammatical forms *difficult / hard to do* and *have a problem doing* in the **natural English** box. You will also probably need to remind learners that this is a hypothetical / imaginary situation, so they will need to use *would* or *might*.

- Make sure that they think about their reasons; this will extend the conversation in **exercise 2**.

- Monitor this activity and give feedback at the end.

listen to this

- Focus the learners' attention on the map and photo of Colin. What do they know about Kazakhstan, and if they don't know anything, what do they imagine it is like? Why might a foreigner go there? You could write these questions on the board for them to discuss, before you play the recording in **exercise 1**.

- In **exercise 2**, it is important that learners do not write in the gaps at this stage. You could give them an example of the kind of information that might be given in gap 1, e.g. *what kind of company?* They can discuss their ideas with a partner if they prefer. See **troubleshooting** on the right.

- As with other listening material in the course, you can adjust the task to suit the level of the group. If you think the task provided will not be sufficiently challenging for your class, you could omit more information in the summary, or omit the activity and ask them to listen and give you their own summary of the recording.

- After they listen in **exercise 3** you could highlight: *come up* = happen unexpectedly, *terrific* = fantastic, *commit yourself to sth* = say you will definitely do something.

Want to know more? Go to **how to ...** teach listening *p.150*.

grammar present continuous and *be going to* + verb

- The use of the present continuous for arrangements can cause problems for some learners. See **language point** on the right.

- Look at **language reference** on *p.165* before selecting additional **cover & check** exercises learners may need for consolidation.

talking about plans and arrangements

- If you feel your learners have done enough listening, you could do the **natural English** box orally without using the recording. Be sure to highlight the stressed words as shown in the answer key. If you feel learners would benefit from some revision of *wh-* questions, you could refer them to **language reference**, unit one, *p.151*.

- In **exercise 2**, once learners have chosen their ideal place, elicit the questions from the class, then give them time to make notes on their own in the answer column. Monitor and help if necessary.

- In order to provide a model for **exercise 3** you could act out part of a conversation with a learner, e.g. ask a learner about their ideal place and respond enthusiastically to demonstrate a typical response, e.g. **A** *So, where are you going exactly?* **B** *Well, actually, I'm going to San Francisco.* **A** *Really? Ooh, that sounds great!* Learners can then do their own conversations in pairs.

giving advice

- You will need to check that learners are using correct verb patterns in **exercise 2**. Either elicit which forms follow the verbs before they write, or go round and monitor.

exercise 1

1 no   2 yes

exercise 3

1 an oil company   5 a hotel
2 next Friday   6 stay in a flat or apartment*
3 one month   7 travel
4 one month

flat (British English) = where people live, often in a block of flats
apartment (British English) = a holiday home, often self catering; also being used for more upmarket flats, especially in estate agents' information
apartment (American English) = where people live, often in a building known as a condominium (or *condo*)

exercise 4

He suggests that she visits him in Kazakhstan.

troubleshooting guiding listening

The activity in exercise 2 is one that you could adapt and use with other listening texts. If you write a summary and omit some of the key information, you can ask learners to think about what <u>type</u> of information could go in the gaps. This will encourage them to think not just about a missing word, but a range of possibilities, which is a more effective prediction activity. Once they have done this, the listening activity itself should be very manageable, even with quite a difficult spoken text. Some gaps are more open-ended than others, e.g. gap 2 can really only be a time phrase, whereas gap 7 could be a range of activities (travel around, learn the language, make friends, etc.).

Want to know more? Go to **how to ...** teach listening (developing the listening skill) *p.151*.

exercise 1

1 The present continuous is used in a and b; *be going to* + verb is used in c.
2 a and b refer to definite arrangements. c is not an arrangement but just a plan / intention.

exercise 3

1, 2, and 5 are also correct in the present continuous because they are definite arrangements. 3 and 4 express intentions only so the present continuous cannot be used.

language point present continuous and *be going to* + verb

Having a choice of forms for plans and arrangements can sometimes cause problems for learners. If this is the case, you could tell them that *be going to* is always correct for plans and arrangements, so when in doubt, they should use that. However, the present continuous is often the preferred form for arrangements made with other people, e.g. seeing the doctor, meeting a friend. They will certainly come across this use in spoken and written text.

nE

How long are you <u>going</u> for?
Who are you <u>working</u> with?
What are you so <u>angry</u> about?

exercise 1

1 for   2 in   3 for   4 with   5 about

exercise 2

When are you leaving?   Where are you staying?
How long are you going for?   What are you going to do in your free time?
Why are you going there?   Is there anything you're worried about?

language point prepositions in *wh-* questions

When the question word, e.g. *how long, who,* is the object of a preposition, it is natural, especially in spoken English, to put the preposition at the end of the clause. Learners find this difficult because it does not happen in other languages very much. They often think that it is too informal or even incorrect. It's important to make clear that it is very natural, and used by educated speakers as much as anyone else.

Want to know more? Go to **Practical English Usage** by Michael Swan, *p.453*.

exercise 1

His main worries are: he doesn't know much about the country; he doesn't know much about the city he's going to, or the local customs; he doesn't speak the language; he might be lonely; he doesn't want to spend all his time working.

reading living in the dark

60 – 70 mins

vocabulary everyday accidents

• When learners have matched the pictures and verbs in **exercise 1**, ask them to say past forms of the verbs to check pronunciation, and elicit which ones double the consonant in the past forms.

• This section has a vocabulary focus, but notice that there is also attention to the present perfect in **exercise 2** to talk about past actions where the results are important or evident now.

• You can do **exercise 3** orally or ask pairs to write sentences. Ask learners to think of one or two things that happened to them recently, describe where and when, and whether there were any consequences.

read on

• Deal with the **language reminder** either by asking learners to look at the box, and going over it with them, or if you prefer, write the two sentences on the board and ask if there is any difference. Look at the **language point** on the right for further guidance. You may not want to interrupt the flow of the lesson by going to **language reference** on *p.165* at this point.

• Elicit one or two ideas for **exercise 1** before asking learners to work together. Then put them with a new partner to say the whole sentences they wrote, so that they get some oral practice of the phrases. These sentences revise the phrases expressing difficulty in the **natural English** box on *p.94*, albeit with different verb forms.

• In **exercise 2**, learners can give a range of answers. In feedback you should be able to elicit a number of vocabulary items they learnt earlier in the lesson.

• In **exercise 4** you could ask for a quick reaction; for further development, see **ideas plus** (discussion) on the right.

expressing your feelings

• Learners need to recognize exclamations in English, and they may be quite different from those in other cultures, as are differences in body language. When they become more proficient in English, they will begin to use these more naturally. Learners should find the activity fun, and they can compare exclamations with the mother tongue.

• There are more exclamations and an activity to practise the present perfect in the book shown below.

Want to know more? Go to **Grammar Practice Activities**, Penny Ur, CUP *pp.239–40*.

exercise 1

1b 2h 3c 4a 5f 6e 7g 8d

regular verbs: trip, step, drop (all three double the consonant), bump, crash, knock, spill (both reg and irreg)

irregular verbs: fall (fell, fallen), spill (spilt, spilt)

exercise 2

We use the present perfect here because something happened recently. We can see the result now, i.e. The woman hit the cup and knocked it over. The coffee is still on the table.

exercise 3

2 The boy has knocked a table lamp over.
3 The young man has fallen off a ladder.
4 The man has tripped over a stone.
5 The man has stepped on the woman's foot.
6 The man has bumped into a lamppost.
7 The waiter has dropped the plates.
8 The cyclist has crashed into a tree.

language point *off, over, into*

Off and *over* occur in the vocabulary in exercise 1, and have different meanings.

off = moving from a higher place to a lower place, e.g. *She jumped off the table. / The book fell off the table.* (from the table down to the floor)

over = something fell / was knocked, etc. from a standing position to a horizontal one on the same surface, e.g. *I knocked the table lamp over.* (it is still on the table, but is horizontal not vertical)

You can demonstrate this distinction to your learners by mime / acting it out.

Into is used with certain verbs to mean hitting or nearly hitting something or someone suddenly. You can *bump / run / crash / drive / walk into* sb or sth. *Bump into* sb can be literal or metaphorical (= meet unexpectedly). Again, the concept of *into* can be demonstrated through mime.

---

exercise 1 possible answers

Customers will probably find it difficult to use their knife and fork / eat their meal. They're going to have a problem pouring drinks / seeing other people in the restaurant. They won't be able to read a menu or a wine list / look into each others' eyes.

exercise 2 possible answers

they can't find things; they spill things; they step on people's feet; they drop things; bump into things; knock things over; they can't tell the difference between things, e.g. raspberry juice and chocolate sauce

exercise 3

1 because it's unique – it's different
2 to help people understand what it's like to be blind
3 you can't light a match or use a cigarette lighter; you ask the waiter for help if you have a problem
4 before the meal, they are often shy and nervous; after the meal they are excited and relaxed

language point *will / be going to*

Learners often find the distinctions between ways of expressing the future very confusing, so it is reassuring for them to know that there are occasions where *will* or *be going to* are virtually interchangeable, and in any case, any fine distinction is not a priority at this level. You can use either form for general predictions. (The **language reference** on *p.165* clarifies that *will* isn't used for predictions based on present evidence, e.g. *Look, it will / is going to rain*.) Learners have already learnt in unit one that *will* cannot be used to talk about plans, and in unit four that *will* is used for spontaneous decisions, offers, and promises. You could copy this table onto the board for your learners if necessary, or elicit it as revision.

	will	*be going to* + verb
general predictions	√	√
predictions (evidence)	x	√
spontaneous decisions	√	x
offers & promises	√	x

---

exercise 1

paragraph 3 *Ow!*   paragraph 6 *Oh, no; Ouch! Oh, no; Oh, dear!*

nE

to express pleasure	*Ah! Great! Ooh!* **Wow!**
to express surprise	*What?* **Oh!**
to express pain	*Ow!* **Ouch!**
to express anger	*Oh no!*
when something bad has happened	*Oh no!* **Oh dear!**

ideas plus discussion

With some classes, you may want to give them the opportunity to develop a more serious and in-depth discussion following the reading text. In this case, you could give them some questions to discuss, e.g.

1 Would this type of restaurant be successful in your country? Why / why not?
2 How does society help blind people in your country?
3 Can you think of other ways life could be made easier for blind people?
4 In what ways is the situation similar or different for deaf people, or those with other disabilities?

 wordbooster

25 – 30 mins

The first part of **wordbooster** is particularly useful before the **how to ...** section,' but the second part on uncountable nouns could be done at any time.

everyday events in the home

- You may wish to introduce the structure *let* sb *do* sth to the class if you think it will be new.
- For **exercise 2**, if you are working in an English-speaking country, you could ask learners to talk about their experiences with home-stay situations, e.g. Does your landlord / landlady let you do these things?

uncountable nouns

- You could teach learners the three rules about uncountable nouns (see **language reference** on *p.166*) by putting them on the board with the examples given, and asking them which examples are incorrect. They can then correct the errors in **exercise 1**.
- In **exercise 2**, if there are other problematic uncountable nouns for learners in your teaching context, you could add these to the list.

how to ... be a good guest!

60 – 75 mins

talk about experiences of staying with other people

focus on and practise ways of asking for and giving permission

listen to a conversation between a student and her landlady

practise introducing questions using **natural English** phrases

role play a conversation with a landlord / landlady

ask for and give permission

- Monitor the conversations in **exercise 1** and tune in to any interesting comments that you can ask learners to share in feedback at the end.
- In **exercise 1**, you have the opportunity to look at cultural differences. If you are familiar with another / other culture(s), you could discuss with learners differences between staying in, e.g. a British or American household, and in the learners' country. For example, using the phone or inviting someone over can vary from culture to culture.
- You could look at the **natural English** box together and practise the phrases, making sure you highlight forms (see **language point** on the right). Alternatively, if this is revision, you could tell learners to shut their books, and elicit four ways of asking for permission to open the window using *could* and *mind*. Write the correct suggestions on the board, then compare with the **natural English** box.
- In **exercise 3** it is important that learners check their answers in the **listening booklet** on *p.30*, so they see a written record of the possible responses to check they have written them correctly.
- Refer learners back to **wordbooster** before they do **exercise 5** to remind them of the vocabulary.

house rules

- In **exercises 1** and **2**, give learners time to read the questions before they listen.
- In the data we collected for this activity, we discovered that intermediate learners found it difficult to introduce their requests into the conversation naturally. They sometimes sounded rather abrupt, even though their language wasn't impolite; these **natural English** phrases help to warn the listener that a request will follow.
- Practising short extracts of written dialogue as in **exercise 4** can be very satisfying for learners. You can see if they want to listen again before they do it in pairs, or you might wish to drill parts of it first.

write a message home

- You could give learners five minutes in small groups to think about what they might say before they write. The writing can be done in class or at home.

exercise 1

invite a friend over
pay the rent late
borrow the iron
hang a picture on the wall
send / receive e-mail messages

video a programme
use the washing machine
move the furniture around
cook a meal for yourself

exercise 1

1 We had **good weather** on our holidays.
2 They gave us some good **advice**.
3 Our accommodation **was** horrible.
4 The **information** we got didn't help.
5 I couldn't do the **homework** last night.
6 We left our **luggage** in reception.
7 The traffic **was** very bad this morning.
8 **There's news** of a bank robbery in Paris.

exercise 3

1 *Yes, sure.*
2 *No, that's fine.*
3 *Yes you can*
4 *No, of course not*

exercise 4

After *Do you mind ...? / Would you mind ...?* we give permission by saying *no*. This is because *do you mind ...?* means *do you have a problem with it?* The answer *no* means *I don't have a problem with it.*

language point asking permission

The phrases in the **natural English** box are all relatively polite, and can be used in situations where you don't know the person you are speaking to very well, or you are asking a friend for something important, e.g. you want to borrow their car. We feel that *would you mind if ...?* is marginally more distant and polite than *do you mind if ...?* but it is not a distinction that has to be highlighted for intermediate learners.

You will need to highlight the forms, in particular *do you mind if* + present tense, and *would you mind if* + past tense. In exercise 4, you will also need to clarify why *no* is used to mean *yes* (see answer key).

exercise 1

1 she dropped a glass
2 no

exercise 2

1 check her e-mails
2 Mrs Clark's husband
3 gives her permission

4 coffee and bread
5 happy

exercise 3

I wanted to ask you ...

ideas plus lead-in

Before learners listen to the recording, you could do a quick warmer. Give them one minute in pairs to think of five things that could go wrong if you are staying in a landlady's house, e.g. you knock something over, you come home late and make a noise. This will lead naturally into the beginning of the recording.

89

extended speaking visitors to your country

60 – 70 mins

practise all language taught in unit

read profiles of different people and the problems they may have learning the learners' own language

discuss and prepare an information sheet for visitors to their country

- It is important at the beginning of this activity to let learners read the left-hand column or tell them what they are going to do in the lesson, or put it on the board. This will enable them to get the whole picture. You should also give them time to look back at the blue **extended speaking** boxes which occur at the end of each section in the unit.

collect ideas

- Use the questions in **exercise 1** if appropriate. If not many foreign visitors go to the learners' town, ask them more generally about foreign visitors to their country. Alternatively, they could discuss where people from their country go for different reasons, e.g. holidays, work, honeymoon, courses, etc.

- Organize the pair work as suggested in **exercises 2** and **3**. Monitor the speaking activity to check learners are including the key information. Have a class feedback on this to be sure that they are ready to go on to the next stage.

discuss in more detail

- This part of the activity focuses on how well the students and Rebecca will learn the language. It raises a number of issues concerning age, gender, motivation, experience, and being alone or with others of the same nationality. In our data, we found that learners often mentioned grammar as a specific problem for foreigners, more than vocabulary, pronunciation, or listening comprehension, which we think are equally important, if not more so. It will be interesting for you to see what your learners say! Give learners plenty of time to think about **exercise 5** and ask you questions if they want. This activity could trigger issues very relevant to the learners themselves.

- Monitor the activity yourself and provide feedback after **exercise 6**. If you like, at the end you can tell learners about your own experience of learning a foreign language and the problems you had.

plan an information sheet

- See **troubleshooting** on the right for guidance on generating ideas.

- With monolingual groups, learners can do the activity as suggested in small groups of three or four. If you have a multilingual group, you could put learners of different nationalities together to exchange information. They will then have to write up their information sheets separately.

- Direct them to the checklist in **exercise 7** and make sure they are clear what to do. You can tell learners that they don't have to cover every topic in the checklist, and if they want to include their own topics, they can.

- It is difficult to judge how long this activity will take. If your group are older or more experienced, it will probably last longer.

- Get each group to do a short feedback on a topic to the class at the end of **exercise 8**.

write an information sheet

- Refer them to the example about Bologna. Different learners in a group could write different sections for the information sheet, and you can collect it the following day and correct it. It could be developed into a mini project, e.g. a booklet for foreign visitors.

feedback checklist

During the **extended speaking** activity, note down examples of …

- **good language use**

- **effective communication strategies**
  (turn-taking, interrupting, inviting others to speak, etc.)

- **learner errors**
  (vocabulary, grammar, pronunciation, etc.)

- **particular communication problems**

Make sure you allow time for feedback at the end of the lesson. You can use the notes you make above to <u>praise</u> effective language use and communication or, if necessary, to do some remedial work.

---

troubleshooting generating ideas

Some learners may find it a little hard to consider some of the topics from an outsider's point of view, especially if they haven't travelled or don't know many foreigners. These learners would be well advised to concentrate on topics where they are recommending places in their town for sightseeing, eating out, and entertainment. However, if you start by brainstorming one of the topics as a class, e.g. public transport, they may well realize the potential within the subject matter. For instance, travel cards vary enormously from country to country, i.e. where you buy them, how much they cost, how long they are valid for, when and where you can use them, etc. You can also ask them to read the text about Bologna as an example of relevant information for foreigners. Some learners in your class may well have travelled abroad or they may be knowledgeable about issues such as behaviour through their acquaintance with foreigners in their own country.

test yourself!

Want to know more? Go to the **introduction** *p. 7* for ways of using **test yourself!**

1 tap sb on the shoulder, call out sb's name, touch sb's arm, whistle at sb, catch sb's eye
2 trip over sth; bump into sth / sb; fall off sth; crash into sth; knock sth over
3 Do you mind if I open the window? Would you mind if I opened the window? Do you think I could open the window?

1 I'd have a problem doing that.
2 Could you do me a favour?
3 I'd advise him to stay.
4 Who do you think is going to win the game?

1 Thank you for the very useful information.
2 How long are you going for?
3 I'm going to the cinema tonight with my sister.
4 Oh no! I've lost my wallet!

nine

wordlist

natural English

vague and exact time
Have you got the time?
What time do you make it?
It's getting on for seven.
Sevenish / eightish
It's around / about six.
Seven o'clock exactly.
Six on the dot.

emotional reactions
I can't stand it.
It drives me mad.
I find it slightly irritating.
It annoys me a bit.
I don't mind it.
It doesn't bother me.

saying how quickly you do things
I do it as quickly as possible.
I do it in a rush / hurry.
I spend a lot of time / ages (doing it).
I like to take my time.

if I was / were
If I was / were younger, the job would be easy.

use of *take*
How long would it take (you)?
It would take (me) about half an hour.
Does it take (you) long to get there?

vocabulary

collocation
use your mobile phone
do crosswords
chat to people on the phone
comb your hair
scratch your head
stare at people
have a shave
have a look at the paper
sing to yourself
put on make-up
get annoyed

wordbooster

words often confused
postpone / cancel
in time / on time
meeting / date
urgent / important
punctual / reliable

prefixes
(il)logical
(in)efficient
(im)practical
(dis)honest
(un)fair
(ir)responsible
(un)pleasant
(dis)organized
(in)convenient
(im)patient

glossaries
hitch / hitchhike (v)
drop sb (= take them somewhere)
pick sb up (collect them in a car)
tractor
give sb a lift
workaholic
in a bad mood
daydream (v)

in unit nine ...

life with Agrippine
cartoon transport
natural English vague and exact time

reading getting nowhere fast
vocabulary collocation
reading What do you do when you're stuck in a rush hour jam?
natural English emotional reactions

listening how quickly do you do it?
natural English phrases saying how quickly you do things
listening people saying how quickly they do things
grammar first and second conditional
natural English if I was / were ...

wordbooster
words often confused
prefixes

how to ... learn English faster
natural English use of take
grammar frequency adverbs and adverbial phrases
listening a teacher talks about her learners' use of English out of class
writing write a learning diary

extended speaking a question of time
collect ideas complete a questionnaire about time
talk about the questionnaire discuss answers and evaluate the results
prepare and write a questionnaire for others to complete
natural English phrases asking about other people's answers

test yourself!
revision and progress check

life with Agrippine   20 – 25 mins

read for pleasure
nE vague and exact time

• Either use the discussion questions at the beginning of the lesson, or take the opportunity to pre-teach some key vocabulary from the glossary, i.e. *to hitch (a lift) / hitchhike, to pick sb up, to drop sb, to give sb a lift.* These are all useful items. You could then ask learners to brainstorm the pros and cons of hitchhiking.

cartoon time
1 because she really wants her mother to pick her up
2 because if she doesn't, Agrippine could get into dangerous situations

---

language point vague language: time and numbers

In unit three *p.35*, we looked at examples of vague language, e.g. *and that sort of thing.* Vague language is also used with numbers and time, when it isn't necessary (or possible) to be exact.

Around, about, and *roughly* all mean *approximately*, e.g. around / about seven; roughly forty, etc.

The suffix *-ish* is used in spoken English with time and numbers, e.g. I'll meet you at sevenish (= about seven); He's thirtyish (= about thirty). It can also be used to describe approximate colour and size, e.g. yellowish, tallish.

Something and *odd* can be used after a number, e.g. He's twenty something (= twenty to thirty); There were fifty odd at the party (= fifty to sixty).

Go to **language point** vague language *p.35*.

---

reading getting nowhere fast

tell stories about getting stuck in traffic

learn verb-noun collocations on the same topic

read an article about traffic jams

express emotional reactions to different situations using **natural English** phrases

lead-in

- Tell learners to cover the text and look at the headline and photo. They can use the photo to deduce some of the words. You can check *rush hour* by asking when it occurs in your town / city. Practise the pronunciation at the same time.

- If you want to do a quick focus on the past continuous in this section, see **language point** on the right.

- When learners are telling their stories in **exercise 3**, monitor and make notes. Listen to see if there is a particularly good story one learner could tell in feedback. Go over some of the language points you noted.

vocabulary collocation

- Do a couple of examples for **exercise 1** with your class before they work alone or in pairs, e.g. *do your hair, do your homework*. Learners won't necessarily come up with the same collocations as the ones in the text (which is fine), and they will find some new collocations when they read the article.

read on

- Give learners time to complete the glossary and task in **exercise 1**, then check the answers. You may want them to do one example, and then conduct feedback, before they work on the other part of the exercise. If necessary, clarify the meaning of *take it easy* = relaxed, not in a hurry.

- For **exercise 2**, tell learners to go through the text and circle the collocations included in **vocabulary exercise 1**. They could write down any new ones. Deal with any problems with new vocabulary, e.g. *do a crossword*.

- In **exercise 3**, learners can go through the text together to say which things they do / don't do. It doesn't matter if they don't drive; they can say what they do when they are in traffic on a bus, tram, etc. or a passenger in a car.

saying what you feel

- When you have checked the answers to **exercise 1**, ask learners to listen and mark the main stress in each line of the dialogue. Go back and replay each line so that they can repeat it as naturally as possible before they practise in pairs.

- Learners should not find the grammar questions in **exercise 2** too difficult, as it is a revision of the grammar in unit six. However, the word *whenever* may be new and is worth teaching, as it would be very natural in the following exercise and the **extended speaking** activity.

- For **exercise 4**, you may wish to encourage the learners to think about specific things that occur and may be annoying in the street in their own country. Provide some prompts to get them thinking.

exercise 1

rush hour = the time in the morning and evening when people are going to and from work / school, etc. and the roads and public transport are very busy

a *jam* = a traffic jam; a long line of cars, buses, etc. that can't move or can only move slowly

stuck = not able to move or escape

language point past continuous

Learners at this level should already be familiar with the past continuous, but **exercise 2** is an opportunity to check the concept and revise it. In the exercise, you can avoid the tense by saying I *was on my way to work / school*, etc. Otherwise, you are likely to need it, e.g. *I was cycling to school, I was driving to work, we were going to the centre*, etc. The most obvious way to revise it is to tell your own story using the framework in exercise 2, including a natural example of the tense. Then draw a timeline on the board and ask learners to indicate the traffic jam (at a definite point in time) and the background to the story / describing the scene before the main event (i.e. where you were going – perhaps a continuous line up to the moment the traffic jam started).

example	*I was driving to visit a friend.*		*I carried on driving.*
— x ——————————	— xxxxxxxxxxxxxxxxxxxx —	——————— x
I left home at 10.00	*I got stuck in traffic for an hour*		*I arrived, but my friend had gone.*

Highlight the form and weak form *was* /wəz// *were* /wə/.

Want to know more? Go to **Practical English Usage** by Michael Swan *pp.417–418*.

Want to know more? Go to the **workbook**, *p.54*.

exercise 1

1 Mr Stressed   4 The philosopher
2 The escapist   5 The workaholic
3 Miss Busy   6 Mr TakeItEasy

glossary

a punctual   c chat
b be in a bad mood   d daydream

exercise 2

get really angry; comb my hair; put on make-up; chat to friends; sing to myself; have a shave; scratch our heads; stare at ourselves in the mirror; do a crossword

ideas plus writing

You could develop a writing activity based on this text. Tell learners to work in groups of four or six, and find a partner within their group. Each learner has to tell their partner what they do in a traffic jam, and the partner writes a short paragraph as in the article, and then they swap roles. Finally, the group get together to collate their information.

You could change the topic if you prefer, e.g. what people do when they are on the beach, or on a long train journey or flight.

exercise 1

1c (strongly negative)   2a (quite negative)   3b (neutral)

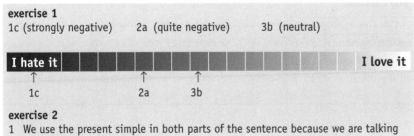

exercise 2

1 We use the present simple in both parts of the sentence because we are talking about what <u>generally</u> happens or how we generally behave in particular situations.
2 You could use *when* or *whenever* here in place of *if*.

listening how quickly do you do it? 65 – 80 mins

talk about how quickly they do things using **natural English** phrases

listen to people talking about how quickly they do things

focus on first and second conditional

talk about daydreams and the pros and cons of various propositions using first and second conditional

glossary

catenation the linking together of consonants and vowels across word boundaries

lead-in

- In **exercise 1**, learners could talk about themselves, and perhaps about members of their family who are different from them. Give them a minute to think of examples of how busy or relaxed they are.

- Ask learners to look at the **natural English** box, then drill the phrases (see **language point** on the right). Point out that *I spend a lot of time / I spend ages* are factual statements, whereas *I like to take my time doing …* means *I enjoy it*, i.e. for pleasurable activities. Highlight the + *ing* form for the phrases on the right, i.e. *spend time + ing, take your time + ing*. *In a hurry* and *in a rush* have the same meaning.

- **Exercise 2** could be done as a class mingling activity.

listen to this

- This listening follows on naturally from the previous section, as learners listen to native speakers talking about some of the same topics.

- After you listen in **exercise 2**, you could highlight: *high-powered* = important job with high status, *hang around* = stay somewhere and do nothing, *muesli* = breakfast cereal with nuts and fruit. If you feel you have done enough listening at the end of **listen carefully**, you could omit the **listening challenge**, or come back to it as a revision activity. Alternatively, you could do **exercises 2** and **3** as a jigsaw listening, if you have the space and facilities. Split your class into two groups, A and B. Group A can listen to Tyler, Julia, and Patience, and group B listen to Jeff and Ralph. They should fill in the table for the people in their part of the activity, then compare ideas and listen again or check against the tapescript if necessary. They then get into A / B pairs to complete the table. This makes the activity more interactive, and the listening less intensive.

grammar first and second conditional

- The examples in **exercise 1** are based on the recordings, so you could go to the **listening booklet** activity on *p.33* before you begin this exercise. You can ask the learners to think about the questions alone, with a partner, or simply go through them with the class. The only disadvantage with the latter is that unless you target weaker learners with specific questions, you may find that only stronger learners shout out the answers, and you won't be certain how many of the class understand.

- When you have gone over **exercise 1**, drill the sentences and focus on rhythm and the contraction *I'd*.

- In **exercise 2**, where learners make up their own sentences, you could ask them to write them down so that you can go round, monitor, and give individual help.

- Notice in **exercise 3**, we are not talking about extreme examples or impossible conditions; examples **a** and **c** are hypothetical or unlikely.

- **Exercise 4** could be done individually or in pairs.

talk about your daydreams

- It's important that learners tick the appropriate answers in **exercise 1**, but that they don't tell anyone.

- Point out the rule in the **natural English** box. You could drill the sentences to focus on the weak forms.

- Monitor while they are writing in **exercise 2** so that you can correct and guide where necessary.

- For **exercise 3**, learners could work in pairs or do a mingling activity. (They are going to work in groups in the next activity.)

it's your turn!

- This activity gives learners the opportunity to use the language in a freer and much more challenging context. Don't expect them to produce perfect sentences; be encouraging about the ideas that they do produce, and help them express their ideas where necessary.

- These topics are related to the theme of time, but you could change them to suit the class.

language point connected speech

The phrases in the **natural English** box include some examples of *catenation* in English. It is important for learners to recognize and practise it themselves so that they are better equipped to deal with connected speech.

in a rush   in a hurry   spend ages   spend a lot of time

You can highlight this form of linking on the board, and encourage learners to link sounds together by modelling the phrases yourself. Learners usually enjoy this sort of practice, especially if you keep it light-hearted.

Want to know more? Go to **Pronunciation Tasks** by Martin Hewings CUP, part 5.

---

exercise 1

1 DeNica: buying a present; she likes to take her time

exercise 2

2 Tyler: eat lunch; in a hurry
3 Julia: tidying up; spends ages
4 Patience: eat breakfast; as quickly as possible / in a hurry

exercise 3

5 Jeff: have a bath; hates to be in a rush / takes his time
6 Ralph: eat breakfast; spends ages

---

ideas plus vox pops

Vox pops are opinions given by ordinary people on a particular subject during a TV, radio, or newspaper report. They provide a natural way for learners to listen to a wide range of voices and accents, and because they are quite short, they don't overtire learners. They can, however, be difficult to tune into, given the variety of voices.

You can produce your own listening activities in a vox pop style. Choose a topic you know will interest your class (perhaps a local issue) and make some short recordings with native or non-native speakers of English. Prepare the interviewees so that they know what the topic is, how long they should speak, and how complex the language should be. Try to make your recording in a small, quiet room which will have better acoustics. Choose the best ones to play to your class; our experience is that not all of them will be usable.

---

exercise 1

1 past simple   4 no
2 could, would, might   5 imaginary
3 present or future

exercise 3

b and *d* will possibly happen; present simple / *will*
a and *c* almost certainly won't; past simple / *could, might*

exercise 4

1 is; will go / could go   4 had; would / could
2 were; would / could tell   5 run; will / might / can catch
3 arrive; will get   6 spoke; would / might / could

---

language point first and second conditional

1 For some nationalities, the most common error is to use *will* in both clauses in the first conditional, and *would* in both clauses in the second conditional, e.g. *If I ~~would have~~ time, I would go and see that play.*

2 Some learners find it difficult to distinguish between first and second conditional: this is because its use depends on the context and the speaker's attitude / point of view, which is not always obvious. In addition, some learners find it hard to live with the fact that both forms may be possible.

3 Some nationalities find it confusing that the tense used in the second conditional is past simple; they may think this suggests past time, which it doesn't, and they may feel a subjunctive form is required, as in romance languages. In fact, the subjunctive is rare in English.

4 The contraction *I'd* (= *would*) here may be misunderstood as *I had*.

 **wordbooster**

This **wordbooster** could be done at any time in the unit before the **extended speaking** activity.

words often confused

- These pairs of words overlap in meaning, so they are easily confused. Learners will have an opportunity to use most of them in the **extended speaking** activity, so the focus here is on clarifying the differences in concept. You may need to give more examples. If in their own language there is one word to cover both concepts, you could point this out.

prefixes

- Prefixes such as *un-*, *in-*, *il-*, *ir-*, and *dis-* can make some adjectives and some verbs negative. Learning prefixes is a quick and easy way for learners to expand their vocabulary.
- After **exercise 1,** drill the words which are difficult to pronounce, e.g. *inefficient, dishonest, inconvenient.*
- For more practice, look at **language reference** on *p.167* and *p.168* and select **cover & check** exercises.

how to ... learn English faster

60 – 70 mins

talk about how long things would take, using **natural English**

focus on frequency adverbs and adverbial phrases

listen to a teacher of English talking about using the language outside the classroom

discuss the ideas

write a learning diary for the week

How long would it take?

- The one-minute warning here doesn't have to be taken literally; the aim is to create a sense of urgency. See how learners are getting on, then give them a ten-second warning. You could do the **natural English** box first before they compare answers.
- Play the recording in the **natural English** box. The aim is to encourage learners to listen intensively. All the forms, with or without brackets, are correct English. These questions are not difficult for learners receptively, but they rarely use them in production at this level, and they are very common.
- Check the concept quickly by asking learners the difference between *How long would it take ...?* (i.e. a hypothetical question) and *How long does it take ...?* (i.e. a factual question).

grammar frequency adverbs and adverbial phrases

- This activity would best be approached as a test-teach-test. See what learners can do in **exercise 1**; they will know most of the words.
- When you go over the answers, clarify the meaning of the unknown items using the line and the way they relate to other adverbs. You could do it as a class activity using the board if you prefer. Check pronunciation, especially the items with phonemic script.
- For **exercise 2**, learners need to treat the adverbs in **exercise 1** as a group, and find only one position where they are <u>all</u> correct. At this point, we are not concerned with whether they can go at the beginning or the end of sentences. For question 1, go over the first example together, then ask the learners to work in pairs on the others. Do question 2 afterwards (beginning sentences with adverbs).
- In **exercise 3**, learners have to produce personalized examples using the prompts.

Want to know more? Go to **how to ...** introduce new language *p.143*.

English out of class time

- The task in **exercise 1** is quite straightforward, but there is a dual purpose to having this list on the page: to make learners aware of the various opportunities for continuing with their English outside class, and to prepare them for the listening in **exercise 3**.
- After learners have discussed **exercise 2**, conduct a class feedback and write up the learners' own new ideas on the board.
- In **exercise 5**, check that <u>each</u> learner has a stated intention to follow up two activities.
- Remember to follow up **exercise 6** in the next lesson. See **troubleshooting** on the right.

exercise 1

1 a d; b c	3 a c; b d	5 a c; b d
2 a d; b c	4 a d; b c	

exercise 1

1 illogical	4 dishonest	7 unpleasant	9 inconvenient
2 inefficient	5 unfair	8 disorganized	10 impatient
3 impractical	6 irresponsible		

exercise 3

1 unfair	3 irresponsible	5 illogical	7 disorganized
2 inconvenient	4 impatient	6 dishonest	8 impractical

nE

no, the words in brackets are not included in the recording

ideas plus mini-project

As a mini-project, you could carry out the six tasks in **exercise 1** in class over a series of lessons, and find out exactly how long each one takes. You could adapt them if you wish, e.g. reduce the fifteen irregular verbs to ten. They are all useful learning activities, and can all be done in learners' own time, so you could be encouraging them to carry on learning beyond the classroom.

exercise 1

1 hardly ever / rarely   2 occasionally   3 quite often   4 almost always

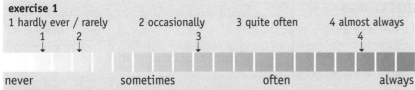

never   sometimes   often   always

exercise 2

1 You can put all the adverbs before the main verb, with the exception of the verb *be*; adverbs go after the verb *be*. (If there is an auxiliary verb, the adverb goes between the auxiliary and the main verb, e.g. *I've never been able ...*).

2 *Sometimes, occasionally, often, quite often* can all go at the beginning. However, *often* and *quite often* are less likely and less natural at the beginning.

exercise 1

1 listening, reading	6 reading, writing
2 speaking, listening	7 listening
3 reading	8 listening
4 listening, reading	9 listening, speaking
5 reading	10 writing

exercise 3

listening

exercise 4

Jackie mentions activities: 1, 3, 4, 5, 6, 7, 8, 9

troubleshooting English outside class

The opportunities for learning English outside the classroom are increasing all the time: satellite TV, the Internet, and increasing use of English in the local environment (adverts, menus, films in original version, greater numbers of English speakers), all make it much easier for learners to access English in their free time. If you can tap into this, and encourage learners to find a medium that interests them, they could make significant progress. It is often through peer advice and suggestion that learners are prepared to try something new.

It is important that you follow this up, so in the next few lessons, ask learners in what ways they have tried to encounter more English outside class.

extended speaking a question of time

60 – 70 mins

complete and discuss a questionnaire about time

evaluate the results

write some questions of their own for others to complete

- It is important at the beginning of this activity to let learners read the left-hand column or tell them what they are going to do in the lesson, or put it on the board. This will enable them to get the whole picture. You should also give them time to look back at the blue **extended speaking** boxes which occur at the end of each section in the unit.

collect ideas

- Get the learners to look at **exercise 1** and the first question of the questionnaire. Then, provide a model yourself. Speak for <u>at least</u> a minute and give examples and reasons for your answers, so that learners will see what is expected of them. Alternatively, look at **ideas plus** on the right.

- Monitor the group work in **exercise 2** to make sure they are doing the task appropriately. Have a brief feedback at the end.

- The thinking time in **exercise 3** is important and will pay dividends when you get to the discussion. Give learners a chance to read and ask you questions about vocabulary. The only new item that hasn't been taught in the unit is *be about to do sth* (= be going to happen very soon).

talk about the questionnaire

- The **natural English** box contains useful language for learners to negotiate their way through the questionnaire and move the conversation on. You could get learners to look at the phrases and drill them.

- Organize the learners into groups for **exercise 4** (three is an ideal size). During the activity, monitor and make notes. Listen to see if there are any interesting answers you can ask learners to share with the class at the end.

- When the groups are close to finishing, give them a two-minute warning, so they know when they have to stop. This activity is likely to take 10 to 15 minutes (if longer, so much the better). Give them time to analyse their scores in **exercise 5**. It is important to point out that they may or may not agree with the results; such questionnaires are not necessarily reliable.

Want to know more? Go to **how to ...** rmonitor and give feedback *p.156*.

prepare your own questions

- Monitor while learners are working in pairs. They should both produce a copy on separate sheets of paper, so that they can each carry out the survey with a new partner.

- If you want an extra writing activity, you could ask learners to write about how they manage their time, based on several questions from the questionnaire.

feedback checklist

During the **extended speaking** activity, note down examples of …

- **good language use**

- **effective communication strategies**
  (turn-taking, interrupting, inviting others to speak, etc.)

- **learner errors**
  (vocabulary, grammar, pronunciation, etc.)

- **particular communication problems**

Make sure you allow time for feedback at the end of the lesson. You can use the notes you make above to praise effective language use and communication or, if necessary, to do some remedial work.

ideas plus making a recording

Find one or two co-operative colleagues or speakers of English, and ask them to think about the first question in the questionnaire. Then, make a recording (in a quiet place), in which you ask them about their answers and ask follow-up questions. Use this in class as a model for your learners, and accompany it with a short listening task to check their comprehension.

test yourself!

Want to know more? Go to the **introduction** *p.7* for ways of using **test yourself!**

1 It's getting on for 6.00; sixish; around / about six.
2 inconvenient; illogical; impractical; irresponsible; inefficient; unfair; disorganized
3 *postpone* = delay / *cancel* = decide an arrangement will not take place; *meeting* = a work arrangement / *date* = a romantic meeting; *on time* = punctually / *in time* = not late; *pick sb up* = collect sb; *drop sb* = take sb in your car to an agreed destination

1 Traffic noise annoys / irritates me a bit.
2 I tidied the kitchen in a hurry / rush.
3 Have you got the time?
4 It doesn't bother / worry me if they arrive late.

1 If I earned a lot of money, I'd get a new car.
2 I could see better at football matches if I was taller.
3 I often do my homework on time.
4 We can go out this afternoon if the weather is nice.

wordlist

natural English

the whole ...
I spent the whole time worrying.
We visited the whole country.
The whole thing was a disaster.

generalizations (2)
Parents tend to worry a lot.
On the whole, I like it.

get + past participle
Several things got stolen.
The glass door got smashed.
I don't know how that vase got broken.

stereotypes
People often say that ...
Actors are supposed to be ...
Teachers are said to be ...

invitations
Do you fancy going ... ?
How about going ... ?
I was wondering if you'd like to ... ?

making and accepting excuses
I'd love to, but (unfortunately) ...
I'm afraid I can't.
I've got to (work tonight).
Sorry, but I (won't be able to come).
Never mind.
That's a pity / shame.
Another time, maybe.

vocabulary

parties
house-warming party
host / hostess
gatecrasher
fancy dress
wedding reception
guest

discussing character
hard-working
caring
honest
tell the truth
liar
corrupt
self-confident
make promises
lazy
patient

mature
sensitive
conventional
loyal

collocation
give sb a lift
babysit for a friend
sort out a problem
pick up a friend from the airport
go and see clients
do revision
deliver documents
go away on business
give a presentation
go to a rehearsal
see sb off at the airport
write an essay

wordbooster

reasons for being late
I missed the bus.
My car had a puncture.
I bumped into an old friend.
The train drivers are on strike.
I got held up in the traffic.
My car broke down.
The alarm clock didn't go off.
I got off the bus at the wrong stop.

suffixes
tolerant / tolerance
confident / confidence
tidy / tidiness
kind / kindness
similar / similarity
stupid / stupidity
honest / honesty
cruel / cruelty

glossaries

boast about sth / sb
a (luxury) cruise
lipstick
nod your head
smash (v)
nightmare
guilty
fingerprint

all sorts

do you get it?   20 – 25 mins

listen for pleasure
vocabulary parties
nE *the whole ...*

- You may need to explain further the meaning of *boast*. For example, you could boast about your new car, or about what a big house you have, or how clever you are.
- The vocabulary (**parties**) leads on from the joke, and some of the items are relevant to the next section about teenage parties.

nE
1 No, I read the whole book.   3 No, she saw the whole thing.
2 No, he ate the whole packet.

parties
1 house-warming party   4 fancy dress party
2 host   5 wedding reception
3 gatecrasher   6 guest

---

ideas plus lead-in to the lesson

For a change of approach, you could make four flashcards, writing on them each of the relationships described in the first activity, e.g. mothers and daughters. Put each card in a different corner of the room, and tell learners to go to the corner which they think is the best relationship. Once there, they work with the others in their group to think of reasons why, and give examples. This will allow them to gather ideas. Then tell them to find someone who chose a different relationship to compare their points of view.

---

reading those teenage years

discuss teenagers

focus on articles and determiners

make generalizations about teenagers and parents using **natural English** phrases

read and discuss an article about teenage parties

describe unexpected events using *get* + past participles

describe and listen to anecdotes about parties

lead-in

- If you have a mixed group of teenagers and adults, you need to decide whether to mix the groups for **exercises 1** and **2**, or to tell all the teenagers to work together. If your class are all teenagers, you could ask them to think about what their parents say about teenagers. Monitor the discussion and listen for interesting comments that learners can share with the class at the end.

grammar articles and determiners

- This is a test-teach-test activity, as most learners at this level will have come across some rules for the use of the definite article before. See **language point** on the right. You can ask learners to compare their answers before going over **exercise 1** and checking the rules in **exercise 2**.

- The **natural English** box follows on logically. When we make generalizations, we tend not to use the definite article (a common source of error). After playing the tape and practising the sentences, give learners a minute to think about whether they agree with the statements in the box.

- **Exercise 3** gives them an opportunity to consolidate the grammar and natural English input through freer discussion.

- **Exercise 5** moves on to look at some common errors with determiners and plurals. You could ask them to look at the **language reference** on *p.169*, as a way of checking their answers, before class feedback. Some errors are characteristic of certain nationality groups, but not others.

- In **exercise 6**, they should be given some freedom to express and develop their ideas. Don't feel you need to keep tight control in this activity.

Want to know more? Go to **how to ...** introduce new language *p.143*.

read on

- Learners have already talked a lot about relationships between parents and teenagers, and parties, so you can go into the text without any further introduction.

- For **exercise 2**, see **troubleshooting** on the right. Ask the pairs to feed back their answers to the class to see if their ideas are similar.

- You'll notice the questions in **exercise 3** include several examples of *get* + past participle. Even if this structure is new, learners should still be able to do the task, as the meaning is fairly clear. However, when you focus on the **natural English** box, you could refer back to the questions. The construction *get* + past participle is used in the common phrases *get dressed*, *get married*, *get changed*, etc. and also here as a form of passive. In this case, it often has a negative connotation, i.e. things going wrong.

it's your turn!

- For **exercise 1**, monitor to see if there are any interesting or amusing anecdotes that learners could tell the class at the end.

- The listening activity in **exercise 2** is meant to be a very light-hearted end to the lesson: for this reason, we haven't laboured it with a lot of comprehension tasks. You can let learners listen with the tapescript if you prefer (see **listening booklet**, *p.36*).

exercise 1
1 –   2 the   3 –   4 –   5 the   6 –   7 –;–   8 the

exercise 2
1 we **don't use** the definite article
2 we **use** the definite article

nE
I think parents tend to worry too much about their teenage children.
On the whole, parents are stricter with their first child than with later children.

exercise 5
1 **Most teenagers** tend to go out in large groups.
2 **Most** teenage boys are more interested in football than the opposite sex.
3 **All teenagers** are allowed to stay out later at weekends.
4 **Most of** the teenagers I know have parties for their friends at their family home.
5 **Some parents** let their teenagers have a party at home and go out themselves.
6 **Most teenagers** don't imagine things can go wrong at their party.

exercise 1 glossary
a lipstick   b nod   c smash   d guilty

exercise 3
Rochelle's party: 1, 5, 6
Zoe's party: 2
Luke's party: 3, 4

language point articles and determiners

This is a huge area of grammar, but we have concentrated in this unit on a few specific areas which prompted a large number of errors in our data for the **extended speaking** activity, **men and women**. Moreover, these errors seemed to occur across the board in terms of nationality. Many nationalities, whether there is an article system or not in their mother tongue, have difficulties with zero article, e.g. *The life is hard*. Most nationalities also made errors with the use of *all, most,* and *some,* e.g *Most of people think that … All people enjoy …*

If you work with a nationality that has additional problems with the article system in English, you can use the **language reference** and **cover & check** exercises on *p.169*, and there is further work on definite versus indefinite articles in the **workbook** *p.59*.

troubleshooting reacting to a text

In the classroom, there is sometimes a conflict between asking learners to react spontaneously to a text (as they would in real life), alongside the need to check learners' understanding of the text, perhaps through a more mundane or artificial task, e.g. comprehension questions. In most cases, we tend to check comprehension before we ask learners to react. Sometimes, however, and particularly with a provocative text, it may be best to give learners the chance to react to the content while it is still immediate, and to worry about detailed understanding later. This is the approach we have taken with this text, and if it is something you haven't done before, you may wish to try it in the future.

listening different groups, different types   70 – 80 mins

glossary

connotation an idea suggested by a word in addition to its main meaning, e.g. positive / negative connotation

vocabulary describing character

- Check the meaning and pronunciation of *stereotype* and *politics / politician*. Ask learners to look at the opinions in **exercise 1**, and deal with the meaning of any new words or phrases, particularly *caring* (= kind and helpful towards people) and *corrupt* (= prepared to use power to do sth dishonest for money or advantage).

- Make sure learners can pronounce the phrases correctly before they compare their ideas with a partner in **exercise 2.** Conduct a short class feedback on their ideas, and again, check their pronunciation.

- **Exercise 3** could be done in pairs, and learners can probably deduce most of the items from context and a process of elimination. Let them use dictionaries if they have them, and check they can pronounce the words in phonemic script before they test their partner.

- **Exercise 4** can be done quickly as a class activity.

lead-in

- Learners can use the language they have just learnt, or any other language they think is relevant. You may wish to elicit ideas for one of the occupations from the class first to check they understand. If you like, you can then go straight into the **natural English** box. Put some of their ideas on the board, and then preface them with the key phrases *People often say that x are …* or, *y are supposed / said to be …* . Practise the phrases, then go back and give them time to think about the other occupations.

listen to this

- **Exercise 1** gives learners the chance to predict, which should enable them to tune in to the three people in **exercise 2** quite easily, even if their guesses were wrong. There are some items which may be new to the learners, and you may wish to highlight these after **exercise 3**: *bad-tempered* = somebody who gets angry easily, *fake* = not real or authentic, *muddle through sth* = do without a plan and not very well, *mess* = a very untidy state, *come across* = meet, *entourage* = a group of people who travel with an important / famous person.

- See **ideas plus** on the right for another way of handling **exercise 5**.

grammar defining relative clauses

- You could put the gap fill sentences in **exercise 1** on the board, and ask learners which words (*who, which, that*) can go in the sentences. They can then complete them in their **student's book** as a written record.

- For **exercise 2**, do the first example with the class, and put the sentence on the board. Then they can do the rest.

- Learners can work on **exercise 3** in pairs, once you have made sure that they know they need to look for appropriate adjectives. They should have enough vocabulary to do each sentence, but one or two new words may arise, e.g. *tolerant* and *optimistic*; *tolerant* reappears in section 2 of **wordbooster**.

- If you want more practice go to **language reference** and do the **cover & check** exercises on *p.170*.

exercise 3
1 sensitive   2 mature   3 patient   4 loyal
5 lazy   6 conventional

exercise 4
insensitive, immature, impatient, disloyal,
unconventional

troubleshooting sensitive issues

In some countries, politicians arouse strong feelings, and many people have a very stereotypical view of them. If this is not the case in the country where you work, or if politics is a sensitive issue which you should avoid, you could adapt the exercise for a different profession or group, e.g. lawyers, car mechanics, the police, doctors, etc. or whatever is likely to arouse strong views, and hopefully conflicting ones, among your learners. However, remember that the aim is to stimulate discussion, not polarize the group, so avoid anything too controversial.

troubleshooting stereotyping

We are conscious of the fact that stereotypes can often reinforce prejudices, but they are a fact of life, and we have introduced the topic to give learners appropriate language (as in the **natural English** box) to describe typical behaviour without sounding rude or dogmatic, e.g. *People say that the French / Japanese / British are / tend to be* ... compared with the rather abrupt *The French / Japanese / British are* ... . Notice the use of *tend to* – a very high frequency verb in spoken and written English – as another way of softening an opinion. This would also be a good opportunity to revise *a bit* and *rather* which are used before adjectives with a negative **connotation** to modify or soften the opinion, e.g. *People often say that supermarkets are rather / a bit impersonal.*

exercise 2
primary school teachers; university students; chat show hosts

exercise 3
1 true   2 false   3 true   4 false   5 true   6 true

exercise 5
DeNica thinks female rock stars have lots of people working for them, but they have isolated lives. Jonathan thinks that rock stars in the 60s and 70s drank a lot and had lots of girlfriends, etc. but rock stars now are clean living, married, and settled down.

ideas plus listening task

You could elicit from the learners their ideas about rock stars and write them on the board for **exercise 5**. They can then use this as a listening task for the **listening challenge**, by comparing the speakers' ideas with their own. This gives the task a more concrete focus and probably makes the **listening challenge** a bit easier to deal with.

exercise 1
1 who / that   2 which / that

exercise 2
1 I only watch TV programmes which / that teach me something.
2 I prefer stories which / that are all about love.
3 I hate drivers who / that go very slowly.
4 I give money to anyone who / that asks me.
5 I don't understand people who / that think the worst will always happen.
6 I often speak to passengers who / that sit next to me on the train.
7 I always thank people for presents which / that they've given me.
8 I don't mind neighbours who / that make a lot of noise.

exercise 3
2 romantic   6 sociable / friendly
3 impatient   7 polite
4 generous / kind / stupid 8 tolerant
5 optimistic

exercise 4
I always thank people for presents which / that they've given me. You can omit *that* because it is the object. The following clause has a subject.

ideas plus extra practice

If you want to provide some extra practice with defining relative clauses and other language points from this section, you could give your learners the following exercise to complete in pairs.

1 People who drive sports cars tend to be

_____.

2 People that eat a lot of fresh fruit are generally

_____.

3 People _____ are very irritating.

4 Books _____ tend to be very boring.

5 TV programmes _____.

They can then change pairs and compare their ideas.

 wordbooster

25 – 30 mins

The first section of this **wordbooster** leads into the **how to ...** section, so is most logical here; the section on suffixes can be done at any time.

reasons for being late

- Learners at this level shouldn't have a problem with understanding this vocabulary but often have problems in producing it correctly. The reasons here will be useful for the **how to ...** section.
- After **exercise 1**, you could give learners a minute to study the correct sentences and test their partner, e.g. **A** I got home three hours late because I ... the last bus. **B** missed.
- In **exercise 2**, point out that their reasons are not limited to those given in **exercise 1**.

suffixes

- You will find suffixes other than the noun suffixes given in **exercise 1** if you go to the **language reference** on *p.170* and *p.171*. You may wish to focus on these and use the **cover & check** exercises, either in class or for homework. For many nationalities, suffixes don't require a lot of explanation, especially by this stage of learning, but learners may benefit from a certain amount of rote learning and practice.
- You could encourage learners to keep a record of these word relationships, and note any pronunciation changes. See **language point** on the right.

how to ... make excuses

65 – 75 mins

talk about inventing excuses in different situations

make invitations using **natural English** phrases

learn common verb + noun collocations

make and accept excuses using **natural English** phrases

listen to a conversation between friends where an invitation is made

role play similar situations in pairs

how about it?

- **Exercise 1** gives learners a chance to discuss some personal situations as a lead-in to the topic.
- When learners have listened and filled the gaps in the **natural English** box, highlight the *-ing* form with *Do you fancy ...?* and *How about ...?*
- The preparation for **exercise 3** can be done orally or in writing.

vocabulary collocation

- When you go over the answers to **exercise 1**, you could also elicit whether the four phrasal verbs are separable or not. (*Pick up, see off,* and *sort out* are all separable here, e.g. *I'm picking up a friend from the airport / ... picking a friend up ...; see sb off* <u>has</u> to be separable; *go away* is inseparable.)
- **Exercise 2** could be done with a partner. Learners could copy the table into their vocabulary notebooks and complete it.

excuses

- Most of the language in the **natural English** box should be revision, although learners may not produce these forms very accurately or fluently. You could tell learners to shut their books, and see which excuses and acceptances you can elicit, feeding in new ones from the box at the end; then let them practise the dialogues in pairs before doing the mingling activity in **exercise 1**. This activity gives learners the opportunity to use the excuses in **wordbooster**.
- You may need to explain *stepson* = your husband / wife's son from a previous marriage, when learners read the summary in **exercise 4** and before you listen, you could pre-teach *works do* = a social event organized by your company.
- After listening, you may want to play the recording again and / or refer learners to the tapescript on *p.38* of the **listening booklet**. You could ask them to find out how Max made his excuse. (*I'd love to, but unfortunately, I've got to prepare a presentation for work.*)

exercise 1
1 missed 2 had 3 bumped 4 on 5 up 6 down 7 off
8 stop

exercise 1
group 1   tolerance, ignorance, confidence, patience
group 2   punctuality, similarity, stupidity, maturity
group 3   tidiness, laziness, politeness, kindness
group 4   honesty, modesty, cruelty, loyalty

exercise 2
-ant adjectives become -ance nouns; -ent adjectives become -ence nouns; maturity (omission of e); tidiness and laziness, y changes to i.

language point pronunciation practice

Encourage learners to say the words in **exercise 1**. You could get them to work in pairs and listen to each other, to find the words where the stress and pronunciation changes between adjective and noun, i.e. punctual, punctuality /pʌŋktʃu'ælɪti/; similar, similarity /sɪmɪ'lærɪti/; stupid, stupidity /stjuː'pɪdɪti/.

nE
Do you fancy going out for a meal tonight?
How about coming over for a drink this evening?
I was wondering if you'd like to see a film?

ideas plus learners' situations

Once they have read the situations in **exercise 1** and thought about them, you could ask learners in pairs to think up another situation where someone might tell the truth or invent an excuse. Put them in groups of four to discuss the given situations, then try out their own situations on each other.

exercise 1
1 give	5 go and see	9 prepare / give
2 babysit	6 do	10 go to
3 sort out	7 deliver / sort out / prepare	11 see sb off
4 pick up	8 go away	12 write

exercise 2
studying prepare a presentation, do some revision, write an essay
work sort out a problem with my boss, go and see some clients, deliver some documents, go away on business, give a presentation
social give sb a lift to the hospital, babysit for a friend, pick up a friend from the airport, go to a rehearsal, see sb off at the airport

language point binomials

These are pairs of words, often very similar in meaning and usually joined by and. They commonly occur together in a fixed order and are best treated as single vocabulary items. In **exercise 1**, go and see is an example of this, as are wait and see and try and do. There are also adjective combinations such as neat and tidy, nice and warm, safe and sound, as well as noun combinations such as law and order, rules and regulations, peace and quiet.

exercise 3
1 There are three voices.
2 Alison is late because of the traffic and parking problems.

exercise 4
Alison invites Max to go to a ~~dance~~ dinner at the Sheraton Hotel on ~~Sunday~~ Saturday evening. He would like to go, but he's got a lot to do this weekend, because he has to prepare a presentation for ~~50~~ 150 people for Monday, and he's busy on Sunday because ~~he's going to his stepson's house~~ his stepson is coming to see him.

extended speaking men and women

60 – 70 mins

discuss statements about the differences between men and women

produce new statements to discuss

record the group's opinions

- It is important at the beginning of this activity to let learners read the left-hand column or tell them what they are going to do in the lesson, or put it on the board. This will enable them to get the whole picture. You should also give them time to look back at the blue **extended speaking** boxes which occur at the end of each section in the unit.

collect ideas

- You could put the statement in **exercise 1** on the board for everyone to think about. Let them compare with each other, but don't do any feedback, because they are going to listen and discuss it again in **exercise 5**.

- Play the recording and go over the answers to **exercises 3** and **4**. The idea of this listening is to give learners a model for the later discussion, so that they can see the need to develop their ideas and justify them. For this reason you will have to allow them plenty of thinking time in the next section. Don't spend a long time on detailed comprehension of this recording, or learners will lose sight of the main aim, which is discussion. You could discuss the answers as a class.

exercise 3
Jonathan agrees with the statement; Julia disagrees with it.

exercise 4
Jonathan thinks men spend longer on the phone because they like using mobile phones. Julia thinks women spend longer on the phone because they like long chats and conversations.

extend the discussion

- Firstly, let learners read the topics and statements in the chart, so that they can ask you if there is anything they don't understand.

- Explain that they should make notes but not write full sentences. Suggest that they think about family, friends, or colleagues to help them answer. Be available to help in case individual learners want to ask you for help, e.g. how to express something.

- Before they start the discussion, learners have to invent their own topics with a partner. Don't worry if there are some learners who haven't come up with two topics; make sure you put them in groups with other learners who have invented discussion statements, then there should be plenty to discuss. If there is another topic learners would prefer to choose, that is fine, as long as it doesn't offend anyone!

- Briefly draw their attention to the **language reminder**; this was an error that occurred frequently in our data for this activity.

- Mixed groups will probably produce more differences of opinion naturally, but if your class is mainly composed of one sex, don't worry. Try to keep the group size to a maximum of four. Listen and monitor, taking notes for feedback later. Bring the activity to an end when most groups are nearly finished; don't let it run on to the point where learners are chatting about other things.

summarize opinions

- Ask the learners to summarize opinions within their group by completing the table, and if you like, elicit these and put them on the board to get a survey of the whole class. People can then comment on the results.

- Do feedback at the end of the activity, commenting on the learners' fluency and accuracy. Be sure to give praise wherever possible, especially where learners have spoken at any length and sustained their discussion.

feedback checklist

During the **extended speaking** activity, note down examples of …

- **good language use**

- **effective communication strategies**
  (turn-taking, interrupting, inviting others to speak, etc.)

- **learner errors**
  (vocabulary, grammar, pronunciation, etc.)

- **particular communication problems**

Make sure you allow time for feedback at the end of the lesson. You can use the notes you make above to <u>praise</u> effective language use and communication or, if necessary, to do some remedial work.

---

ideas plus writing a summary

If you want to provide learners with an opportunity to write about one of the topics, you could ask them (perhaps for homework) to write a short summary of their group's views. Here is an example:

Women spend longer on the phone than men.

In general, the people in my group tended to agree with this statement, but for different reasons. Enrico thought it was true because women like to gossip more than men. Carla and Silvia said it was because women work harder at relationships. On the whole, men use the phone for practical reasons.

---

test yourself!

Want to know more? Go to the **introduction** *p.7* for ways of using **test yourself!**

1 get held up in traffic, have a puncture, oversleep, your car breaks down, the buses / trains are on strike, bump into someone, get off the bus at the wrong stop
2 patience, honesty, tidiness, cruelty, punctuality, confidence, maturity
3 impatient, dishonest, insensitive, immature, lazy, corrupt, intolerant, cruel, etc.

1 I worked the whole afternoon.
2 The window got smashed.
3 Do you fancy coming for a drink?
4 I'm afraid I'm busy tonight.

1 Most students are very hard-working.
2 I can't understand people who speak fast.
3 Parents don't always understand teenagers.
4 Nurses are said to be very caring.

---

eleven

wordlist

natural English

have (got) sth on, with sth on
He hasn't got anything on.
I haven't got my glasses on.
The lady with the green hat on.

giving opinions about issues
I think it's OK to ...
I don't see any problem if ...
I don't think it's right to ...

which clauses
She invited all of them, which was kind of her.
We lost the match, which was disappointing.
They got up at 5a.m., which was crazy.

changing plans
I was hoping to ..., but in the end ...
I was planning to ..., but I ended up ...

uses of tell
You can't tell what's happening.
You can tell by their faces.
It's hard to tell (how old she is).

sequencing
Which one do you think comes first?
This one could be the earliest / the most recent.
This one must come before this one.

vocabulary

describing a picture
In the foreground / background ...
On the (far) right / left-hand side ...
In the middle ...
In the top / bottom left-hand corner ...
You can just see ...

wordbooster

word building
retire / retirement
achieve / achievement
regret (n), (v)
believe (in) / belief
fail / failure
grow / growth
elect / election
solve / solution
satisfied / satisfaction
successful / success
political / politics
proud / pride
famous / fame
wealthy / wealth
ambitious / ambition
poor / poverty

time expressions
towards the end of the film
at the end of the film
next month
the following month
shortly after (the wedding)
soon after (the wedding)
during (the war)
throughout (the war)
last year
in the last year

glossaries
horrendous
you can say that again ☺
get changed
remove
replace
improve
fit (v)

life with Agrippine   20 – 30 mins

read for pleasure
nE *have (got)* sth *on* / *with* sth *on* (= *wearing*)

Photo booths are common around the world, but if they don't exist in the country where you teach, you may need to explain what they are before learners read the cartoon. An alternative lead-in would be to ask learners these questions: *Have you ever had a photo taken professionally? If so, when and why? What was it like?* There are many occasions when this is done, e.g. baby photos, school photos, ID cards, weddings, etc. See also **ideas plus** below.

cartoon time
They realize they look terrible but don't want to admit it is them.

---

ideas plus photos

Photos make wonderful source material for a wide range of classroom activities, and many learners take and keep photos or have sets of photos of their own. You could exploit this by asking learners (in the previous lesson) to bring in four or five photos of people or places that are important to them. Start the lesson by talking through a little selection of your own photos that mean something to you, then put learners in small groups to show and talk about their own photos. If anybody doesn't have photos, they can listen to other people. You could do this as an introduction to this or other sections in this unit.

Want to know more? Go to **how to ...** introduce new language (try it out) *p.145.*

---

reading the camera never lies

find differences between photographs
read an article about changing photographs
give opinions using **natural English** phrases
focus on passives and practise them through dictogloss
talk about photos using *look, look like, look as if*

lead-in

- Give learners a minute or two to think about the differences between the photos in **exercise 1**. You could give them some information about the people, but it isn't essential (three of the names occur in the reading text). The people in the photo on *p.127* are, at the time of going to print (from left to right): Robin Cook (Leader of the House of Commons), Tony Blair (the Prime Minister), John Prescott (Deputy Prime Minister and First Secretary of State), and Gordon Brown (the Chancellor of the Exchequer).

- Avoid doing feedback on the answers at this point, because learners are going to read the text to find the differences.

read on

- For **exercise 1** you could tell learners to circle or underline the differences between the photos when they read the article. Let them compare with a partner.

- When you deal with the language in the **natural English** box, you will need to focus on intonation and sentence stress.

  I think it's <u>OK</u> to make people look more attractive.

  I don't see any <u>problem</u> if newspapers change pictures.

  I don't think it's <u>right</u> to take pictures of celebrities on holiday.

- For **exercise 3**, you could take in some photos from magazines and newspapers which relate to the questions, e.g. of adverts, famous people, riots, etc. to stimulate the discussion.

grammar passive forms

- **Exercise 1** makes use of the text to highlight the form and meaning of the passive. **Exercise 2** focuses on the form and pronunciation of different tenses of the passive. Make sure that learners are pronouncing the weak forms and contractions accurately through a class drill, or pair drilling as you go round.

- Notice that **exercise 3** is really a practice activity for passives in the form of a *dictogloss* (see **want to know more?** below). It includes some high frequency passive examples, e.g. *was born, was educated, was offered*, within the context of a personal biography, and these forms will be useful for learners in the listening section when they create their own life stories. You can expect that when learners do stage 3 of the dictogloss, i.e. reconstructing the text, they will have to think about whether to use active or passive forms, and they could make errors, e.g. they may try to use passive forms for *grow up, leave*, etc. When you get to stage 5, you can ask them to compare with the **listening booklet** on *p.40*, but at the end you should still go over the tenses used in the passage. If necessary, check understanding of these forms, as illustrated in exercise 1.

- The activity in **exercise 5** provides some speaking practice, and continues with the theme of photographs which have been altered. It also provides further (but limited) practice of the passive forms.

Want to know more? Go to **how to ...** introduce new language (dictogloss) *p.146*.

grammar *look, look like, look as if ...*

- For **exercise 1**, do the first example as a class, then learners can work together on the rest.

- In **exercise 2**, learners may not know how to express the final rule, (i.e. the word *clause*) but if they say *followed by a verb*, they have understood. It is worth pointing out that learners often understandably confuse these forms, and produce examples such as ~~he looks like mad~~.

- You could demonstrate **exercise 3** by writing a sentence on the board about someone in the class. Draw a blank line instead of the person's name and then ask the class to guess who it is. Then learners can either write individually, or in pairs if you prefer, and try their sentences out on other pairs.

exercise 1 glossary
1d 2c 3a 4b
The differences are: one man was removed; the background was darkened; the man on the left was moved closer to Tony Blair; the red plastic was removed; they put in a bottle of champagne; Gordon Brown's serious face was replaced with a happy, smiling face.

exercise 2
1 they used a computer program
2 to improve the quality; to make people fit on the page
3 a people believe that photographs reproduce reality
  b there's no problem with improving things a bit

language point giving opinions

Learners often pick up phrases to introduce opinions such as *in my opinion* or *from my point of view*. These are not easy for intermediate learners to use and can sound both stilted and rather opinionated. For this reason, we have provided some introductory phrases in the **natural English** box which are more neutral in style, but easy to learn and very natural. Furthermore, they are not the kind of phrases that learners at this level will usually produce unprompted, so you will need to highlight them.

exercise 1
1 We are more interested in what happened to the pictures than who changed them.
2 the passive form; was darkened, was moved, was also removed, was replaced, was chosen, was decided

exercise 2
Phones and faxes **are** /ə/ made here.
Her old house **is being** /ɪz ˈbiːɪŋ/ sold.
The letter **was** /wəz/ sent yesterday.
I've been /aɪv bɪn/ offered the job.
The report **will be** /əl biː/ finished later.

exercise 5
picture 1 1 Stalin, the head of the secret police, and two other men; 2 the head of the secret police was removed; 3 because he lost favour with Stalin.
picture 2 1 Princess Diana and Dodi Fayed; 2 Mr Fayed's head was rotated; 3 to make it seem as if they were kissing; this would be a much more sensational picture.

language point passive forms

Short passive forms, where the agent is not mentioned, e.g. *My bags were stolen*, are much more common than 'long' passive forms in which the agent is mentioned, e.g. *My bags were stolen by two young boys*.
Passives are relatively common in written English, especially in academic prose, but with a few exceptions, they are relatively infrequent in conversation.

exercise 1
1 both photos on *p.146*
2 Diana and Dodi on *p.148*
3 Stalin in the first photo on *p.146*
4 the men in the second photo on *p.146*
5 Stalin in both photos on *p.146*
6 Diana and Dodi in the first photo on *p.148*

exercise 2
1 *look* + adjective   2 *look like* + noun   3 *look as if* + clause

ideas plus commenting on photos

As an alternative to **exercise 3** you could ask learners to choose one or two photos of their friends / family that they brought to class which their classmates haven't seen or talked about yet. In pairs or groups of three, they can swap photos and make (positive) comments about the people in the photos, e.g. *He looks nice / cheerful. She looks like a teacher*, etc. They can respond to each others' ideas about the photos, e.g. *Yes, he is. That's my best friend, Carlos. Actually, she's a doctor. She's my cousin, Maria.*

Want to know more? Go to **how to …** activate vocabulary (using visuals) *p.140*.

 wordbooster

25 – 30 mins

This **wordbooster** is best used at this point in the unit as both parts will be useful for the listening section and the **extended speaking** activity.

word building

Exercise 1 would be a useful homework exercise, leaving you more class time to go over it in the next lesson and give learners more oral / pronunciation practice.

time expressions

These phrases will be very useful for the listening section and the **extended speaking** activity. Some are problematic because of L1 transfer, e.g. *last year, in the last year*, or overlapping meaning, e.g. *during* and *throughout* (see answer key). Discuss the first example together before learners work in pairs. See **ideas plus** on the right for oral practice.

exercise 1

a regret   b wealth   c achieve   d pride
e retire   f elect   g poverty   h ambition

exercise 2

verb	noun	adjective(s)	noun
retire	retirement	satisfying / ied	satisfaction
achieve	achievement	satisfactory	
regret	regret	successful	success
believe (in)	belief	political	politics
fail	failure	proud	pride
grow	growth	famous	fame
elect	election	wealthy	wealth
solve	solution	ambitious	ambition
		poor	poverty

language point

1 satisfaction
2 retire
3 achievement; proud
4 regret
5 success; wealthy
6 poverty

---

exercise 1

1 *towards the end of the film* = in the later part of the film
at the end = the final scene, the conclusion of the film
2 If this month is January, then *next month* is February. *The following month* is the one after the month you've mentioned (in the past or future), e.g. *I was in Rome last May, then the following month I went to ...* (i.e. June).
3 they have the same meaning
4 *throughout the war* = from the beginning of the war right through to the end of the war
during the war can have the same meaning, but it can also mean a time / a moment between the beginning and end of the war
5 *last year* = the year before this one
in the last year = during the twelve months leading up to now

---

language point collocation

Some of the items in the table have specific lexical and *grammatical collocations* which you could highlight as you go through the answers to **exercise 1**.

*famous **for** sth*   *proud **of** sb / sth*   ***live / die in** poverty*
*a **huge** success*   *retire **from** a job*   ***get** a lot of / great satisfaction **from** sth*

For extra practice, you could give learners these sentences to complete with words from the table.

1 As a policeman I got a lot of _____ from helping people.

2 She decided to _____ in her early sixties because of poor health.

3 My greatest _____ was learning to speak Japanese. I'm very _____ of that.

4 My biggest _____ is that I didn't stay in the navy. That was such a mistake.

5 His business was a huge _____ and the family became very _____, with houses all over the world.

6 Her life changed when she lost all her money and sadly, died in _____.

---

ideas plus practising time expressions

After completing their sentences in **exercise 2**, you could ask learners to find a partner. They read their sentence beginnings in a different order and ask their partner to guess the ending. Alternatively, you could do this as a mingling activity.

listening looking back over a lifetime

talk about people's biographies

listen to a person's future life story (imagined) and discuss it

focus on *which* clauses for adding comments and opinions

invent their own future life story

talk about changing plans using **natural English** phrases

tell a partner their life story

lead-in

- Start by teaching *biography* and *autobiography*, then go on to the exercise. You could ask learners if they have read any autobiographies recently, and what they were like. You could even bring in one or two to add authenticity and ask learners if they have read them or would be interested in reading them. You could also give them a list of famous people from their own country and learners can say whose biographies would interest them.

listen to this

- You need to set up this situation very clearly because it is an unusual type of autobiography. You could demonstrate it first to the class by telling them that you are going to describe your life until now, and then invent the next thirty to forty years. Briefly tell them your life story so far (three or four sentences) and then your invented life. You could ask them to tell you where they think the invented part begins and explain that Elly is going to invent her future life too. Then go on to **exercise 1**. Before you listen, you could explain that *GCSEs* are public exams taken by British students at the age of sixteen.

- **Exercise 2** is similar to the summary exercise in unit eight (see **troubleshooting** *p.85*). If you are highlighting the connectors as suggested in **language point** on the right, you could do this after exercise 2, and then ask learners to shut their books and reconstruct the story from the time connectors on the board. Before you listen in exercise 2, you could pre-teach: *be into* sth = be interested in / like something, *a big break* = sudden opportunity to do something and be successful, *household name* = somebody famous / that everybody knows.

- You could do **exercise 5** as an open class activity, or in pairs.

- When you practise the *which* clauses in the **natural English** box, model the intonation, pausing before *which*, and stressing the adjective.

- You could direct learners to the **listening booklet** on *p.40*, to find other examples of *which* clauses. They will find that there are other constructions following *which*, i.e. not just *which* + *be* + adjective (e.g. *they had their own furniture business, which did really well*).

- In **exercise 6**, they can use any appropriate construction and you could do this as a telepathy exercise. Learners work with a partner, but don't speak to them or look at what they are writing. They have to complete the sentences with a comment clause, trying to imagine what their partner is writing, and put the same. They then compare to see who has great telepathy.

it's your turn!

- In **exercise 1**, make it clear that learners do not have to include information about all the prompts. These are just designed to give them a framework and some suggestions. They can write notes, but discourage them from writing the biography as a text, or it will sound stilted when they tell it to a partner. The terms to do with military service are there partly because this is part of many people's experience around the world, but also because they come up in the **extended speaking** activity. See **troubleshooting** on the right.

- When you have done the **natural English** box, you could give them a minute to see if they can incorporate it into their invented autobiography.

- Monitor the activity in **exercise 2**, and make notes for feedback. If some learners finish early, pair them up with a new partner to retell one of their stories. Give learners feedback at the end, and plenty of encouragement if they have managed to speak continuously for any length of time.

- For **exercise 3**, we have suggested a short extract to write up, but if the activity has gone well and learners are keen, they could write their whole autobiography.

lead-in

1 Venus Williams (US tennis player)
2 Salvador Dali (Spanish artist, died 1989)
3 Ayrton Senna (Brazilian racing driver, died 1994)
4 Nelson Mandela (Ex-President of South Africa)
5 Hilary Clinton (US Ex-President's wife)

exercise 1

She was born in Toronto, Canada; she's an only child. Her parents were rich and they had a furniture business. They moved to England when she was three. She did well at school and went to university to study economics.

exercise 3

1 her family's furniture business
2 an actress
3 drama school
4 Tom (her husband)
5 a part in a TV soap opera
6 films / movies
7 retired
8 a Mediterranean island

exercise 4

1 She was offered a part in a major Hollywood movie.
2 She won an Oscar for Best Actress at 70. She thinks this is her greatest achievement.

language point time connectors

The gap fill summary in **exercise 2** provides a number of time connectors in sequence which would be useful to highlight or revise with your learners.

After university ... she soon realized that ... While she was there, she ...
In her thirties ... Later she ... She ... in her mid-fifties when she ...

In the recording, Elly twice uses the construction *It wasn't until x happened that ...* . If you feel your class needs a further challenge, you could highlight and practise this structure.

nE

I was hoping to work in television, but in the end I got a job in radio.
I was planning to travel a lot, but I ended up getting married and settling down.

troubleshooting reducing the level of challenge

The learners have had a lot of input leading up to the final activity. To make **it's your turn!** less demanding, you could do one of the following:
1 Do the activity, but omit the **natural English** box on changing plans.
2 Ask learners to tell the first part of their life story, i.e. up to now, then tell them to prepare their ideas for the invented part for homework, and do the speaking activity in the next lesson.
3 Set the whole activity up as a homework exercise. Learners should make notes on their ideas for their future and plan the first part too. In the next lesson, do the **natural English** box, then they can do the speaking activity.

how to ... talk about a picture

65 – 80 mins

artistic tastes

- Check learners understand and can pronounce the vocabulary in **exercise 1**, then give them a chance to discuss their ideas.

vocabulary describing a picture

- The meanings of the phrases in **exercise 1** are fairly transparent and learners should be able to do the activity through a process of deduction and working together. The problems are more to do with form (see **language point** on the right).

- For the practice stages in **exercises 2** and **3**, you can ask learners to carry on until they can describe the parts of the picture without looking at the phrases.

grammar modal verbs of deduction

- If your learners have difficulty with the concept of *must / can't* here, you should focus on the idea of something being a logical explanation, or the most logical explanation. With *might* and *could*, you are talking about logical possibilities. Do the first example in **exercise 1** together, then ask learners to try the rest alone and compare with a partner afterwards.

- *Must* /mʌst/ is stressed with this meaning. Practise the sentences using modal verbs to check your learners' pronunciation.

- You could provide extra reinforcement here by doing a 'test your partner' activity. Student A (with their book open) should say an **a** or **b** sentence. Student B should say what it means.

- For **exercise 3**, learners can either work in pairs, then tell the class, or work alone and then compare with a partner. You could ask learners to write the sentences if you prefer so that you can check individuals have understood and can use the forms. Then give them an opportunity to express their views in **exercise 4**.

- When you look at the **natural English** box together, you could ask learners to think about how this meaning would be translated into their language, or whether *tell* might be translated differently in the three examples.

- **Exercise 5** provides further practice of the forms. Remind learners that they can use the phrases *They could well be ... / It could well be ...*, etc. to make deductions.

- If you feel your learners need a further challenge, you could introduce and practise modal verbs of deduction in the past, using the **workbook**, *p.69*.

it's your turn!

This activity gives learners the opportunity to put everything they have learnt into practice. You may find it works best if half the class choose one picture, and the other half choose the other; they can then pair up for **exercise 2**.

exercise 1
1 In the top left-hand corner ...
2 In the background ...
3 The man on the far left-hand side ...
4 In the middle ...
5 The man on the far right-hand side ...
6 In the foreground ...
7 In the bottom right-hand corner ...

exercise 3
In the foreground, there are some men sitting round a table. In the background, you can see some men lying on beds. The man on the far left-hand side is looking thoughtful. The man on the far right-hand side is picking up some cups. The people in the middle are making sandwiches. In the top left-hand corner you can just see a table; in the bottom right-hand corner you can see three mugs.

---

language point describing pictures

This language is extremely useful for First Certificate speaking test, but there are a number of linguistic pitfalls for intermediate learners:
1 Many languages don't use the modal verb *can* (learners say ~~I see~~ ... and not *I / you can see* ...).
2 Learners find *on the right / left-hand side* a mouthful; they tend to say ~~the right / left side~~.
3 They may get the prepositions wrong, e.g. they say ~~in the left-hand side~~.
4 They often don't know the phrases *in the foreground / background*.
5 The use of *just* meaning *barely* may cause problems, although in unit three they met *I can just remember* ... in the **natural English** box, *p.40*.

---

exercise 1
1 ad; bc   2 ac; bd   3 ac; bd   4 ad; bc

exercise 2
1b   2b   3b   4b

Paintings A and B are both by Stanley Spencer (1891–1959), a British artist many of whose paintings reflect his wartime experiences. He was a hospital orderly during the First World War. A is called *Tea in the Hospital* and B is *Village Life, Gloucestershire*.

exercise 3 possible answers
The man on the bed on the right might be looking at a photo of his wife.
The man picking up the cups can't be very badly injured.
The man eating sandwiches must be hungry.

---

language point common verbs

Common verbs such as *tell*, *see*, *give*, and *leave* are very familiar to learners, so they often assume they understand them. In so doing, however, they can overlook important meanings of common verbs that are actually new to them, and may not have a direct equivalent in their own language. *Tell* meaning *recognize* is one example of this.

other examples

see = understand (*I see what you mean.*)
see = find out (*I'll ask him and see what he says.*)
leave = forget (*I left my hat on the bus.*)
leave = allow sth to remain (*Leave your coat there.*)

The paintings are both by the contemporary British artist, David Hockney, and the first one is called *Mr and Mrs Clark and Percy*. It was painted in the 1960s. This couple were friends of the artist, and were both fashion designers. The other painting by Hockney is of his parents, and dates from a later period.

---

ideas plus personal pictures

A possible approach to **it's your turn!** would be to tell learners the day before that they should bring one or two pictures to class with them; something that they are able to describe. It should be a picture that they like, e.g. a postcard of a painting, or something from an artbook, if they have one. This will make the activity more personalized. Alternatively, you can bring a number of postcards / pictures of your own to class and learners can select their favourite. (It is easy to get pictures off the Internet, e.g. www. altavista. com, or a search engine, e.g. yahoo.com then follow the links to arts.) Once they have described their picture, you can ask them to write a short description, i.e. giving the title, date, and artist, describing the picture and making deductions about it, and finally, giving their opinion. This could also make an interesting classroom display or project book.

extended speaking a life in pictures

50 – 60 mins

- It is important at the beginning of this activity to let learners read the left-hand column or tell them what they are going to do in the lesson, or put it on the board. This will enable them to get the whole picture. You should also give them time to look back at the blue **extended speaking** boxes which occur at the end of each section in the unit.

collect ideas

- You need to start **exercise 1** by pointing out that all the photos are about the life of one person – who is a real person – and that the aim of the activity is to organize the pictures and work out what happened in the person's life. Give learners plenty of time to study the pictures. Some of them contain quite a lot of detail which is useful to the overall story. Don't be tempted to tell them who the person is.

- When they have had enough time to think, feed in the language in the **natural English** box, which will be very useful in the next activity.

- For the pair activity in **exercise 2**, encourage the learners before they start to describe the photos in as much detail as possible, before deciding on the order. Go round and monitor, making notes for feedback. Don't tell them if they are making wrong guesses, though if you like, give learners a clue by asking questions, e.g. *What is the date of that picture?* or *Do they look like members of the same family?* You should also be available to help learners if they need particular vocabulary.

- Allow at least ten minutes for this stage of the lesson. Don't do class feedback at this point.

develop the story

- Here, learners change from description to narrative, i.e. they must try to tell the person's story. Let them have one go at this in **exercise 3**. If you like, put two pairs together to compare their versions of the story so far, as this will give them more practice and a chance to exchange ideas.

- In **exercises 4** and **5**, each learner gets some new information which should help to make more sense of the pictures. Give them time to think about how to incorporate the information, then tell their partner.

find out the facts

- Before you listen in **exercise 6**, you could pre-teach *a distinguished career* = very successful, *stand as a candidate* = present yourself as a candidate in an election, *euthanasia* = helping people to die without pain when they are very old or ill. What new information learners discover will depend on what they deduced in the earlier activities.

feedback checklist

During the **extended speaking** activity, note down examples of …

- **good language use**

- **effective communication strategies**
  (turn-taking, interrupting, inviting others to speak, etc.)

- **learner errors**
  (vocabulary, grammar, pronunciation, etc.)

- **particular communication problems**

Make sure you allow time for feedback at the end of the lesson. You can use the notes you make above to praise effective language use and communication or, if necessary, to do some remedial work.

test yourself!

Want to know more? Go to the **introduction** on *p.7* for ways of using **test yourself!**

1 *She looks* + adjective; *He looks like* + noun; *They look as if* + clause
2 belief, failure, success, growth, election, achievement
3 satisfactory, political, success, achievement, ambitious, poverty

1 He must know them.
2 Her bike was stolen.
3 He can't be Spanish.
4 I don't see any problem if papers change stories.

1 The books have been sent / were sent.
2 I saw him last year.
3 The man on the left of the photo.
4 She helped me, which was kind of her.

twelve

wordlist

natural English

what a ... !
What a disaster!
What a nightmare!
What a terrible thing to happen!

realize, remember, find out
I suddenly remembered (that) I'd forgotten ...
She realized (that) she'd already met ...
I found out later (that) I'd seen ...

numbers in phrases
a ten-cent coin
a ten-pound note
a five-pound phone card
a two-thousand-dollar reward

actually
He looks old, but actually he's only 32.
A Could I borrow the car?
B Actually, I need it today.

asking for clarification
I didn't understand the bit about ...
Could you explain the bit about ... again?
I'm sorry but I didn't understand what / why / how ...

vocabulary

driving
reverse
overtake
pull out
park (v)
slow down

money
wallet
purse
cashpoint
safe
lend / borrow
win / lose money
inherit
earn
invest money in sth

wordbooster

shopping
a sale / the sales
overcharge
refund (n)
deposit
receipt
bargain
exchange sth

phrasal verbs with back
ask for sth back
take sth back
send sth back
get sth back
come back
go back
give (sb) sth back
pay sth / sb back

glossaries
brand new (adj)
show sth off
tear sth off
disaster
sleeve
rubbish
funfair
budget (v)
bear in mind

money matters

do you get it?   20 – 30 mins

> **listen** for pleasure
> **vocabulary** driving
> **nE** *What a ...!*

- In the lead-in to the joke, explain the phrase *if money were no object*, i.e. if you were rich and money wasn't a problem. Tell learners that they don't necessarily need to choose a brand or make for each one, e.g. they may want to say *I don't care what brand of perfume I wear.* They could then compare with a new partner and justify their reasons.

- You could ask learners to look at the glossary and decide in which picture / context each vocabulary item could be used. Then tell them to talk about the pictures in pairs.

- When you have done the **natural English** box, you could ask learners to brainstorm other phrases with *What a ...+* noun, e.g. *What a shame / pity / nuisance / pain / mess.* They could then think what situations might prompt each of these phrases.

> **driving**
> 1b   2e   3a   4c   5d

> **language point** *brand, make, model, type*
> These words overlap in meaning.
> *brand* = a type of product made by a particular company, usually everyday products such as drinks, foods, cleaning products, e.g. *What brand of coffee did you buy? I don't like that brand of toothpaste.* Not to be confused with *brand new* = completely new.
> *make* = types of machinery or equipment, e.g. *What make of car does he drive? There are many different makes of computer.*
> *model* = more specific information about a *make*, e.g. *What make is it? It's an Apple Macintosh. What model? An iMac.*
> It is possible to avoid these distinctions by using *type / kind*, e.g. *What kind (or type) of car / perfume is it?*

listening tell me what happened

listen to stories about a lost wallet and some keys

focus on the past perfect simple

use natural English phrases with the past perfect simple

develop a narrative around a framework using **natural English** phrases to bring it to life

tell the story to a new partner

lead-in

- The first activity sets the scene for the listening, and could be done as a whole class activity or in pairs.

listen to this

- The warning in **exercise 2** refers back to the **lead-in**: *Be more careful!* Before you listen in exercise 2, you could pre-teach: *pick* sb's *pocket* = steal something from somebody's bag / pocket. After listening you might want to highlight: *gosh!* = an exclamation of surprise, *what a cheek!* = exclamation of surprise when somebody has behaved badly.

grammar past perfect simple

- **Exercises 1** and **2** are diagnostic, so let learners work together and see what they already know. You could ask them to work on the two exercises at the same time, then do feedback. If learners have problems with this concept, be prepared to use a timeline to illustrate the meaning of sentence 2, i.e. a line showing three consecutive actions in the past: he lost the wallet, he got home, he realized. Alternatively, you could use **cover & check** exercise 12.1 in the **language reference** on *p.173*, as a concept check. When dealing with the form in **exercise 2**, you could focus on and practise the contractions in **exercise 1**, sentence 2b.

- Learners can work alone or together on **exercise 3.** When you go over the answers, clarify any points where learners have problems. For instance, in sentence 3, you may need to explain that both are correct, because when *before* or *after* are used, the past perfect is optional if the meaning is already clear.

- In the **natural English** box, learners are listening for the weak form of *that* /ðət/. As it is very common in English to omit *that* in these clauses, encourage learners to practise the sentences without *that* to reinforce the point.

- The section finishes with another story. This provides further listening practice, consolidates the past perfect, and introduces the use of direct speech in narrative, which is the focus of the next section.

story-telling

- If there is little time left in the lesson, we suggest you come back to this section in the next lesson, and do a game or revision activity here instead.

- In order to get the most out of **exercise 1** and do it well, learners will need quite a lot of time. Give them time to read the basic story about the neighbour, then explain that they are going to make the story more interesting or dramatic. Start off together looking at the first question, *What was he like?* and get learners to think up different ideas. Then in pairs, they decide on their answer, and carry on with the rest of the activity. Monitor the pair work offering help and advice, and make notes for feedback.

- For **exercise 2**, you can tell each pair to get on with this when they are ready. Tell them to practise it more than once; they have to be able to tell it without looking at their books (though they can make notes if they like).

- For **exercise 3,** reorganize learners into different pairs to tell their stories, and monitor again. At the end, you could ask the class to tell you which details or developments in the stories they liked most. Give feedback on the content and language learners used.

exercise 1

1 an Italian restaurant
2 good; he had a really good meal there
3 he went home

exercise 2

because somebody had taken the money and left a rude note in his wallet

exercise 3

1 When Sam arrived home, he didn't have the wallet.
2 correct
3 His wallet contained his name, address, phone number, and £50.
4 The man rang two days later.
5 He said, *I'll send it to you*.
6 When Sam got his wallet back, there was no money in it.

language point *could have done*

In the true / false questions in **exercise 3**, question 2 contains the structure *could have done*. Learners should be able to work out what this means, as they looked at present deduction in unit eleven, *p.131* (past deduction is also covered in the **workbook** *p.69*).

exercise 1

1a   2b   3b

exercise 2

1 The past perfect is formed using *had* (*'d*) + past participle.
2 We use the past perfect in these two examples to show that a past action preceded another past action.

exercise 3

1 'd left   4 was having; had gone
2 'd had   5 locked
3 both are correct

nE

1 no   2 yes   3 yes   4 yes

listening challenge

Sally's husband had the other set of keys. Her daughter arranged for a taxi to collect the keys from her husband and take them to the house. The taxi driver posted the keys through the letter box.

language point past perfect simple

For some learners, the past perfect is not particularly problematic, especially where they have a similar form in their language. However, there is a danger that, having introduced the tense, learners overuse it. In fact, the past perfect is most common in fiction, and is not very frequent in conversation.
It is worth pointing out (as in **exercise 3**, sentence 3) that the past perfect isn't always needed if the sentence includes *before or after,* and the meaning is clear.
There are a number of form issues which can cause problems:
– the contraction *'d* may be difficult for learners to hear, e.g. *I'd done it*.
– they may confuse *'d = had* with *'d = would*

Want to know more? Go to **Practical English Usage** Michael Swan *pp.426–428*.

ideas plus writing

As learners already have a clear framework for the story, and they only need to add in further details, this is a very achievable writing activity for intermediate learners. You could ask learners to write their versions for homework, as this would be quite a time-consuming class activity.

reading attitudes to money

65 – 80 mins

learn and use money vocabulary and **natural English** phrases containing numbers

read and discuss an article about pocket money

discuss issues related to giving children money

glossary

semantic (adj) the meaning of words and phrases

syntax the way words and phrases are put together to form sentences

vocabulary money

- Make sure learners know how to pronounce the items in **exercise 1**, then practise saying the words. See **language point** on the right.

- For **exercise 2**, if necessary, look again at unit two, **troubleshooting** (find someone who …) on *p.25*. This activity should take about ten minutes. Monitor and make notes for feedback on language at the end.

- Learners should know many of the verbs in **exercise 3**, but they are a common source of error owing to *semantic* overlap and mother tongue transfer, e.g. *lend* versus *borrow*, *win* versus *earn*. Demonstrate the activity with an example. Learners will probably need time to work alone, then compare and practise with a partner. Check learners' pronunciation of *earn* /ɜːn/ and *inherit* /ɪnˈherɪt/.

- When you go over the answers, highlight one or two important grammatical collocations on the board, and get learners to note them down, e.g *spend money on sth, invest money in sth; borrow / inherit money from sb*. You *pay an electricity bill*, but you *pay for sth*, e.g. *pay for your electricity, a meal*, etc.

- For **exercise 4**, it would be helpful to set this up on the board. Tell learners this is information from someone's finances, and put a table on the board as in the exercise. Look at the first example (*borrow £100 from someone*) and ask them which column it should go in. Learners can then copy and work together on the rest of the table. Refer them to the irregular verb list on *p.175* if necessary.

- Explain the language point in the **natural English** box; this is a very common feature in English, and the *syntax* here is often different from other languages. Then do the activity, but demonstrate it first yourself.

read on

- It is important that you don't lead in to this reading activity with personalization, as learners get the opportunity to talk about pocket money in **it's your turn!**. **Exercise 1** is a prediction activity which leads learners into the text and sets up certain expectations. Don't give them the answers at this stage, as they have to find them in the text.

- Give learners a couple of minutes to think about their ideas for **exercise 5** before they work with a partner.

it's your turn!

- If your class contains some parents, you must first decide whether you want the parents to work together as a group, or to mix them with non-parents. Either way, there should be some differences in experience. Give learners time to think about **exercise 1**, and be available to help them with vocabulary, etc. You could also ask them whether other members of their family gave them pocket money, e.g. grandparents or older brothers and sisters.

- You could demonstrate the one-minute speaking activity yourself by talking about your experience as a child or as a parent. Tell learners to listen and think of questions to ask you at the end, and then answer them. By this stage, learners should have a clear idea how to do this activity within their small groups. Keep groups to a maximum of three or four.

- During **exercise 2**, move the activity along for different groups where necessary, and make notes for feedback at the end. Ask one or two learners to tell the class any interesting points that emerged from their discussion.

exercise 1

1	wallet	3	piggy bank	5	safe
2	cashpoint	4	purse		

exercise 3

find £10 in the street
lend someone £100 to buy a CD player
invest £3,000 in a new company
lose your wallet with a £50 note in it
win a £2,000 prize
spend £150 on clothes
pay a £50 phone bill
inherit £2,000 from a relative who's died
earn £40 in overtime this week

exercise 4

money coming in (+)		money going out (−)	
borrowed	£100	lent	£100
found	£10	invested	£3,000
won	£2,000	lost	£50
inherited	£2,000	spent	£150
earned	£40	paid	£50

They are in credit (by £800).

exercise 3

1 (My 13-year old and 10-year old) generally spend it on sweets or save it.
2 (My son Michael) will get £1 a week, £1.50 if he keeps his room tidy.
3 I opened bank accounts for them, so that they could learn to save.

exercise 4

a	Claire Scott	d	Claire Scott
b	Claire Scott	e	Adrian Butler
c	Mary Carter	f	Mary Carter

language point money vocabulary: British and American English

There are several issues to do with meaning here.

British English	American English	
purse	*coin purse* or *change purse*	= a small bag for coins
wallet	*billfold*	= a small case for bank notes or cards
handbag	*purse*	= a bag often carried by women for money, keys, etc.

There are a number of words for *cashpoint*: *cash machine*, *cash dispenser*, *ATM* (especially Am E) and *hole in the wall* 🙂 (Br E).

ideas plus writing

These short texts are a useful model for a personalized writing exercise on memories of childhood. You could provide a framework along these lines:

– how much pocket money you received at different ages
– what you spent it on
– what your attitude to money was, e.g. Were you a saver or a spender?
– any specific information you think others may find interesting.

If you set this activity as homework after **it's your turn!**, learners will have had a chance to discuss the issues. Another useful idea would be to do a general revision of money vocabulary at the end, taking vocabulary from the first part of the section and the reading texts.

troubleshooting cultural differences

Although pocket money is quite a common concept in many cultures, it isn't necessarily universal. If you teach in a country where it is not part of the culture, you should first decide if the topic will engage your learners. If you feel that it won't, you could develop a discussion around other money issues which are relevant; you are in the best position to decide what they are. Possibilities might include: saving money, state pensions, personal pensions, state subsidies, etc.
If pocket money <u>is</u> common in the country where you teach, you also need to consider whether money generally is a sensitive topic for class discussion. In any case, make it clear that learners don't need to reveal their personal finances to others!

 **wordbooster**   25 – 30 mins

> This **wordbooster** is best used at this point in the unit as the vocabulary will be useful in the **how to ...** section.

shopping

- Learners should be able to complete **exercise 1**, given the context and what they already know. When you go over the answers, you will probably need to reinforce the meaning, and practise the pronunciation of the words in phonemic script in particular.
- **Exercise 2** gives learners the opportunity to practise through personalization.

phrasal verbs with *back*

- These phrasal verbs have been grouped together because the particle *back* has a common meaning when it is part of a phrasal verb. See **language point** on the right.
- Remind learners that they will need to change the word order with some examples.

how to ... say the right thing in a shop   60 – 70 mins

> **focus** on plural nouns
>
> **complete** a questionnaire about what to say in a clothes shop
>
> **listen** to a conversation in a clothes shop
>
> **focus** on **natural English** in the conversation
>
> **role play** a situation in a clothes shop

grammar plural nouns

- If you think learners will know the vocabulary in **exercise 1**, you could do this as a memory game. Give them one minute to remember everything in the pictures, then with a partner, write down the twelve words. You may find that they are unsure about several items, which will create a need for them to know the words in English. At this stage, whether they have labelled the picture or done the memorization activity, you can go round and monitor how many of them they wrote as plural nouns with an *s*. Then go over the answers, and make sure that they write and say all the words with an *s*. You don't need to deal with the grammar at this point.
- If you don't go to the **language reference** after **exercise 3**, you will need to point out that plural nouns take a plural verb, and with items of clothing we often use *some / a pair of / two pairs of* before the noun. See **language point** on the right.

in a clothes shop

- You could set up **exercise 1** without the **student's book**. Tell learners they are shopping for clothes, and have to think what to say. Explain the first situation in the table, i.e. *What does the assistant ask you?* and elicit learners' ideas. Put several on the board, and correct them if they are inaccurate or unnatural. Then tell them to look at **exercise 1**, and do the rest with a partner. If they can think of several answers, so much the better, but don't give them the answers (they are in the listening in exercise 3).
- Bring the class together, elicit their ideas for the situations, and put them on the board.
- For **exercise 2**, you can either ask them to tick phrases they wrote or look for the ones on the board. Before you listen, you could pre-teach: *give* sb *a shout* = call somebody, *How are you getting on?* = What progress are you making?, *tight* = too small to be comfortable (opposite = *loose* /luːs/).
- Replay the recording for **exercise 3** and pause at appropriate points to give learners time to write. You can either elicit new sentences on to the board, or ask learners to compare what they wrote with the **listening booklet** on *p.42*. Help with any phrases that learners didn't know.
- You can model the language in the **natural English** box for learners to repeat before they practise in pairs.

exercise 1
1 receipt
2 a sale / the sales; bargain
3 exchange
4 overcharge
5 refund
6 deposit

exercise 1
1 went back
2 took back / took the dress back
3 send back / send the radio back
4 gave me my money back / gave me back my money
5 paid it back / gave it back
6 came back

language point particles in phrasal verbs

1 Sometimes, particles do not change the meaning of the verb in a phrasal verb, e.g.
save (*up*)   *stand* (*up*)   *hurry* (*up*)   *sit* (*down*)   *lie* (*down*)

2 Sometimes, particles add a particular meaning to the verb in a phrasal verb as with *back*, e.g. *get **back**   go **back**   put sth **back***

3 Very often, however, particles change the meaning of the verb radically, and don't have an identifiable meaning, e.g. *take up* (*a hobby*) = start
take over (*a business*) = take control of

exercise 1
1 trousers
2 jeans
3 pyjamas
4 shorts
5 tights
6 socks
7 boots
8 sunglasses
9 gloves
10 underpants
11 knickers
12 slippers

exercise 3
glove, slipper, sock, boot

exercise 4
1 I've got a new pair of sunglasses / some new sunglasses.
2 He bought three pairs of trousers.
3 These shorts are too small.
4 Have you got (some / any / a pair of) jeans like this in size 14?
5 Where are my underpants?
6 His clothes don't look very fashionable.

language point plural nouns

The main difficulty for many learners is that some plural nouns in English are not plural in their language, e.g. *un pantalon* (singular) in French is *trousers* (plural) in English. If you wish, you could also point out that plural nouns in English are quite common in other areas as well as clothing.
examples

tools, e.g, *scissors, pliers, shears, tweezers*
general nouns, e.g. *goods, clothes, resources, refreshments, facilities*

It would be a good idea for learners to keep a record in their notebooks of plural nouns like these that they encounter.

exercise 3
2 I'm just looking.
3 Where can I try it on?
4 I'm afraid it doesn't fit very well.
5 I don't think it suits me really.
6 I'll take this one.
7 Could you wrap them up for me please?

extended speaking shopping stories

60 – 70 mins

- It is important at the beginning of this activity to let learners read the left-hand column or tell them what they are going to do in the lesson, or put it on the board. This will enable them to get the whole picture. You should also give them time to look back at the blue **extended speaking** boxes which occur at the end of each section in the unit.

collect ideas

- You may decide that in order to give your learners time to think of a shopping story, you will tell them what they are going to do <u>the lesson before</u>. This means that even if they can't think of a story of their own, they can ask a friend or family member for a story.

- The listening activity in **exercise 3** is designed to give listening practice, but also to provide a narrative framework which the learners can use or adapt for their own stories. Start by asking them to look at the picture and guess what the context of the story is. You could pre-teach: *stunning* = extremely attractive / beautiful, *price tag* = ticket showing how much something costs. When they have read questions 1 to 5 in the table, play the recording. It has been divided into two parts because it is quite long.

- After **exercise 4**, you could let learners listen with the tapescript, but if they have understood the gist, don't spend too long on this, as the aim of the section is speaking. Give them a chance to react to the story. Do they think it is silly, funny, believable? (It is, in fact, true.)

exercise 3

2 when she was getting married   4 she saw a lovely hat but couldn't afford it
3 a hat to go with her pink dress   5 the hat was reduced in the sales

exercise 4

6 yes; her husband cut two holes in the hat and put it on a horse's head   7 the speaker thought it was funny

prepare your story

- The preparation of the stories could take a little while; don't hurry learners here, as the more confident they are about the story, the better it will be. Be available to help them with vocabulary or expressions, and make sure that learners aren't writing out the story; it won't sound natural if they read it aloud. Tell them that their story should last between one and two minutes. Make sure that they are very familiar with the guidance in the checklist. If they can't think of a real story, they can invent one.

tell your story

- Before learners work with a partner, it is very important to emphasize that they <u>must</u> learn each others' stories, as they are going to tell both of them to a different partner afterwards. To help them clarify details in their partner's story, you can first go over the language in the **natural English** box, which will reinforce the idea of checking that they understand the story.

- Try to make sure pairs cannot hear each others' stories. Monitor during this speaking activity to make sure that learners are doing the task correctly, and make notes for feedback.

- Make sure learners understand the instructions for **exercise 7**. The stories have to sound plausible told by either speaker, so if, for instance, a man has to tell his partner's story about buying a pair of high-heeled shoes, he will have to pretend it is his girlfriend's story, for example. They need to make these changes as they are repeating their partner's story.

- At the end, see how many people guessed the story correctly, and how they knew. If there is one particularly good story, the learner could tell it to the class. Give feedback on language use.

write your story

The framework again reinforces the idea of structuring the narrative, and if learners can add a new idea to their written story, it will give their partner a motivation to read. This writing stage is probably best done out of class time. Collect the learners' written work at the end and correct it.

exercise 9

1 in the Bahamas   4 they had given her two left shoes   6 no
2 on the last day of her holiday   5 it wasn't solved   7 negative
3 a pair of shoes as a souvenir

feedback checklist

During the **extended speaking** activity, note down examples of …

- **good language use**

- **effective communication strategies**
  (turn-taking, interrupting, inviting others to speak, etc.)

- **learner errors**
  (vocabulary, grammar, pronunciation, etc.)

- **particular communication problems**

Make sure you allow time for feedback at the end of the lesson. You can use the notes you make above to <u>praise</u> effective language use and communication or, if necessary, to do some remedial work.

> **ideas plus** collect ideas
>
> Instead of using Elspeth's story, you could tell learners your own story. The important thing is that it should aim to follow the framework given in **exercise 3**, which would allow you to use the questions for comprehension and guidance for the learners' speaking activity. It may be that your own story will be culturally familiar for the learners as well. Alternatively, you could familiarize yourself with Elspeth's story and tell it as if it were your own / your sister's experience.
>
> **Want to know more?** Go to **how to …** teach listening (live listening) *p.153*.

test yourself!

Want to know more? Go to the **introduction** *p.7* for ways of using **test yourself!**

1 shorts, tights, underpants, knickers, pyjamas, jeans, sunglasses
2 go back, come back, get sth back, give (sb) sth back, pay sth / sb back, ask for sth back, send sth back, take sth back
3 borrow, lose, lend, spend, find, win, invest, pay, inherit, earn

1 When I arrived, John had (already) left.
2 Where can I try this on?
3 It doesn't fit (me).
4 I got a refund.

1 I suddenly realized where I'd met him.
2 A ten-pound note.
3 He spent the money on the car.
4 Oh, no! What a disaster!

teacher development chapters

how to ... activate vocabulary

1 What do we mean by 'vocabulary'?

In **natural English**, vocabulary development is prominent in a number of places. For instance:

- glossaries highlight key lexical items in all of the written and spoken texts
- lexis is the basis of the five or six **natural English** boxes in each unit
- there is a separate section in each unit for vocabulary building called **wordbooster**
- there are additional exercises and activities devoted to vocabulary development in each unit.

Vocabulary is often grouped in different ways for teaching purposes.

topic areas

Individual words have been organized within a particular topic area and sometimes linguistically as well. For example:

- adjectives describing transport and journeys, e.g. *safe, dangerous, frustrating, unreliable*
- music vocabulary, e.g. *group, orchestra, conductor, lead singer, solo artist.*

collocations

Even with individual words, further practice activities usually illustrate how the selected items often collocate in a wider sense; they may not be adjacent pairs but they often co-occur in certain contexts, e.g. Simon Rattle was the *conductor* of the Birmingham Symphony *Orchestra*; buses are *unreliable* in big towns, and this can be very *frustrating*.

lexical collocations

Most of the time though, the focus is on adjacent collocation and longer lexical phrases, reflecting the now widely-held view that much of our language consists not of individual words combining uniquely in each utterance we make, but of combinations of smaller or larger chunks of language which recur frequently and fairly predictably. Typical lexical collocations include:

- verb + noun, e.g. *join a club, do a degree*
- adjective + noun, e.g. *great fun, loud music*
- adverb + adjective, e.g. *happily married, incredibly easy.*

grammatical collocations

There are also combinations often described as grammatical collocations:

- verb or adjective + preposition, e.g. *depend on, interested in*
- preposition + noun, e.g. *for a while, in my twenties / thirties*
- verb + particle, e.g. *pick sth / sb up, get on with sb*
- noun + noun and compound nouns, e.g. *television programme, bus stop, swimming pool.*

lexical phrases

Lexical phrases – sometimes whole sentences – can be fairly fixed, e.g. *never mind, that's a pity;* or they can allow significant variation, e.g. *to a great / large / limited / lesser / some extent.* Phrases can also be idiomatic, i.e. they are difficult to understand from the constituent parts, e.g. *break the ice; for the time being;* or they can be fairly transparent, e.g. *at first, the whole thing.* It is just as important for learners to 'notice' and practise this second group of fairly transparent phrases. The same concept may be expressed in a different way in the learner's first language, but even if it is expressed in the same way, the learner still needs to know this is the case by having it pointed out.

These are examples of phrases included in the intermediate level of **natural English**.

Never mind.
That's a shame.
Nice to meet you.
Excuse me, is anyone sitting here?
Does it take long to get there?
That sounds (great / awful / interesting).
(It / That) doesn't (really) appeal to me.
There's something wrong with the (TV / cooker / phone).
I'm thinking of (going to Australia / doing French).
The most important thing is to (stay calm / keep warm).
I don't know much about (architecture / cookery / hypnotism).
(Swimming, riding,) and that sort of thing / and things like that.
I'm not too keen on (tennis / rock music / prawns).
Shall we go on to (the next one / number 3)?

---

think![1]

Look at the phrases in **bold** below. Write down two or three of the most likely words that could go in each gap. Do you think these phrases are suitable for intermediate level, or not?

1 We **had a** _____ **time** in Paris.
2 It was terrible – **the whole thing was a** _____ .
3 They **had no** _____ **but to** wait for the next bus.
4 The course was **a waste of** _____ .
5 I didn't need to worry about money any more, which was **a** _____ **off my mind.**
6 It could be a 'p' but **it's hard to** _____ .

---

go to **answer key** *p.142*

colligation

If collocation describes the lexical company that a word keeps, then colligation describes the grammatical company a word keeps. For example, the verb *to bear* (as in *bear a child*) is almost always used in the passive, e.g. *I was born in Paris*, so it wouldn't make sense to present it in any other way. Some of the lexical phrases in the book are presented so as to exhibit their colligational features. In the list of phrases on *p.136*, *I'm thinking of -ing* is presented as a phrase in the continuous form because that is the most frequent way it is used, and *keen* appears first in a negative construction because that is also how it is commonly used.

2   Why does vocabulary need to be activated?

In the past, we tended to assume that practice of new lexis was not only desirable but essential for successful acquisition to take place. More recently, that assumption has been questioned, partly on the grounds that production puts learners under pressure. While they are busy retrieving and articulating items from memory in order to communicate a range of different meanings – and all within real time – this may actually inhibit or interfere with successful acquisition.

There is a degree of stress involved in productive practice, and we should certainly be aware of how much we can or should expect from our learners when they are experimenting with new language. This is particularly the case when the time between language input and learner output is quite short. Productive practice, however, can take many forms, from controlled exercises to freer activities. It is part of the teacher's expertise to graduate the different forms of practice so that learners are not confronted with activities that are frustrating or unduly stressful. Productive practice should be challenging, but above all, it should be achievable. We wouldn't (and indeed cannot) claim that productive practice necessarily leads to acquisition, but we do believe it can perform a very positive role in the classroom.

think!²

Think of at least three arguments in favour of productive practice of vocabulary, then read on.

1   For many learners the classroom is the only place where they receive feedback on their ability to pronounce phrases in isolation, and within utterances, to an acceptable standard. Over time, productive practice should promote fluency, and improve learners' pronunciation. It doesn't matter how much language a learner has acquired if they are incomprehensible to listeners.

2   Pronouncing (and repeating) a word or phrase and fixing the sound and stress pattern in our heads is one of the ways in which we store words in the memory and are able to retrieve them when needed.

3   When we create opportunities for learners to use and re-use new language, we are compensating for the lack of exposure that many learners suffer from when they are learning English for a few hours a week in their own countries. These learners won't meet new vocabulary four, five, or six times by chance – or however many times it is felt that people need to meet a word before acquisition is

most likely to take place – so productive practice may be important in helping to retain new items.

4   Productive practice doesn't just mean repeating ten or twenty words or phrases. It is an opportunity for learners to use and recycle a much wider range of language, some of which will have been quite recently encountered and won't have been fully acquired. Freer productive practice is, therefore, giving learners an opportunity to consolidate and acquire much more than just a narrow band of target language.

5   Most learners want to use and experiment with new language. With an engaging activity in a supportive classroom, learners can get enormous satisfaction from successfully sustaining conversation in English. While nobody should be forced to speak, for most learners it is motivating and builds confidence – two key ingredients, in our view, for successful language learning.

6   Last but not least, productive practice has 'face validity'. Learners expect it and may feel disappointed or even cheated if they don't have opportunities to practise new language.

3   'Exercise' versus 'activity'

think!³

You are going to read about the distinction between vocabulary 'exercises' and vocabulary 'activities'. Look at this extract from **natural English**. How are exercises 1 and 2 different?

1   **Complete the sentences with these words. Compare with a partner.**

a sale / the sales exchange	refund (n) /'ri:fʌnd/	receipt /rɪ'si:t/
bargain /'bɑːgɪn/	overcharge	deposit /dɪ'pɒzɪt/

1   Do you normally keep the _____ for things you buy? If so, why?

2   Do you often buy things in _____? What is the best _____ you've ever found?

3   If you go back to a shop because you aren't satisfied with something you bought, is it generally easy to _____ it for something else?

4   Is it common for shop assistants to _____ people by mistake?

5   If you take something back, are there shops where it is difficult to get a _____? Have you ever asked for one? What happened?

6   When you buy something, do you ever have to pay a _____?

2   **Ask and answer the questions in groups.**

from **student's book unit twelve** *p.140*

Exercises to test and practise vocabulary are very familiar to all teachers. Use the material in any coursebook or supplementary book, and you won't be able to complete a single language lesson without coming across one or more of the exercise types below. As you read, tick ✓ the ones you use most often. Can you explain why you use some types more often than others?

- ☐ gap fill sentences or dialogues
- ☐ matching exercises, e.g. words and definitions, sentence halves, stimulus and response, etc.
- ☐ jumbled words in phrases, e.g. 1 time / nice / a / have!
  2 get / soon / better / I / you / hope
- ☐ substituting words of similar meaning, e.g. phrasal verbs:
  1 She <u>recovered</u> from the illness very quickly.
  2 He <u>returned</u> the goods to the manufacturer.
- ☐ choose the correct word / phrase from a selection of two, three, or four possibilities
- ☐ identify / label pictures or parts of things
- ☐ complete tables, e.g. word building tables, collocational grids, etc.
- ☐ complete word spray diagrams, e.g.

go   abroad /əˈbrɔːd/

- ☐ oral drills / dialogue practice for pronunciation practice and repetition of forms
- ☐ transformations, e.g. She doesn't like Bach very much.
  = She's not very _____ .
- ☐ games, e.g. one learner defines words / phrases for their partner to guess.

vocabulary exercises

Vocabulary exercises tend to be very controlled, testing the meaning and / or form of items. They usually have a specific answer which is 'correct' or 'incorrect', and they often perform the function of reinforcement. But exercises can offer further benefits:

- they can provide useful written records, (spray diagrams, visuals, and tables can be attractive storage systems)
- they sometimes involve other language and skills, e.g. transformations help develop the ability to paraphrase, an essential communication strategy
- they allow learners time to assimilate new forms and meanings without the external pressure of trying to communicate ideas.

With the exception of games, they all have one thing in common: <u>they can all be done alone</u>, as self-study activities. In class, teachers may and often do bring exercises to life by encouraging learners to work on them co-operatively in pairs or groups, or work individually before comparing and discussing their answers. Getting learners to talk <u>about</u> the items is a valuable activity, but getting them to use the items in communication is a different matter.

vocabulary activities

Let's compare this with vocabulary activities. These can be controlled or less controlled, but the difference is that activities have <u>a communicative goal</u> as well as a linguistic goal, and for this reason they require learners to interact with each other; giving opinions, sharing experiences, exchanging information. The onus is on the learner to be 'creative', but this need not be on a big scale, nor should it be frightening. The results will be more unpredictable, and perhaps less amenable to 'correct' or 'incorrect' answers.

merging exercise and activity

You will, of course, find examples in which exercise and activity merge. For instance, if you ask learners to complete sentences, there will be an element of creativity but within quite controlled limits, e.g. asking learners to complete the sentences below in their own words, using *hopefully*, *surprisingly*, or *fortunately*.

1 I'm going to spend six months in Germany;
_____

2 I didn't have any money with me;
_____

3 My uncle usually forgets my birthday;
_____

4 It's a difficult situation, but _____

from **student's book unit six** p.73

Our feeling is that learners generally need both exercises and activities, and the weakness of some vocabulary materials in the past is that they have tended to concentrate on the former at the expense of the latter. If you only have exercises, the accumulative effect may be that vocabulary is taught for its own sake with no language use in mind, and learning then becomes rather one-dimensional. With a little thought, however, it is possible to see the potential for both an exercise and an interactive activity from the same basic material. (See **think!**[3] p.137.)

think![4]

How might you transform these sentences into both an exercise and an activity for intermediate level learners?

cinema habits

1 If I'm watching an English film, I don't like to see the subtitles; I prefer films which are dubbed.
2 When I go to the cinema, I tend to ring and book in advance.
3 It's very common for the audience to clap at the end of a film in my country.
4 I always read the film reviews before I decide to go and see a film.
5 My favourite films are thrillers and romantic comedies; I'm not very keen on westerns.
6 I prefer to sit in the back row at the cinema.

go to **answer key** p.142

4 Activity types

There are a number of ways in which you can encourage learners to activate words and phrases, but among the most common are: personalization, using visuals, sorting and ranking activities, and creative activities / role play.

In practice, some of these activities overlap. Let's look at each one in turn.

a personalization

Personalization involves learners talking about their lives, their backgrounds, their personal experiences, and their opinions. Most learners are happy to talk about themselves, and this is the most accessible store of information they have. You obviously have to be careful about certain topics in some learning contexts, however, and you should always make it clear that your learners should only disclose what they want, and no more.

1 You can use **sets of questions** (often containing topic-related or linguistically-related vocabulary) which enable learners to personalize in pairs or small groups. The shopping activity opposite (unit five, *p.63*) is one example, and you will find another in unit five, (see **vocabulary exercise 4**, *p.61*) where the words or phrases in bold can be pre-taught or checked first, before learners discuss the questions and give personalized answers.

2 **Questionnaires** are a valuable source of vocabulary practice. The example extract below starts at exercise level as learners focus on the linguistic aim, i.e. choosing the correct verb to match the *syntactic*[1] pattern, before they move on to discuss what they themselves would do in each situation.

questionnaire

1 You sent a present to your 14-year-old cousin, and she hasn't phoned or written to thank you. The next time you see her, two weeks later, she doesn't even mention the present.

Would you:

a _____ her you're upset?

b _____ to introduce the subject of the present into the conversation?

c _____ to say nothing?   tell

d *your own idea*   decide   try

2 Your 16-year-old brother tells you he's going to do a bungee-jump, without telling your parents.

Would you:

a _____ that it's dangerous?

b _____ him not to do it?

c _____ him that you will tell your parents?

d *your own idea*   advise

warn   explain

from **student's book unit seven** *p.82*

syntactic[1] go to **glossary** *p.142* for numbered items

3 Learners can talk about **things happening around them** and in the learning environment. For example, they can use *have (got) sth on* (= *be wearing* sth) to describe their classmates' appearance, or give two true and two false statements for others to verify.

4 They can give **opinions** about sentences which contain lexis you want them to activate. In the example below, after looking at the meaning of the vocabulary items in these statements about politicians, they have to agree or disagree with them.

> They're hard-working and caring /ˈkeərɪŋ/.
>
> They're mostly honest /ˈɒnɪst/ and tell the truth.
>
> I think they're all liars /ˈlaɪəz/ – and they're corrupt /kəˈrʌpt/ too.
>
> They often make promises they don't keep.

from **student's book unit ten** *p.118*

5 Learners can **amend sentences** (containing target vocabulary) so that they are true of themselves. Look at this example where learners fill the gapped sentences with an appropriate verb and then personalize them.

shopping

1 **Fill the gaps with a form of the verbs from the box. Sometimes two verbs are possible.**

pack	do	wait	order
attract	stand	push in	go
serve	put	get	

1 I get angry if shop assistants talk to each other while they're _____ customers.

2 When I _____ shopping for clothes, I always take a friend with me.

3 I don't always _____ the shopping; I take it in turns with the people I live with.

4 When people are queueing in a shop, it's not acceptable for others to _____ .

5 In some shops you can wait for ages trying to _____ someone's attention.

6 With some shops, you can _____ goods over the phone and they deliver them.

7 In supermarkets, shop assistants help you _____ your goods into carrier bags.

8 You have to _____ in a queue for about fifteen minutes in some shops.

2 **In groups, make the sentences true for you in your country.**

from **wordbooster, student's book unit five** *p.63*

6 Learners can talk about people they know using words and phrases they have studied. They can develop their *discourse*² around the questions and give more information about the people. For example:

---

1 Read the questionnaire. Notice the phrases in bold. Mark the stress on the words in *italics*.

Do you know anyone who ...

1 ... is **training to be** a doctor or a nurse?
2 ... **works** *freelance*?
3 ... is **looking for** a job?
4 ... **works for** a *multinational company*?
5 ... is *retired*?
6 ... is *unemployed*?
7 ... **works in** the *computer industry*?
8 ... **runs their own** *business*?
9 ... has recently **given up their job**?
10 ... has a job which *involves* **a lot of travelling**?

2 Write the name of someone you know next to each question, if possible.

3 In small groups, say more about the people you thought of in exercise 2.

from **student's book unit one** *p.16*

---

b using visuals

Visuals are an indispensable aid for dealing with meaning at exercise level and can be used for controlled or free practice. They are common in coursebooks.

controlled practice

Where learners are asked to describe what they see in a picture, they will be practising target language in a controlled way, as in the exercise below.

---

1 Look at the pictures for 30 seconds, then shut your book. Tell your partner what everyone's wearing.

examples   There's a man wearing a suit.
            There's a woman wearing jewellery.

suit /suːt/	shorts	evening dress
tracksuit /ˈtræksuːt/	jewellery /ˈdʒuːəlri/	sandals
trainers /ˈtreɪnəz/	T-shirt	
tie /taɪ/	top	

from **student's book unit five** *p.61*

---

freer practice

When they are giving a reaction or interpreting pictures, for instance, then they are using visual materials as an 'activity'. For example, the exercise above continues in the following way:

---

2 Say who looks:

casually dressed	smartly dressed	scruffy ⓖ /ˈskrʌfi/
trendy	elegant	

If you provide two paintings and ask learners to say which they like / dislike / prefer / are not very keen on, etc. there will be different views, and there will be interaction and reaction. If you give them a set of pictures of things happening in the street and ask them to comment on whether they don't mind / are annoyed / irritated by them, etc. you also have differences of opinion which will stimulate discussion as well as vocabulary use.

free and controlled practice

At a more factual level, you can find pictures which are similar but different. Put learners in pairs and give each one a picture. Together – and without looking at each other's picture – they have to find the differences between their pictures. This has an element of both exercise and activity: on the one hand, it may be an opportunity to practise language in quite a controlled way. On the other, learners will be reacting, agreeing, clarifying, and possibly contradicting each other.

c sorting and ranking activities

Sorting and ranking activities also provide opportunities for personalized practice. Putting lexical phrases in a logical chronological order (as in the activity below) is a useful initial test of understanding, and the chunks can be memorized and practised orally. However, they need to be put to use. If you ask learners to think about someone they know (perhaps a family member) who did some or all of these things, they can adapt the phrases to describe the chain of events in that person's life. As with the activities above, what makes something interactive in class is a difference in either opinion, information, or experience. This provides the incentive for learners to listen to each other.

---

1 Put the stages in a logical order. Compare with a partner.

- [ ] you **look after** the baby
- [1] you **find a job** in the computer industry
- [ ] you **carry on working** for a few months
- [ ] you **settle down** and decide to **start a family**
- [ ] you **have a baby**
- [ ] you **go back to work**
- [ ] you **take six months off** work
- [ ] you **get married**

from **student's book unit six** *p.73*

---

think!⁵

1 Imagine you are going to use the activity below with an intermediate group. Which items would you need to check first for meaning and/or pronunciation?

A good friend is moving abroad and gives you his personal possessions (see below). What would you do with them, and why? **a** give the thing(s) away to friends / relatives, **b** throw them away, **c** sell them, or **d** keep them for yourself. Put a, b, c, or d.

- ☐ photo albums of his family and friends (including you)
- ☐ a collection of CDs including classical, jazz, rock, and pop
- ☐ a portable TV
- ☐ a fairly new full-length leather coat
- ☐ a pair of brand new walking boots, size 43
- ☐ a large collection of paperback novels
- ☐ a set of 12 encyclopaedias dating from the 1920s
- ☐ a pile of old comics
- ☐ a large, antique wardrobe

2 Try doing this sorting exercise yourself. Be sure to think about your reasons. When you've finished, put yourself in one of your learner's shoes, someone of a different age, sex, and background. What do you think their answers would be, and would their reasons be the same as yours?

go to **answer key** p.142

d creative activities / role play

There are many simple ways of getting learners to use vocabulary creatively. It can happen at sentence level in quite a controlled form, and may draw on personal experience. In the activity below, learners have to match the sentence halves (based on the context of what one might wear to a restaurant). Then they think up their own examples for a different context.

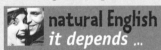

natural English
it depends ...

1	It depends who	a	I'm having dinner with this person.
2	It depends what kind of		
3	It depends why	b	I'm meeting.
4	It depends how well	c	the weather.
5	It depends if / whether	d	restaurant I'm going to.
6	It depends on	e	I know the person.
		f	I'm going there straight from work or not.

NOT It depends who ~am I~ meeting.

Say the complete sentences.

3 You're going to a wedding and you need to buy something to wear. With a partner, think of five sentences beginning *It depends ...*

from **student's book unit five** p.61

Learners can work in pairs to invent stories using words and phrases from a lexical set they have just studied, or they can integrate them into short dialogues, or even role plays (see **try it out** below).

try it out vocabulary role play

I've devised a set of role cards based around different topic areas which I use to teach and activate vocabulary. Learners do most of the work themselves and they are very active and involved.

1 I write the role cards (see two examples below), in which I incorporate about half a dozen key words and phrases on each card. I sometimes highlight these in bold.
2 I give one role card to each pair. They use dictionaries to check the meaning and pronunciation of new items; they have to understand the items well enough to explain them to others and I make that clear to them. I monitor this stage carefully and check with pairs that they understand the items. They learn the information on their cards.
3 Pairs then split up and find a new partner. They have to tell them about their holiday, using the new vocabulary and explaining it where necessary, The listener has to react appropriately with interest and sympathy, and possibly ask questions. The listener then talks about their holiday.
4 At the end, we have a round up. Which holidays would they personally enjoy, and why? And then we produce a written record of the vocabulary from all the role cards.

My learners find it a very enjoyable and challenging way to learn and use new items.

David Scott, Sydney, New South Wales.

Role card 1

You've just come back from 6 weeks of **trekking** in the Himalayas. You **had an absolutely fabulous time**. The people were extremely **welcoming**, the food was really **delicious** and the **accommodation** was **basic but comfortable**. And of course, you **got a lot of exercise**. You now **feel very fit** and you would recommend this holiday to anyone.

Role card 2

You've just come back from a holiday which was **an absolute nightmare**. Five weeks crossing the Simpson Desert in Australia on a **smelly** camel. You never want to see one again. The **scenery** was really **monotonous** and the food you were given by the guides was **absolutely revolting**. What's more, you **got bitten** by some nasty insects because no one told you to bring **insect repellent**. The **camping equipment** provided by the guides was inadequate and the tents were **cramped and uncomfortable**. Never again.

conclusion

In this chapter, we have looked at:
- what we mean by 'vocabulary'
- ways vocabulary can be grouped for teaching purposes
- the advantages and disadvantages of 'exercises' compared with 'activities'
- a variety of ways in which learners can activate vocabulary.

Most of the example activities can be found in the **student's book**, but these ideas can be adapted for use with materials which you have devised yourself. Next time you use a vocabulary 'exercise' with your learners, consider whether you can transform it into an activity and use it for productive practice.

follow up

Lewis M 1997 *Implementing the Lexical Approach* LTP (chapters 6 and 7)

Lewis M ed 2000 *Teaching Collocation* LTP (chapters 8 and 9)

McCarthy M 1990 *Vocabulary* Oxford University Press

Gairns R and Redman S 1986 *Working With Words* Cambridge University Press

answer key

think![1] *p.136* possible answer
1. great, good, terrible, etc.
2. disaster, nightmare, mess
3. choice, alternative, option
4. time, money, effort
5. weight, load
6. tell, say, judge

The phrases in 1, 2, 4, and 6 are all included in the intermediate level of **natural English**. We feel that sentence 3 is syntactically difficult for intermediate learners and would sound odd alongside the rest of their language output. Sentence 5 is both informal and idiomatic, and not, we feel, a priority at this level.

think![4] *p.138* possible answer
If you highlight and preteach the key vocabulary items to do with cinema going, e.g. *subtitles*, *dubbed*, *book in advance*, etc. or remove them and create a gap fill, you can turn this into an exercise where learners focus on the vocabulary.

If you ask learners to adapt the sentences to make them true for them, and <u>to give their reasons</u>, they will have ideas to communicate to others about the sentences. These steps will produce a communicative vocabulary activity. This is one possible answer; you may have thought of others.

think![5] *p.141*
1. Unknown items at this level might be:
   get rid of, portable, leather, pile / set / collection of ... , brand new, paperback, comics, wardrobe.
   Pronunciation difficulties might include:
   album, encyclopaedia, antique, wardrobe.
   You may also want to point out the phrase *keep things for yourself*, which may be transparent in meaning but would not be a phrase learners would normally produce themselves.
2. If you suspect that different learners will react differently to these questions, you have the basis for a good communicative activity.

glossary

syntactic the adjectival form of *syntax*, meaning the way words and phrases are put together to form sentences.

discourse the use of language in speech or writing in order to produce meaning

how to ... introduce new language

1 Criteria for introducing language successfully
2 Ways of introducing new language
   a   using visuals
   b   using texts
   c   using examples
   d   test-teach-test
3 Dealing with 'transparent' language

1   Criteria for introducing language successfully

Part of a teacher's role is to draw learners' attention to language areas, principally grammar and lexis, which are new or partly unfamiliar to them. Traditionally called 'presentation', this is sometimes now referred to as 'consciousness raising', i.e. bringing to conscious awareness features of the language that learners may have encountered but not noticed. Whatever approach is used, we need to remind ourselves that the language we select and decide to focus on is not necessarily what our students will learn (although they may learn other things). Nevertheless, in selecting and introducing new language, our aim remains the same: to choose an approach that will create the most favourable conditions for effective learning to take place. How can we do this?

We feel there are four criteria which will aid effective learning:

– introduce language economically and clearly

– make the language focus clear

– make the language focus memorable

– use approaches that are appropriate for the group.

Let's look at these in turn.

introduce language economically and clearly

Perhaps the single most important criterion for success is being economical. If you are introducing new language and conducting your class exclusively, or even largely in English, learners at intermediate level will find this demanding and tiring, and consequently their attention span will be limited. So, keep it brief, and where possible, keep it simple.

Unfortunately, brevity is often in conflict with clarity and truth. If you rush through a language focus in order to save time, your learners may be left confused; and if you distil information down too much, it may be over-simplified and not sufficiently accurate. Obviously there is a balance that needs to be struck here, and this is a key issue you have to consider, not just at the planning stage, but throughout the lesson as new language arises incidentally from other activities.

---

think![1]

A teacher has decided to focus on the meaning and use of these degree adverbs: *fairly, quite, pretty, rather*. Do you think these explanations have achieved the right balance of truth and clarity for <u>intermediate</u> level? Are any explanations too inaccurate or too detailed for this level?

1   *Fairly* means more or less the same as *quite*. If something is *fairly good* then it is *quite good*. They mean that something isn't <u>very</u> good but it is *better than OK*. *Quite* is the more common of the two words.

2   *Quite* sometimes mean *fairly*, but it can also mean *completely* or *absolutely*. So, you can say that a question is *quite difficult* or *fairly difficult* to answer, but you can also say that an answer is *quite wrong*, which means it is completely and totally wrong. You can't say that an answer is *fairly wrong*.

3   *Pretty* means the same as *very*. If a film is *pretty interesting* then it is *very interesting*.

4   *Rather* is also similar in meaning to *quite* and *fairly*, but not always used in the same way. When we use *rather*, we sometimes show surprise – something is better than we thought. For example: *The food at the hotel was rather good*. = I am a bit surprised perhaps because it's often not very good.

go to **answer key** *p.149*

If you are conscious of the fact that you sometimes struggle to preserve this balance, one way round the dilemma is to divide up your input into smaller more manageable chunks. A policy of 'little and often' is actually one we have generally adopted in **natural English**; if learners need a particular use of the present perfect to achieve a specific communicative goal, we may decide to focus on that use without feeling bound to examine all the other uses of the present perfect at the same time or within the same unit (as books sometimes do if they are driven by a pre-selected grammar syllabus). In his excellent book, *How to Teach Grammar*, Scott Thornbury also points out that being economical enables the teacher to fulfil another criterion for successful learning to take place, which is:

The rule of use: teach grammar in order to facilitate the learners' comprehension and production of real language, rather than as an end in itself. Always provide opportunities for learners to put the grammar to some communicative use.

Want to know more? Read **How to Teach Grammar** by Scott Thornbury *(p.153)*.

go to **follow up** *p.149*

make the language focus clear

This is a maxim that is easy to say but more difficult to achieve. How do we know if something is clear? Usually it is quite easy to see after the damage is done and confusion reigns, but how do we pre-empt this? One way is to try and learn from our mistakes. If something hasn't worked, go back over it again and try to identify where and why it might have gone wrong. This can be painful, but it happens to all of us. We don't expect our students to learn the language effectively without making mistakes, so why should we imagine that we can teach the language effectively without occasionally making mistakes? So, try to look upon it as part of the learning process in getting something right. If you are brave enough, you can show the lesson to another teacher you trust for their opinion.

make the language focus memorable

If you want learners to remember something, make it as memorable for your learners as possible. 'Chalk and talk' may be enough for some learners some of the time, but you are more likely to be successful if you can engage learners' interests. That means:

– using your special knowledge of the group to contextualize language within relevant and motivating topics and situations

– sometimes adapting the topics and situations in the coursebook you are using

– making as much use of the learners as you can; exploit personalities within the group when creating contexts or giving examples (in a sensitive manner), especially if they can be humorous; use actual samples of language from the learners where relevant

– choosing texts and contexts that are in the news or contemporary and relevant to the group.

However satisfactory your coursebook may be in general terms, this is where you can build in a layer of interest and motivation beyond anything a book can provide.

use approaches that are appropriate for the group

Whatever approach you use, it has to be appropriate for your group of learners. Age, level, culture, and learning background are all factors that will influence your choice of approach, although it is important to retain an open mind and not simply assume that one or other approach won't work. A pop song may not seem the most appropriate vehicle to present new language to a group of middle-aged businesspeople, but it may just turn an ordinary lesson into something quite different and special. It is important, therefore, to try out different approaches with your learners and monitor how well they are received. Ask the learners themselves what they have liked or enjoyed. Some teachers may think this is putting their head on the block, but if you are teaching adult learners and consult them in this way, they are unlikely to react negatively to you as a teacher, even if they do respond with a clear preference for one approach you have used over another.

2   Ways of introducing new language

a using visuals

It is obvious that with learners at beginner or elementary level, pictures, realia, diagrams, etc. are immensely useful because:

– they are often the most economical way of dealing with the meaning of new vocabulary items and structures

– if they are clear, they will also free you from the need for sometimes lengthy explanation or concept checking

– they often serve as useful prompts for practice

– they are appealing to most learners, and can make language more memorable.

With learners of intermediate level onwards, pictures can be particularly useful diagnostically. If you ask small groups to label the items / furniture in a picture of an office, you and they will quickly be able to identify what they already know and what they have yet to learn, and they may be able to help each other with unknown items. Realia such as *timelines*[1] and *clines*[2] can provide a framework for checking understanding as well as a written record of meaning, as you will see in this example.

1   Match 1 to 3 with a to c in the **natural English** box. Where does each pair of phrases go on the line?

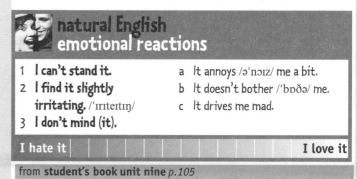

natural English
emotional reactions

1	**I can't stand it.**	a It annoys /əˈnɔɪz/ me a bit.
2	**I find it slightly irritating.** /ˈɪrɪteɪtɪŋ/	b It doesn't bother /ˈbɒðə/ me.
3	**I don't mind (it).**	c It drives me mad.

I hate it | | | | | | | | | | | I love it

from **student's book unit nine** *p.105*

think![2]
Which items might you introduce on these clines for intermediate level learners?

1	baby								pensioner
2	boiling								freezing
3	it's definitely true					it definitely isn't true

go to **answer key** *p.149*

Visuals are very versatile: they provide a focus when you are working with the whole class from the board or OHP, but are equally valuable to prompt and encourage learner interaction in pair or group work. They often play an important role in establishing context, which directly or indirectly may clarify meaning. An example in **natural English** is where learners have to talk about some pictures of people meeting for the first time, and then match appropriate conversation openers with the pictures.

go to **student's book unit one** *p.13*

timelines[1] go to **glossary** *p.149* for numbered items

try it out family photos

I use a selection of photos of my family going back about sixty years, but you could use a contemporary selection only. I find these sets of photos incredibly useful for teaching or practising a range of grammatical structures and vocabulary at different levels. Learners are often fascinated by the photos (particularly the old ones) and some classes have brought in their own sets of family photos.

Among other things, I've used them for:
- physical descriptions (appearance, clothes, etc.)
- describing people's lives (X works for / has worked for / has been studying ..., etc.)
- comparing (comparatives, modifiers, superlatives)
- narrating (X used to ... was doing X before Y, etc.)
- deducing (X could be Y's mother, must have been ...)
- relative clauses (That's the uncle who got married three times / whose wife was a night club singer)

One class produced a wall display of their photos which we used often in language practice and speaking activities.

Liz, Hungary

b using texts

Texts can be written or spoken, and either scripted, authentic, or semi-authentic, i.e. guided or adapted. All texts are a potential source for language work. It may be that the language you focus on is in the text itself, e.g. asking learners to find all the words and phrases relating to money in a news text. In other cases, you may be asking learners to identify or notice certain language features, and this may involve some analysis and probably language use. These language features may be grammatical structures, individual words, or lexical phrases. You will find a focus throughout **natural English** on features of spoken English in listening texts, and often in reading texts too, as the articles selected for this level are often in an informal style and include spoken or informal written features.

Alternatively, the target language may not be in the text itself, but be prompted by the content of the text, e.g. a text about someone's very bad morning leading up to an important interview: he forgot to set the alarm, didn't have a clean shirt, didn't have time to shave, got on the wrong train, arrived an hour late for the interview, etc. From this context, the teacher can first give examples of what the person *should* or *shouldn't have done*, then move on to elicit further examples from the group.

Texts are popular for language focus, and reading texts in particular can be 'adult' in approach. Long texts, however, can be time-consuming, and it is important that learners are not weighed down by the text itself; if they don't grasp the gist of the text, they will probably be in no mood to focus on language in it! Written texts have an advantage over recordings in that learners have time to focus on and absorb the written word, and for many learners, reading in English is easier than listening. If they are to focus on language in recordings, a tapescript is essential. You will find the tapescripts and accompanying exercises in the **listening booklet** will enable your learners to focus on spoken English features more easily.

focusing on language

Let's look at a couple of specific ways of focusing on language in spoken and written texts.

In this first example, learners have already listened to the recording and been through the different stages to aid their understanding. Look at this extract from the **listening booklet**. Learners are asked to find out about collocation, form, and pronunciation, then compare with the **natural English** box (see below) which provides a written record of what they have noticed. They then practise the language.

a   Look at the tapescript. Find the words *advantage* and *disadvantage(s)*.

b   How are they pronounced?

c   What preposition often follows these words?

d   Which words come before *advantage* and *disadvantage(s)*?

from **listening booklet** exercise 6.3 *p.21*.

natural English
talking about advantages and disadvantages

The main advantage of working in the family business is ...
Another advantage is ...
The disadvantage of my situation is ...

With a partner, use the phrases to talk about the advantages and disadvantages of working for a very big / very small company.

from **student's book unit six** *p.75*

In this second example, learners read three short letters and replies from a spoof problem page. There is a comprehension check, a brief vocabulary focus, and an opportunity to react to the text in groups. Learners then move on to a focus on rules about adjectives and adverbs: they can infer the rules, using the examples following each rule, and complete the gaps in the rules. They look back at the text to identify the use of underlined phrases containing adjectives and adverbs. Finally, they select the correct form in personal questions, and go on to use the forms in production.

1   Read the rules. Fill in the gaps with the words *adjectives* or *adverbs*.

adjectives and adverbs

1   We often use _____ to modify nouns, e.g. a *casual* shirt, a *big* house.

2   We often use _____ to modify verbs, e.g. he walked *casually*, listen *carefully*, he speaks *fast* (*fast* can be an adjective or adverb).

3   We modify <u>certain</u> verbs (e.g. *be, seem, look, sound, feel, become, get*) with _____ , e.g. that looks *interesting*, he seemed *angry*.

4 We often use _____ to modify past participles, e.g. *well* made, *badly* written.

5 We use _____ before certain _____, e.g. *terribly cold*, *incredibly stupid*.

2 In A/B pairs, A read out an underlined phrase in the article in **read on**, and B match it with a rule in the box. Swap roles after five phrases.

example 'unbelievably lazy' = rule 5

from **student's book unit five** *p.60*

---

try it out dictogloss

Dictogloss (or grammar dictation) is a very useful way of highlighting language forms either for revision or introducing structures. You need a short text (not more than six lines) in natural English, containing at least a couple of examples of the target language, e.g. past perfect, passive forms, *have* sth *done*.

Explain the procedure to the class before you begin.

1 Introduce the topic to stimulate interest, perhaps through discussion.
2 Read the text at natural speed with slight pauses, so that learners can get the gist. (You could use a recording.)
3 Re-read / replay the text. This time the learners can note down key words.
4 In small groups, learners write out the text using their notes. The text does not need to be identical, but must convey the same ideas, and should aim to be accurate. Monitor, but don't correct at this stage.
5 Together, learners call out suggestions and decide on one version for the teacher to write up, or learners from different groups take turns to write on the whiteboard.
6 Give them copies of the original text (or write it on the board). It is important that they identify any differences and decide together if their version is correct. During this stage, you will need to focus on any problems arising with the target language in the text.

Want to know more? Read **Grammar Dictation** by Ruth Wajnryb for a more detailed description of this approach and a wide range of texts.

go to **follow up** *p.149*

c using examples

Teachers in the past often used to present their learners with a rule and then ask them to apply it (known as the grammar-translation approach). A more common practice nowadays is to proceed in the opposite direction: present examples of language use and then ask the learners to infer the rule (or rules) for themselves. A common example of this, usually referred to as 'guided discovery', is utilizing the learners' knowledge of one concept in order to help them to work out the rules of use of a new (or less familiar) concept that is closely related in meaning. For example, in **how to ...** talk about your past in unit three, learners work in pairs and tell each other about periods in their life based around a series of sentence stems such as, *When I was younger ...* or, *When I left school ...* or, *When I first got married ...* . After this, they listen to some native

speakers talking about similar periods in their lives, and they complete these sentences (see the sample (underlined) answers):

1 Listen to some people talking about art. Complete the sentences.

1 When I was at primary school, we used to write stories and then draw pictures to go with them.

2 When I was a child, I used to enjoy painting lessons at school, but I never liked going round art galleries.

3 When I left school, I started a History of Art course at university, but I didn't finish it.

4 I remember when I was younger, I drew pictures of my family all the time. My mum really loved that.

5 When I was in my early twenties, I worked in a museum for six months.

Having first checked their answers, they then answer the following questions which are designed to help them to infer the difference in use between the past simple and *used to* + verb.

3 Answer the questions.

1 Two of the speakers say *used to* in their sentences. What do they mean?

2 Look at the other sentences. When is it possible to say *used to* + verb in place of the past simple?

3 How do you pronounce *used* in sentences 1 and 2? Practise saying the sentences.

from **student's book unit three** *p.41*

An opportunity to put the grammar to communicative use is provided towards the end of the lesson.

A contrastive approach like the one above can be very economical, but if you are trying to clarify a rule without the use of contrast, you should have a good range of examples so that learners can discern a clear pattern of use leading to a particular rule, as in the example below.

1 Circle the *-ing* forms in these sentences. What kind of word comes before *-ing*?

1 One advantage of speaking English is that it helps you get a job.

2 You should never give up your job before finding another one.

3 You should borrow money from friends or family instead of going to the bank.

4 You shouldn't set up a business without doing a management course first.

5 You should apply for jobs immediately after leaving school or university.

6 The disadvantage of working in only one company is that you don't get enough variety of experience.

from **student's book unit six** p.75

The main advantage of a guided discovery approach such as those above is that learners are not spoon-fed a rule; they have to work it out for themselves. This means they are involved in the learning process – active participants and not casual bystanders – and they have to expend more mental effort and do more mental processing. This extra effort and involvement should make the learning experience more meaningful to them, and more memorable. When learners are doing this together, there is the added benefit of a speaking activity with a real communicative aim and a high degree of motivation. Adults usually like this approach, because it treats them as intelligent human beings and makes use of their adult analytic capabilities; for younger learners it may be less appropriate.

There are, however, potential drawbacks. If the rule in question is particularly 'messy', e.g. trying to differentiate some of the many different ways of expressing the future in English, or if the examples have been stripped of too much of their surrounding context, learners may end up with a very partial and inaccurate rule, or they may be confused and frustrated. It pays, therefore, to provide as much of the context as you possibly can, and, of course, to choose your examples carefully.

---

think!³

How could you finish each of these sentences to illustrate the difference in concept between a and b in each case?

1 Show the difference in meaning between the past simple and *used to* + verb.
   a I used to go to the cinema _____
   b I went to the cinema _____
2 Show a difference between present perfect simple and continuous.
   a I've painted the room and _____
   b I've been painting the room and _____
3 Show the difference between these connectors.
   a I worked hard at school, although _____
   b I worked hard at school whereas _____

---

go to **answer key** p.149

d test-teach-test

Although the title of this chapter is *how to … introduce <u>new</u> language*, it is increasingly the case from intermediate level onwards, that it is difficult to make assumptions about what learners will or won't know. And a glance at any series of coursebooks will immediately illustrate that a significant percentage of the language introduced at intermediate level is, in fact, a refining and development of structures already introduced at pre-intermediate level; and at upper intermediate level a very high percentage of language under the spotlight has already been introduced at intermediate level.

using a diagnostic approach

When this happens, you can make more use of a diagnostic approach, i.e. find out how much learners know first, and take that as the starting point for further development and consolidation. Psychologically, it also makes good sense to give learners an opportunity to demonstrate what they actually know and understand first. For some, there are few things more irritating than to have to sit through a lengthy presentation of language they already know (or think they know). Sometimes, of course, initial testing may demonstrate that the learners don't, in fact, have a very firm grasp of the target language you assumed they might know. If this is the case, you will obviously have to retrace your steps and proceed more slowly in the 'teach' part of the cycle, but you can do so in the knowledge that your learners should now realize why there is a need to examine or revisit this particular area of language.

At intermediate level, test-teach-test is often a suitable way to approach the present perfect simple. In the example below, an assumption has been made that learners will be familiar with the form and name of the target structure, having almost certainly encountered it at pre-intermediate level. The 'test' is to find out how well they can distinguish it from the past simple in certain contexts.

1 Look at the speech bubbles on *p.147* and answer these questions.

1 Underline the verbs in the questions. What tense are they?

2 Is the man asking about experiences happening before now?

3 Is he asking <u>when</u> things happened?

4 Look at the woman's answers. All the *a* answers are in the present perfect. Why?

5 All the *b* answers are in the past simple. Why?

6 Circle the words *before*, *ever*, and *just*. Which word means:
   – at any time in your life?
   – at a time before this particular occasion / on a previous occasion?
   – recently / a short time ago?

2 With a partner, ask questions 1 to 3 but give your own answers.

from **student's book unit one** *p.15*

Once learners have either confirmed their understanding or newly arrived at a working hypothesis of the rule, they need an opportunity to test it out (in this instance we have used a correction exercise), followed by an opportunity to put it to more communicative use, as below.

1 Complete the sentences about yourself.

think of ...

somewhere interesting you've been

I've _____ .

someone interesting you've met

I've _____ .

something unusual you've **eaten**

I've _____ .

something you've just **done** in your work/studies

I've just _____ .

something you'd **like** to do

I've always wanted _____ .

a **sport** you've never done

I've never _____ .

2 Work in groups of three. Use the prompts in **exercise 1** to talk about yourselves. Ask and answer questions to find out more.

from **student's book unit one** *p.15*

3 Dealing with 'transparent' language

When we search for language that will help our learners to express themselves more effectively, we usually assume we are looking for new and unfamiliar language. But this is not always the case. With some examples of collocation and lexical phrases, learners will be familiar with the individual words and be able to make sense of the whole, but would not express themselves using these phrases unless they had been pointed out. For example, an intermediate learner might well understand that *I had a good time at the party* means *I enjoyed the party*; but it is much more likely that they would use the latter. *Have a good / great / bad / awful time* is not usually part of their productive repertoire, and it deserves to be.

The transparency of this language means that you will probably not need to devote much time to checking that it is understood. The extent to which this is the case will, of course, depend on the learners' mother tongue. Once it has been highlighted, learners need the opportunity to use it. For this reason, you will find that short practice activities are generally provided, as in this example.

natural English
talking about memories

I **can remember** <u>learn</u> **-ing** <u>to swim</u> very clearly.

I **can just remember** <u>learn</u> **-ing** <u>to ride a bike</u> .
   = I can remember, but only a little

I **can't remember** <u>learn</u> **-ing** <u>to tie my shoelaces</u> **at all.**

Listen and complete the sentences. Practise saying them.

2 Look at the pictures. Can you remember learning to do these things? Tell a partner, using phrases in the **natural English** box.

from **student's book unit three** *p.40*

think!⁴

Look at the underlined phrases and structures.

a Which would need to be checked in terms of meaning with your intermediate learners because the meaning is not obvious or easily guessable?

b Which would your learners understand because they are transparent, but probably not use?

1 When I got there at 7.30, Richard <u>had left</u>.

2 <u>I find it very difficult to</u> speak English on the phone.

3 <u>I spend a lot of time</u> sitting in traffic jams.

4 <u>I don't know very much about</u> politics.

5 Could you <u>give me a hand</u> with my suitcase?

6 I was busy this afternoon – <u>I had my hair done</u> and then I went shopping.

go to **answer key** *p.149*

conclusion

In this chapter, we have discussed:

- the various criteria for introducing new language successfully

- four ways of introducing new language: using visuals; using spoken and written texts to focus on language or to prompt target language; using examples in a 'guided discovery' approach; and using a diagnostic approach (test-teach-test) to find out what your learners know before introducing new language

- the importance of focusing on 'transparent' language at this level, i.e. common phrases which learners will probably understand but not use correctly.

Examples can be found throughout the **student's book** in the **natural English** boxes.

answer key

think![1] *p.143*

1 There are shades of difference between the meanings of *fairly* and *quite*, but we feel it is simpler and clearer not to worry about the difference at this level, and accuracy is not seriously compromised.

2 This is truthful but we doubt it is necessary for the learners at this stage. Truthfulness here could interfere with clarity, simplicity, and understanding.

3 This explanation is over-simplified (*pretty* is not synonymous with *very* even though it can mean that), and it also omits the fact that *pretty* is largely used in spoken English.

4 There are various nuances of meaning connected with *rather*. This explanation doesn't go into detail on this, but it does a fair job, in our view, of explaining the general meaning but also with some sense of the slightly different shade of meaning it often conveys. It isn't complete, but neither is it inaccurate.

think![2] *p.144* possible answers

1 toddler; child; teenager / adolescent; adult
2 hot; warm; lukewarm; cool; cold
3 it's probably true / it's likely to be true; it could / might / may be true; it's unlikely to be true / probably isn't true

think![3] *p.147* possible answers

1a ... every week, but I don't go very often now.
1b ... twice last week.
2a ... put the furniture back.
2b ... I think it'll look nice when it's finished.
3a ... I didn't do very well in my exams.
3b ... my brother was incredibly lazy.

think![4] *p.148*

1 (a) With very little context here, learners might think *had left* means the same as *left*. We feel this concept would certainly need checking, unless your learners have an obviously parallel structure in their language.

2 (b) We think many learners will understand this, but not use it. Indeed, in our data, we found they were much more likely to say *For me (it) is very difficult* ... . It's worth pointing out this more natural construction.

3 (b) Again, this is transparent for most learners, but many would say *I pass time* ... or avoid this construction altogether.

4 (b) The meaning is transparent here, but again, this is not always how intermediate learners would express the idea. In our data, learners often said *I know (a) little about* ... .

5 (a) In some languages, there is a similar idiom. However, it is possible with some language groups that the meaning could be unclear and would need checking.

6 (a) For most intermediate learners, this structure is not transparent. They are often unaware that it is a kind of passive structure suggesting a service to be paid for. Learners can confuse it with active and perfect tenses. It would certainly need checking.

glossary

timelines a diagrammatic way to illustrate tenses, using a line (see *p.95*)

clines a diagrammatic way to illustrate a progression from one end of a spectrum to the other (see *p.95*)

follow up

Thornbury S 1999 *How to Teach Grammar* Longman (worth reading in its entirety)

Carter R, Hughes R, and McCarthy M 2000 *Exploring Grammar in Context* Cambridge University Press

Batstone R 1994 *Grammar* Oxford University Press

Wajnryb R 1990 *Grammar Dictation* Oxford University Press

Harmer J 2001 *The Practice of English Language Teaching* Part 5 Longman

how to ... teach listening

1 Why is listening difficult?

There are certain global problems that can arise in almost any situation where learners are trying to understand what is being said to them.

- The speaker is talking too fast and the listener doesn't have time to process the incoming information. After one or two sentences, the listener is floundering.
- The listener is struggling with the speaker's pronunciation – words are all strung together, the accent is unfamiliar, the delivery is unclear, etc.
- The speaker uses language unknown to the listener and this causes a breakdown in communication. The listener is no longer concentrating on the message but thinking, 'What did that mean?'

In addition to these general problems, there are other more specific ones.

think!¹

Imagine you are living in a foreign country, learning the language. Assume you are intermediate level. Which of the following would you find difficult, and why?

1 On a packed train, three people sitting behind you are chatting; you're trying to understand them.
2 You're listening to the words of a pop song.
3 You've just started a course at a language school. The director is giving all the students a ten-minute welcoming speech.
4 Your teacher announces your class is going to have a listening test, hands out the test paper and turns on the tape recorder.
5 You're sitting with your landlady watching TV. It's a programme about medieval literature which she needs to watch for her degree course.
6 You ask your landlady why there is a transport strike tomorrow, and she explains it to you. The reasons aren't simple.

go to **answer key** *p.155*

the classroom context

A further factor in terms of difficulty for learners is that created by the classroom context (e.g. situation four above). Apart from teacher talk and the occasional use of video, most listening is probably provided by audio cassettes. While these often do provide interesting and valuable listening material, there are obvious drawbacks:

- absence of body language
- lack of visual context, i.e. learners can't see where the speaking is taking place
- lack of opportunity to interact with the speaker by asking them to repeat or slow down
- poor sound quality or acoustics.

Finally, it can be harder to motivate learners to listen to disembodied voices. However, cassettes are the easiest way to provide a variety of listening material with a range of different voices. In section 4, you'll find ways of overcoming the difficulties mentioned.

2 Features of natural spoken English

When you listen to natural spoken language, whether it is English or any other language, there are many features which distinguish it from most forms of written language. Firstly, conversation is very rarely planned; it doesn't always progress in a clear linear way, as scripted language does. Other speakers in conversation will take it in different directions from those the original speaker intended, and there will be frequent digressions. We also tend to repeat ourselves and use more language than is necessary to convey our ideas. This is not a sign of an uneducated or poor speaker, simply a reflection of the way people communicate.

think!²

Can you think of other characteristics of natural, informal speech? Note them down, then compare with the list below.

features of natural speech

- discourse is usually unplanned, with frequent digressions
- repetition and redundancy (saying more than is necessary to convey a message)
- loosely structured or unfinished sentences
- false starts (begin a sentence, abandon it, and start again)
- ellipsis (words are omitted, but the meaning is clear, e.g. *Ever been there?*)
- speaking over one another when there are two or more people involved
- hesitation
- use of lubricators and fillers, e.g. *well*, *you know*, *let me see*
- reliance on a small number of simple *discourse markers¹*, e.g. *and*, *so*, *but*
- more informal lexis
- less emphasis on grammatical accuracy
- pronunciation is less 'clear' with differences from phonemic representations in dictionaries

discourse markers¹ go to glossary *p.155* for numbered items

think!³

Look at this extract from a listening passage in the **student's book**. Which features from **think!**² can you identify?

> **S: Sophie; B: Brian**
>
> S   We've met before, haven't we?
> B   Yes, I'm really sorry, I don't remember your name.
> S   Sophie.
> B   Sophie. That's right, yeah.
> S   And you're Brian, aren't you?
> B   Yep, yep, yep, yeah.
> S   Yeah, yeah. We did the, er, we did that other course last year ...
> B   That's right, yeah. (Yeah.) It was about this time of year too, (yeah) actually, wasn't it, yeah.
> S   And I seem to remember you'd just had a kid, hadn't you?
> B   Yes, that's right, yeah, yeah, little girl.
> S   Little girl. How is she?
> B   She's very well. (hmm) Yes, yes, growing really quickly ...

from **welcome unit** *p.6*, **listening booklet** tapescript 0.1 *p.2*

go to **answer key** *p.155*

3   What type of listening do learners need?

Is it better to build our learners' confidence by playing examples of carefully graded and scripted English? Or should we expose them to the type of authentic English you have just looked at, which they would have to get used to in the real world? If our aim is to prepare learners to function effectively in an English-speaking environment, it is hard to justify a strict diet of carefully scripted English which bears little resemblance to natural, spontaneous speech. This doesn't mean, however, that we throw our learners in at the deep end, and allow them to become demoralized as they try to cope with authentic English.

select appropriate listening materials

We need to provide our learners with listening which is largely authentic, but selected and graded so that comprehension is achievable. These are some of the ways in which we can do this.

- Choose speakers with a naturally slow and distinct delivery, as they are easier to follow. Slight differences in accent are not significant and add to the exposure that learners get.
- One voice is easier to follow than two (and two than three).
- In terms of content, straightforward information, stories told in chronological order, and predictable conversations, e.g. at a ticket office, make comprehension easier in the early stages of learning.
- Choose topics which are familiar and relevant to the learners' environment. This makes listening easier.
- Being able to see the speaker(s) and their body language helps considerably. This is a disadvantage of audio cassettes whether you are listening to scripted or unscripted recordings. (See **Teacher talk** *p.153*.)
- Keep recordings short, or play longer recordings in extracts.

Want to know more? Read **Teaching the Spoken Language** Brown G and Yule G. go to **follow up** *p.155*

So, if we choose listening passages carefully, and adjust comprehension tasks accordingly, we can prepare learners for real-life listening with much more confidence. Far from being discouraging, it is immensely satisfying for learners to be able to feel they can take on a piece of 'real' listening and get something out of it.

However, this doesn't exclude a role for scripted material, which can be used to provide a focus on new language, as a model for guided practice, and to highlight particular features of pronunciation.

select a variety of listening materials

Above all, learners need variety as their listening ability develops. In selecting listening materials, bear these points in mind. Learners need to:

- be prepared for language spoken in a range of locations and situations
- listen to dialogue as well as monologue
- have short sound bites and gradually develop their ability to follow longer extracts
- cope with casual conversation along with more animated discussion
- be able to follow people of different ages with different accents, and so on.

think!⁴

Which of these listening materials would be most relevant to your learners, and why?

- a recording of the day's news
- the pop song *Wonderful tonight*, by Eric Clapton
- information about the volume of shipping in The English Channel
- extract from an interview with a Hollywood actor
- a very short ghost story
- an interview with someone who collects antiques
- an amusing anecdote about a teacher the learners know
- a phone conversation in which someone is buying an airline ticket

4   Developing the listening skill

working at macro level

In most situations in the real world, we don't listen without some idea of what we are listening to, so it is unrealistic, and certainly unhelpful, simply to turn on a tape recorder and tell learners to listen to a conversation and answer questions on it at the end. You can prepare your learners for listening in various ways.

- Set the scene by telling them who is involved and broadly what the listening is about, e.g. *You are going to hear a husband and wife discussing their holiday plans*. A picture could perform a similar function.

- You can ask the learners to discuss the topic before listening, e.g. learners tell each other how quickly they do certain everyday things (have lunch, have a shower or bath, etc.), before listening to native speakers describing how quickly they do the same, or similar activities (see unit nine *p.107*; **listening booklet**, tapescript 9.2 *p.32*).

- Learners can predict the content of what they are going to hear, e.g. learners listen to a conversation in which someone arrives late. Learners have to think of three reasons why people are often late, then listen to find out if they guessed correctly (see unit ten *p.121*; **listening booklet**, tapescript 10.7 *p.38*). You can also ask learners to predict the attitudes or opinions of people they are going to listen to if you first provide some background information about them.

- You can pre-teach key vocabulary. This not only helps by reducing the burden of unknown lexis, but will probably give learners a fair idea of the topic of the listening. We wouldn't recommend doing this on a large scale though, as learners have to get used to coping with unknown lexis. Words and phrases which may well be new to intermediate learners and could be pre-taught, are highlighted in the lesson plans.

- You can preset questions, or let learners preset their own questions – assuming, of course, they know the topic of the listening.

Whichever of these you choose, the aim is broadly similar:

a to provide a framework for learners to make sense of the listening

b to give as much help as is necessary (but not more than that) to ensure the listening will be comprehensible

c to create a reason / motivation for listening.

tune in to the voices and context

In section 1, we looked at some of the problems involved in listening to an audio cassette which are not a problem in face-to-face conversation, e.g. the lack of visual clues to assist understanding. Moreover, most listening materials contain a strange set of voices which do require some adjustment (a process John Field describes as 'normalisation') before attempting a challenging comprehension task. These difficulties have perhaps been underestimated in teaching materials, and that is why we have included **tune in** as a step in many of our recordings. This is a short extract, usually from the beginning of a recording, which learners listen to before they hear the main extract and before doing the comprehension task. The aim is to help learners to tune into / adjust to the speakers' voices and the context. For example:

---

tune in

1 (8.3) You're going to listen to Colin on the phone to a friend, Diana. Listen to the beginning of the conversation.

   1 Did Colin expect Diana to ring?
   2 Does he sound pleased?

from **student's book unit eight** *p.94*,
listening booklet tapescript 8.3 *p.28*

Here, the context is established before listening through some pictures and a description in the instructions. Learners are eased into the listening by a fairly undemanding task which focuses on the voices. In addition, they only hear a very short extract (about ten seconds), just enough to acclimatize to the voices and context.

keep tasks focused

When learners are listening, it is unfair and unrealistic to expect them to be reading eight, ten, or twelve questions at the same time, or writing quite lengthy notes on what they are listening to, or trying to absorb a lot of information which they will then be expected to regurgitate immediately after listening. To keep the focus clearly on the development of the listening skill, it is, therefore, important to keep the task relatively simple and avoid too much reliance on other skills.

- If there are questions, restrict the number and keep them short.

- If there is a table or grid to fill in, make sure very little writing is involved.

- If you are asking learners to recode the information, keep to two or three main points.

With a listening passage in which an opinion is expressed, the simplest and arguably the most realistic task is to ask learners to react. Do they agree or disagree with the opinions they heard?

set realistic tasks

One of the points made earlier about natural listening is that it contains a fair amount of repetition and redundancy. This means that listeners can usually allow their attention to drop at certain points in the listening without necessarily losing any of the key information. This fact should be borne in mind when we are setting tasks. If a task tests comprehension of every phrase or sentence in a passage, it probably means the passage itself is fairly unnatural, or we are pushing our learners into a listening habit which is artificial and unhelpful. Different types of listening material call for different levels of attention – in the case of announcements, attention may need to be constant and intensive – but for most situations, we need to develop positive, confidence-building listening habits which will promote a sense that learners can get something out of natural English without understanding every word or phrase.

give the listeners control

As with many things in life, confidence often has a lot to do with feeling in control; and for many learners this is definitely not something they feel with most classroom listening. You can counteract this by handing over control of the tape recorder to the learners. Give one of them the power to stop the tape if they or others don't understand, or tell learners to raise their hand or call out if they want you to stop and replay a section of the tape. This is, after all, a course of action that is often open to us in the real world – we can sometimes interrupt people and ask them to slow down, repeat something, etc. – but more importantly perhaps, it may be a necessary stage in the learners' development before they can feel they are fully independent listeners.

working at micro level

Understanding spoken language at a micro level is more to do with features of pronunciation (sounds, *stress*[2], and *intonation³*), recognizing words and phrases within a stream of speech, and recognizing cohesive devices which link *utterances⁴*, e.g. *anyway, actually, soon after that*, and indicate the direction of the discourse.

dealing with pronunciation

Pronunciation is often treated in two ways. Firstly, you can deal with it in specific, tailor-made pronunciation activities, e.g. *minimal pairs⁵* exercises, *phonemic script⁶* focuses, indicating stress patterns in word families, intonation on *wh-* questions, etc. Secondly, listening extracts themselves can be used to focus on pronunciation features. In **natural English**, the main source for micro-level understanding is the **listening booklet**, where you will find discrete pronunciation activities on individual sounds, word and sentence stress, and intonation.

You will also find that we have used the unscripted recordings as a source for noticing specific features of pronunciation in natural speech. For instance, question a below focuses on the weak form of *are*.

> a Look at Diana's questions which have been underlined. How does she pronounce *are*? Listen again. Practise saying the questions.
>
> b Look at Diana's responses. She responds to Colin's news with surprise and excitement. Circle the phrases she uses, as in the examples. Practise saying the phrases.

from **listening booklet** p.29

Tapescripts of unscripted English allow you to focus on features of natural English, whether these are pronunciation, lexis, discourse markers, etc. For too long they have been buried at the back of coursebooks, and are often under-exploited. In question b above, the focus is on natural responses which might otherwise go unnoticed, e.g. *Wow! That sounds exciting! Hey, that's great!*

You can use scripted listening material to introduce new language and, at the same time, work on your learners' ability to recognize the presence (or absence) of words within a stream of speech. Here is an example from a **natural English** box.

natural English
use of *take*

How long would it **take** (you) to do that exercise?
It would **take** (me) about half an hour.

Does it **take** (you) long to get there?
No, not very long.

Listen. Do you hear the words in brackets?
Practise the phrases.

from **student's book unit nine** p.110

All these discrete exercises focusing on pronunciation and new language contribute to learners' listening competence, but need to be accompanied by the development of the macro listening skills discussed earlier.

5 Teacher talk

Some of the most valuable and meaningful listening practice your learners will get is through listening to you. There are several reasons for this.

- Most of the time, there is a real purpose to the listening; learners need to listen to you in order to be able to answer a question, carry out an instruction, understand an explanation, etc.

- There is also a high degree of motivation because they will probably be more interested in listening to something, e.g. a story told by you (someone they know), than by a stranger on a tape recorder.

- It is very realistic listening practice, as your presence not only gives learners important visual clues, but also the opportunity to interrupt and ask for repetition, clarification, and so on. This will often be the case in real-life listening situations, and it is vital that learners gain practice in asking the kind of questions they will need to check understanding or appeal for help.

Teacher talk is particularly useful when introducing the topic of a lesson or to provide a speaking model for learners to follow.

> **try it out** live listening
>
> Think of something that happened to you or someone you know which links in with the theme / topics you are teaching, e.g. in unit two, you could tell learners about a brilliant or disastrous holiday you had. If possible, make it an anecdote that would generate ideas for learners to produce their own. It should take about 60 to 90 seconds to tell.
>
> - Practise the story in your head. Make notes if you like, but don't write a script to read aloud; it will be less natural.
> - Plan how you'll get the learners to tune in to the story (could you use photos? souvenirs? travel brochures? postcards?).
> - Decide if you need to pre-teach one or two key items.
> - Decide on a listening task for learners.
> - Arrange the seating in the classroom in a horseshoe around you, if possible, to make the atmosphere informal.
> - Tell the learners they can stop you to ask questions about your experience or if they don't understand.
> - You can record the story as you are telling it so that you and the learners can refer back to it if necessary.
> - Do *feedback⁷* at the end on the task you set.
> - Then give learners a framework and time to think of their own anecdote to tell others in small groups.

Want to know more? Try activity 1.5 in **Listening** White G

go to **follow up** p.155

6 Frequently asked questions

How often should I play the recording?

In **natural English**, recordings are broken down into short extracts of about twenty seconds to a minute and a half. You should be able to replay recordings or parts of them several times if necessary. There are two main reasons for replaying a section:

- The learners want to hear it again. Give them the opportunity to tell you.
- You have good reasons for replaying it: you have evidence that the learners haven't understood it (even when they think they have); you want to focus on a phrase or utterance for language practice; you want to give them the chance to listen and follow the tapescript, etc.

Most importantly though, you need to be aware when they are saturated. Very short sections of a recording for intensive language focus can easily be replayed several times, but learners will become exhausted and possibly bored if you play a long recording too many times.

What if they don't understand it?

Fine. This should happen sometimes, otherwise there is no challenge for the learners. However, when you find there is a big gap between what you expect the learners to understand and what they actually understand, alarm bells ring for any teacher, no matter how experienced they are. This situation can arise the first time you play the recording. If the learners can't understand the gist, you may need to allow more time for tuning in. Simplify the initial task. You could:

- change the initial task slightly to make it easier
- give learners a little more information about the context, then replay it
- let them read the first few lines of tapescript to tune in.

Once you move on to more intensive listening comprehension, you may sense that the problem is unknown language. In this case, you could teach one or two relevant phrases, then replay the recording.

It's vital to clarify that the learners don't need to try to understand every word. Make it clear that much of the time you're helping them to understand the gist of what they hear (as they do in L1), but that sometimes they need to focus on particular phrases, especially where they cause a communication problem.

If the language is known to them, but they are unable to decipher it in natural connected speech, they will need to develop this ability. Look at the way one teacher tackled it in **try it out**, opposite. Do you do this with your learners?

---

try it out helping learners decipher speech

Learners listened to recording 8.3 and did the **tune in** and **listen carefully** activities. I then wanted them to pick out the utterance, *Are you going to do any travelling while you're there?* from the recording to focus on the language in it later.

1 I replayed the question, asking them to listen for any words they understood. This was to give a positive feel to the task. They compared with a partner. I asked them to shout the words out, and wrote the ones they knew on the board, leaving spaces for missing words.

    Are you going – – – travelling – – – there?

2 I played it again and they compared with their partner. I encouraged them to guess and then listen again.

3 The class then called out the missing words and I wrote them up. The only problem was *while*. I got them to guess, and they came up with *when*, which was good.

4 They listened again, and talked about why it was hard (weak forms, contractions, the phrase *do any travelling*).

5 They practised saying it as on the recording – to help them with fluency and to make the connected speech more memorable.

I usually only do this once in a listening activity.

Janet, London

go to **listening booklet** tapescript 8.3 *p.28*

When should I use the tapescript?

We have suggested a stage in the listening section where it is appropriate to look at the tapescript (this is usually at the end of the **listening challenge**). If the learners usually look and listen right from the start, however they will find it very difficult to become self-reliant as listeners, and you won't know how much they have understood of the recording.

Learners do find it very satisfying to listen and follow the tapescript. It can often fill in missing pieces of the jigsaw for them, and each learner may get something different from the activity. One thing you can do is to focus on a short extract only; perhaps a few exchanges of dialogue which they can listen to with the tapescript, then practise with a partner.

Tapescripts are a great resource for self study. You can train learners to skim the tapescript for particular types of language (as you'll see in the **listening booklet** exercises). If learners have access to the student's CD, they can listen and follow, repeat, and practise 'shadow reading', i.e. listen and read along with the speaker.

conclusion

In this chapter, we have looked at:

- the reasons why listening can be difficult, both inside and outside the classroom
- the features of natural spoken English which distinguish it from most written language, and which learners at this level often find challenging

- criteria for selecting appropriate materials which should help build learners' confidence
- ways of developing the listening skill at a macro level, e.g. giving learners the opportunity to 'tune in' to the context, and setting realistic, focused tasks; and at a micro level, i.e. dealing with discrete language items, such as pronunciation or new lexis
- the importance of teacher talk in the classroom.

If you have never used 'teacher talk' activities before with your learners, do experiment with them. You should find them very rewarding for both you and your learners.

answer key

think![1] *p.150* suggested answers

1 Background noise and the fact that you can't see the speakers' body language and mouths make understanding extremely difficult. Eavesdropping is difficult even in L1 in these circumstances, and native speakers take time to tune in: the topic and cultural references may be unfamiliar, people may be talking over each other, using completely natural and ungraded language, private jokes, etc. Perhaps the most difficult context of all of them.

2 Although motivating, song lyrics can be difficult to follow where sounds are distorted, and language may be non-standard.

3 Some of the content of the speech will be predictable, which helps comprehension, and there is visual support. However, you may find it hard to concentrate for ten minutes.

4 Most learners will feel varying degrees of nervousness in this situation, which can inhibit their ability to understand. You may feel exposed and worry about the teacher's disapproval of your performance; this may affect your self-esteem.

5 This may well be a topic outside of your experience or interest, and is likely to include a high level of specialized vocabulary. There will be cultural references which may be hard to follow.

6 The explanation may be difficult to follow for cultural reasons, or specific language items may be unfamiliar. (However, you have the opportunity to interact with your landlady when you don't understand, which will be more motivating and less tiring than listening to a speech.)

think![3] *p.151*

- repetition, e.g. *yeah*, *yep*
- informal lexis, e.g. *kid*
- hesitation, e.g. *er ...*
- false start, e.g. *we did the, er, we did that other course ...*
- fillers, e.g. in this text *yeah, yeah*, and *that's right* are partly used as fillers
- overlap, a limited amount with *yeah* and *hmm*
- pronunciation, e.g. lots of contractions
- ellipsis, e.g. the omission of the pronoun and auxiliary verb (*she's*) in *Yes, yes, growing really quickly; ... yeah, little girl.*

glossary

discourse markers words or phrases which hold phrases and sentences together in speech or writing, e.g. *and*, *so*, *in other words*, *What's more*, etc.

stress the position within a word, phrase, or sentence on which the emphasis is placed in speech

intonation tone of voice expressing meaning and attitude

utterances the act of expressing something in words

minimal pairs two different phonemes in which the sounds are very close or are difficult to distinguish for many learners, e.g. *ship* /ɪ/ *sheep* /iː/

phonemic script a system of symbols devised to represent each single unit of sound in the pronunciation of spoken English; usually represented in dictionaries following a word entry, e.g. *book* /bʊk/

feedback information given to learners following an activity about their performance

follow up

White G 1998 *Listening* Oxford University Press

Ur P 1984 *Teaching Listening Comprehension* Cambridge University Press

Anderson A and Lynch T 1988 *Listening* Oxford University Press

Field J 1998 *The Changing Face of Listening* in English Teaching Professional (6 Jan)

Brown G and Yule G 1983 *Teaching the Spoken Language* Cambridge University Press

how to ... monitor and give feedback

1 What is monitoring, correction, and feedback? Why is it necessary?

Monitoring is concerned with observing learners when they are engaged in pair or group work activities, and feedback is providing learners with information on their performance. Feedback consists of error correction and praise for what learners have achieved (linguistically and communicatively). It can also be a platform for further new language input arising out of the activity.

Monitoring and feedback should also take place during individual writing tasks, but this chapter is devoted specifically to spoken English.

why monitor?

Teachers need to monitor for various reasons. Here are two:

- You need to check that learners understand the activity / task and are fully engaged in it.

- You need to notice how learners are performing in order to provide the most useful feedback.

---

think![1]

Think of three more reasons why you should monitor. Then read the list. Tick ✓ the ones you thought of, and put an asterisk * by any that are new.

- ☐ You need to be aware of how learners are interacting with each other. Noticing good or bad group dynamics is clearly relevant to future activities.

- ☐ You need to know when an activity has run its course and should be brought to an end.

- ☐ You need to be available to deal with learners' queries about language or the activity.

- ☐ Learners expect you to monitor. They see it as an important part of your responsibility, and if they sense you aren't listening to them or that you aren't interested in what they have to say, this could have an adverse effect on their motivation or their relationship with you.

- ☐ With monolingual groups in particular, you need to check that learners aren't using their own language <u>unnecessarily</u>.

---

why give feedback?

Feedback has been associated largely with error correction, but that is only one reason for its use. Equally important is the opportunity it gives the teacher to praise learners for effective language use, and discuss how well they achieved their communicative goals and contributed on a personal level. In some cases, it will lead into a new cycle of language input arising out of the activity. This input can be some of the most useful and memorable language you teach, and many learners view feedback as one of the most crucial parts of their learning experience.

2 Why do learners make errors?

Some writers distinguish between performance mistakes and competence errors. Mistakes are 'slips' made due to carelessness, tiredness, or inattention: the learner knows what he / she should have said, and is capable of correcting the mistake, e.g. *I haven't made my homework ... no, sorry, I haven't done my homework*. Errors, however, occur because the learner has not yet learnt the rule which helps them to produce the correct form, e.g. *I picked up it*. Alternatively, he or she is applying the wrong rule, e.g. *She spoke to me friendlily*, or doesn't yet know a specific item, e.g. *The stone smashed the car's front window*, where the speaker means *windscreen*.

In practice, there is clearly a degree of overlap between the two. From experience, the teacher will often know whether learners are capable of correcting themselves or not, as long as they are familiar with the learners' mother tongue and background.

Although errors in the past were considered something to be avoided, it is now widely recognized that they are an essential part of progress, and that 'getting it wrong' is often a step along the road to 'getting it right'.

the causes of error

As you read the causes of error below, think of examples from your own teaching and language learning experience.

- L1 transfer: learners 'translate' from their mother tongue.

- False friends are a classic example: *librairie* (French) looks like *library*, but means *bookshop*.

- Collocations and phrases may come across inaccurately: *I did it by my own; he lost the bus and had to walk*.

- Grammatical structures may not transfer directly: *I want that you go* rather than *I want you to go*. In addition, forms in one language may not convey the same meaning in English: *Se ha cortado el pelo* (Spanish); *He's cut himself his hair* should be *He's had his hair cut*.

- All aspects of pronunciation are problematic, e.g. misplaced stress on vocabulary items; inaccurate phoneme transfer; non-standard rhythm and intonation.

- Negative transfer: this can also occur from other languages the learner knows, e.g. a Swiss person whose first language is German, but also speaks French could experience interference from both languages when learning English.

- Overgeneralization: learners try to use a rule which doesn't apply, e.g. adding -ed to an irregular verb form (*she taked my book*); or adding -s to make a plural (*womans*).

- Errors induced by teaching or teaching materials: as teachers we all have to provide simplified rules or explanations, and occasionally, learners will make assumptions based on these which turn out to be incorrect. For instance, if you tell your class that *weak* is the opposite of *strong*, learners may assume that if they can say *a strong accent* they can also say *a weak accent*. Such errors are to some extent inevitable.

- The desire to communicate overrides accuracy: when learners become more concerned with conveying their message, many will be less able to monitor the accuracy of their language, or will produce non-standard / incorrect forms through communication strategies. This is something which can be viewed positively as long as it isn't overused, e.g. using circumlocution to express an unknown word (*I need a thing for open this wine bottle*: a corkscrew) or using a more general word if they don't know a specific term (*table* instead of *desk*, *ticket* for *fare*, etc.). In such cases, you can praise your learners for their communicative skill, but also use the opportunity to teach them the item they didn't know.

3 What sort of errors do learners make?

Here are some categories of error in spoken English:

- grammar morphology (e.g. tenses, plurals, etc.) and syntax (e.g. word order, verb patterns, etc.)
- lexis: words and phrases
- style / appropriateness
- discourse organization: the way text is connected
- pronunciation: sounds, stress, rhythm, intonation.

---

think!²

The extracts below are taken from recordings of intermediate learners made during the piloting of role plays or extended speaking activities in the **student's book**. Match the highlighted errors in bold with the categories above. Each error may involve more than one category. (Not all errors in the extract are highlighted.)

1 A telephones B, whom he doesn't know, to invite her to give a talk at the weekend English course.

A Hello?
B Hello. Miss Anna Sinclair (1)?
A Yes.
B This is Franco (2) and I am a student of Oxford Academy. I'd like to ask you if you could participate to (3) a conference we are going to organize for the school and all of us students.
A Oh, that sounds very interesting, but I don't know. I have to check in my agenda (4). When is (5)?
B Well, actually, we have two weekend of conferences. I mean there will be two conferences: one on Saturday afternoon and one on Sunday afternoon.
A Do you know the time?

B Each will be one and a half hours more or less. It depends on you because if you need more time we can (6). We are planning now the situation. Let me you inform (7) about the topic.

from **unit four** (extended speaking) p.55

2 Roberta (Italian) is telling Ceyhan (Turkish) about her home town; their teacher is listening.

R My town is a very little town near the sea, there isn't underground station, but there is the bus, or the taxi, the taxi are (8) not very cheap, but the bus are (9) cheap, the ticket (10), you can buy ticket (11) in the machine near the bus station (12).
Teacher Do you mean the bus station or the bus stop?
R No, no … at the bus stop, every stop …
C How much are tickets?
R In pounds 50 pence, bus ticket for one travel (13). The bus ticket is very cheap. For call in public call box is necessary (14) the coin or card, you can buy phone card in the post office or where tobacco, … or post office or tobacco shop …

from **unit eight** (extended speaking) p.101

go to **answer key** p.161

4 When is feedback and correction appropriate?

It is clearly not sensible to interrupt learners continuously with praise or correction, so the timing of feedback is important. Praise is often the most suitable starting point for feedback at the end of an activity. With error correction, you often have three choices:

- correct it on the spot
- correct it at the end of the activity
- do nothing if it is not a high priority.

If you decide to correct, the timing will be influenced by these factors:

- Is correction appropriate at this stage in the lesson? If learners are engaged in a free exchange of opinions, it may be less inhibiting to wait until the end of the activity. During a more controlled or accuracy-based task, correction may seem less obtrusive.

- Is it a serious error in the sense that it has caused a breakdown in communication? If so, correction may be necessary for the activity to continue effectively. Can you deal with it quickly and effectively, or will it take a lot of time? If the latter, then you should wait till later.

- Is it relevant to one learner or the whole group? If it is only relevant to one person, it may be better to talk to them when they are working individually, so that you don't waste other people's time.

- Who made the mistake? Some learners want correction and feedback more than others, and some respond to correction more positively than others. In theory, you may feel you should treat all learners the same, but in practice this is not always practical or desirable. It is important to be equally fair and responsive to all your learners, but that doesn't necessarily mean dealing with them all in the same way.

make time for feedback

It is important to build a feedback stage into your lesson after a freer speaking activity, and leave sufficient time for it. We've made the mistake ourselves of coming out of class and saying, *the learners talked so much, I didn't have time to do feedback*. There is no doubt that many learners expect to complete the cycle of learning with feedback, and it can turn a good speaking activity into a valuable learning experience. On occasion it may be appropriate or necessary to give feedback in the next lesson, or before doing a similar activity – so keep your notes even if you run out of time – but bear in mind that it will have more impact when it directly follows the activity.

---

think!³

Your intermediate class are working in small groups on a freer speaking activity, and you overhear the following exchanges. Would you:

- definitely correct / intervene on the spot?
- leave it for now, but come back to it later?
- do nothing?

1 A I think it's not important telephone every day, because you have nothing to say.
  B Yes, but your parents like to listen to your voice and to know everything is OK.

2 A If you want to travel by bus every day, it's a good idea to buy a ... um ... a ... .

3 A I don't know the name, but when terrorists take one person and ask the family for money, I think the family must never pay this money.
  B And if the terrorist kill this person?
  A I know it's terrible, but ...

4 A What do people wear to the theatre?
  B Well, they mustn't wear smart clothes.
  A Really? In my country it's the opposite; you have to wear smart clothes.
  B No, I mean you can wear what you want.

go to **answer key** p.161

---

5 Ways of monitoring

class management

When you monitor a student-centred activity, you need to be as unobtrusive as possible.

- If you walk round the room and stand directly in front of a pair or group of learners, they will soon direct their comments at you and start asking you questions. Standing behind learners is more sensible, as it allows you to hear what is being said without becoming the centre of attention and without having eye contact with learners. Your presence may even go unnoticed.

- Standing up makes you very visible, so we would recommend sitting down at least part of the time. If the classroom layout allows it, you can position your chair where you are able to see and hear something from a number of pairs / groups in the room, then you can move elsewhere to monitor other groups (with a large class).

- Try not to attach yourself too closely to one group, or you may not realize that the rest of the class have finished the activity and are now doing nothing. Sitting in or near the centre of the room (where you can see and hear most things) minimizes this problem, and enables you to home in on a specific pair or group at a strategic moment and pick up the most relevant and useful contributions from different learners in the class. In practice, of course, it may be quite impossible to hear everything that is said, especially if the activity has been successful and generated a lot of noise. The important thing, however, in terms of classroom management, is that the group feel you have monitored fairly and closely.

making notes

What do you actually do while you are monitoring? Obviously, you need to be available to help if necessary. For the rest of the time, many teachers like to jot things down for later feedback. We find it helpful to do this by dividing the page into different sections. First you need a section for praise, e.g. noting down effective use of language and/or effective communication strategies. Then a section devoted to errors, which can be further sub-divided into 'grammar', 'vocabulary', and 'pronunciation'. You could also consider one further section for errors causing a breakdown in communication. In this **teacher's book** in each **extended speaking** lesson plan, you'll find a feedback checklist which you can photocopy and use for making notes.

There are several advantages to organizing your comments in this way.

- You can see at a glance whether you are paying equal attention to positive and corrective feedback.

- With errors, you will notice whether your comments tend to pick up one type of mistake rather than another. And if that is the case, is it because your learners are more prone to one type of error than another, or is it a reflection of you as a teacher being more conscious of and sensitive to certain types of error? We have found this technique helps us not to become too narrowly focused; one area that can get neglected at this stage is pronunciation.

- Feedback is more systematic. If you jot things down randomly, you are more likely to feed them back randomly. Writing them down in clear categories tends to avoid this; you can provide lexical feedback in one chunk and pronunciation feedback in another.

- Where one category seems to have the most useful and relevant points, it makes sense to restrict your comments to the one area. Learners may find this more memorable.

In certain activities, e.g. presentations, you may want to make individual notes for each learner. You can then either give personalized feedback, or even, if appropriate, give each learner a copy of your notes to look at and discuss with you later. This may be useful if you are short of time, and learners usually appreciate the personal attention.

Keeping your monitoring notes will provide a 'real' on-going record of how your learners are performing in freer spoken English activities. It's not a complete record but is arguably one of the most useful ways to make informal assessments of their progress.

using a tape or video recorder

If these resources are available, you can use them to introduce some variety into monitoring. Some learners are nervous the first time they are recorded, especially using video, but they soon get used to it and most enjoy being able to see and/or listen to themselves. It certainly makes an activity more exhilarating and potentially more memorable. Short recordings can be played back on the spot, but longer recordings do need to be watched and/or listened to after the lesson, so you can make notes on the learners' performance and select short interesting extracts to play back. (Don't abuse this luxury by playing back over-long sections.) You need to remember that this can be a sensitive area, so make sure before you play something back that there is nothing which might potentially embarrass any of the learners in the class. With video, ask them first if they are happy for it to be shown.

try it out

Peer monitoring and feedback is another variation to try with your class, but you should only consider it when they know each other reasonably well. It hands control to the learners and involves them fully in making the activity more effective.

1 Look at the two role cards on *p.144* and *p.148*.
2 Divide the class into threes. Student C in each group is going to monitor the activity, using the role card below.
3 When the role play has finished, A and B should say how they felt it went; student C should then give their feedback. Monitor the groups to see how effectively this is working.
4 Change roles: either A or B should take student C's role. Repeat the procedure twice.

Learners often need to do this type of feedback two or three times before they can do it effectively. Repeating the same role play with different roles does mean that learners have a chance to improve.

Don't be discouraged if it doesn't work very well the first time. To train learners how to do it, you could play the whole group a recording of a pair from a different class doing a similar type of role play, and give them questions to guide them.

student C

You are going to listen to the phone conversation role play. Afterwards you will talk to students A and B about how it went. While listening to the conversation, think about the following:

– Does each person express their ideas clearly in general?

– Are there any problems or areas of confusion? If so, what?

– Is there any way the conversation can be made better? How?

from **student's book pairwork** *p.144* and *p.148*

think!⁴

Look at the extract from our data of learners doing the extended speaking activity in unit ten. (Learners were not pre-taught any language.)

a What would you praise?
b Can you see one or two particular areas you would correct?
c Is there one particular language point you would teach?

D: Question 2 – *Women are much better liars than men* – definitely.

A: Agree.

C: No doubt.

B: I disagree. I'm a girl but I'm not good for a liar.

A: But think in general, all woman tell lies.

C: But the mans tell lies too.

A: But the woman are better telling lies.

C: It's true in your case?

A: I tell white lies. It depends of ...

C: The basic situation to this point is when the woman or man are ... unfaithful. This is the best situation. I think the woman is very good ... because in this situation the woman don't feel guilty about ... in general the man feel more guilty.

A: No, I'm disagree with you.

B: I think when woman make a liar they didn't feel nervous or embarrasses or face become red. If men become liar, they feel nervous.

A: OK ...

(They later go on to discuss the next topic.)

C: Number three – *When men and women suffer from the same illness, men take twice as long off work.* Three is OK.

A: I'm agree with this.

B: I disagree.

D: Why?

B: Because I reckon that one man and one woman both got ill ... the woman take the medicine and lie down on the bed, but the man don't care about that. Maybe they go out they go to their job. I think the man is ... I think woman take longer.

D: I disagree.

A: We are completely disagree with you.

C: I reckon that the man in general are more hungry for attention. You know like a kid. When the man is ill, it is a good opportunity to look for attention.

D: When a man get illness, they act like children.

B: I think it depend on the personality.

from **student's book unit ten** (extended speaking) *p.122*

go to **answer key** *p.161*

6 Ways of giving feedback

Once you have collected and selected your data, you'll need to give feedback. It is a good idea to vary the way you give it so that learners stay interested. Making it game-like or competitive introduces an element of fun.

think!⁵

Read the possible procedures below. Put a tick ✓ for the ones you use, an asterisk * for those you would like to try, and a cross ✗ if you don't think they are suitable for your learners.

☐ Give learners a minute to think. What were they pleased about in the speaking activity they just did? Is there any single area they could have done better? Then they compare in their groups, or tell you.

☐ Start by giving the class some positive feedback on what the learners achieved, communicatively or linguistically. Praise particular things they said that were stimulating, interesting, risk-taking, or funny. If you then move on to correction, you will have created a positive climate in which to approach it.

☐ Use your board. Write up a mixture of correct and incorrect language that you noted down (up to about ten short examples). Ask learners either individually or in pairs to identify the ones which are right, and correct the rest. Go over them as a class together. Be sure to allow plenty of time for this important stage. Some teachers deal with the errors anonymously; others ask learners if they can identify their own errors, and then give them a chance to correct themselves before anyone else does. Experiment to see which approach works best with your groups.

☐ You can also use an OHT for the language feedback. If you prefer, provide learners with a photocopied handout to work from. This might mean delaying feedback to the following lesson though, which could be less motivating. On the other hand, it may mean that the speaking activity finishes on a 'high', and they are able to look at the language afresh in the next lesson.

☐ If your learners have taped themselves, you could listen to the recordings, then select short, useful extracts from them for feedback. You could also transcribe short passages for them to look at (or ask them to do it). There is no denying, however, that this can be very time-consuming on your part, and might be most useful for one-to-one teaching or very small groups only.

try it out gamblers anonymous

I've done this with classes where there is no taboo or restriction on the concept of gambling, but it wouldn't be suitable in every teaching context.

To make a language feedback exercise more fun, divide the class into small groups, and tell them they are going to bet on whether they have got each sentence right. (If your exercise has a mix of correct / incorrect sentences, then obviously they have to identify the correct ones and change the others.)

Each group starts with 100 points, and they bet each time on a sentence. They can bet 10, 20, or 30 points. If they are correct, they add the number of points to the total, but if they lose, they deduct the points they have bet. If you want

to make it more demanding, tell them that if they're wrong, they lose twice the number of points they have bet.

I've also used this with potentially quite dull gap-fill exercises to liven them up – and it certainly does. It works for me with all ages.

Gil, Rio de Janeiro

try it out self-correction

If you have facilities for learners to record themselves, e.g. a language laboratory or study centre, you can try this self-correction activity. It is surprisingly motivating!

1 For homework, learners should think up a story / anecdote (about two to three minutes) guided by a model you give them, e.g. something that happened in childhood, at a party or wedding. They shouldn't write it down.

2 In class (or a language laboratory), learners record their story on a tape individually. (This can be done with a partner listening.)

3 They listen to their recording and make a quick evaluation: what went well? what might they improve? (If they are really unhappy with the recording, they can do it once more.)

4 They listen again and write a transcript of what they said. As they write, they can make any changes to improve it in terms of accuracy, expression, or organization. They can also change it from a spoken text into a written one, i.e. omit spoken phrases such as *anyway*, *the thing was*, etc. They can also ask you for help.

5 When they are satisfied, they give it to you. Hand it back in the next lesson with positive comments and any further corrections.

6 They memorize their final version and tell it to another learner.

Francesca, Italy

conclusion

In this chapter, we have discussed:

- the importance of monitoring spoken English and giving feedback
- why learners make errors
- common causes and categories of error
- ways of monitoring student activities and recording your findings
- when and how to correct
- ways of conducting class feedback, including recording your learners, and peer monitoring and feedback.

You can select ideas which will suit your class, but we hope you will also try some new ideas to introduce variety and make feedback an important and memorable learning experience. Your learners will welcome some correction, but remember how important praise is to them.

answer key

think!² p.157

1 style: normally we say *Miss Sinclair* or *Anna Sinclair*. It would also be more likely, but not essential, to say *Is that Miss Sinclair?* Perhaps a further style error.
2 style: he needs to give his full name, e.g. *My name is ...* ; you wouldn't normally use *this is* to a stranger.
3 lexical: wrong preposition, and it would be rather formal. More common is *take part in* or *give a talk at*.
4 lexical: it should be *diary*.
5 syntax: it should be *When is it?*
6 a discourse problem: the speaker is trying to use ellipsis and it doesn't work. It should be *if you need more time, we can provide it*.
7 style (too formal) and error of syntax: the word order is wrong.
8 and 9 morphology : the nouns should be plural.
10 and 11 morphology: these should be plural nouns too.
12 lexical: the speaker means *bus stop*.
13 lexical: it should be *journey* not *travel*.
14 syntax: the word order is wrong. It could be a lexical error as well. *You need* would be more natural.

think!³ p.158 possible answers

1 We wouldn't correct *important to telephone* on the spot; learners are engaged and communicating. Afterwards, however, there is a useful point to make about adjectives commonly followed by a full infinitive: *important / useful / happy / necessary to do...* .
2 In this situation the learner is struggling to find the right word. If their group can't supply it, we would intervene and give the word *travel card*, particularly if they will need the word again in the activity.
3 Here we would note that it would be useful to teach the items *take sb hostage* and *demand a ransom* afterwards. The learners understand each other and there is no communication breakdown at this stage. We wouldn't correct the minor errors, e.g. the speaker has either omitted a plural form on *terrorist* or third person *-s* on *kill*.
4 There is a communication breakdown here: speaker B is clearly confusing *mustn't* and *don't have to*. In this case, you could intervene and correct on the spot. You should monitor for this error amongst other groups as it may be a common error, and you would therefore need to deal with it at the end in class feedback.

think!⁴ p.159

a We would praise the general communication in this activity. Learners are expressing ideas quite clearly (and in places taking risks), responding naturally to each other, and really listening to each other. There is good use of expressions, e.g. *act like children, hungry for attention, tell white lies*.
b A consistent error throughout is that learners don't seem to know how to use zero article + plural noun for things in general, e.g. *men are ... women tend to be ...*, so you have errors like *I think woman take longer / when the man is ill / in general the man feel more guilty*. This is something that ideally could be anticipated and pre-taught.
They also misuse the verb *agree*, e.g. *I'm agree / I'm disagree*: this is almost certainly L1 translation.
c A point we would teach in feedback is use of *(tell a) lie / (be a) liar: I'm not a very good liar / I'm not very good at telling lies*. (Errors include ~~make a liar / become liar / better telling lies~~.)
You could also feed in other ways of making generalizations: *Generally ... Men tend to ...* .

follow up

Thornbury S 1999 *How to Teach Grammar* Pearson Education Ltd (chapter 7)

Swan M and Smith B eds 2001 *Learner English* Cambridge University Press

Nolasco R and Nolasco L 1987 *Conversation* Oxford University Press (chapter 5: Feedback)

Bartram B and Walton R 1991 *Correction: A Positive Approach to Language Mistakes* LTP Publications

Tanner R and Green C 1998 *Tasks for Teacher Education* Pearson Education (unit 12: We all make mistakes)

Ur P 1996 *A Course in Language Teaching* Cambridge University Press (module 17: Giving feedback)

how to ... do free speaking

1 Types of free speaking activity

Free speaking activities may be designed with an underlying linguistic aim, but their first priority is to promote fluency through an activity in which learners have to achieve a communicative goal. There are many different types of free speaking activity; here is a selection of the most common. As you read, try to think of an example of each one from your own teaching experience.

planning and creating activities

An example is the **extended speaking** activity in unit two, where learners have to decide on the location, size, and facilities of a holiday complex. Another activity with a creative end product might be planning and producing an advertisement or a radio news report.

go to **student's book unit two** pp.30–31

problem-solving activities

A common form of these are case studies, e.g. learners read about the different choices facing a person who has recently been made redundant, or the choices facing a working couple who have just had a baby, as in unit six. Their task is to evaluate the different courses of action suggested, and decide on the best one. A shorter activity might involve two learners with busy diaries who are trying to find a time when they can meet.

go to **student's book unit six** pp.78–79

describing activities (people, places, events)

Learners may have to describe their home town to someone who has never been there, or describe their best friend and why they like them. In unit eleven, learners describe a picture. The description might be part of another more extended activity, for example, a role play in a police station where someone has to describe something that was stolen from them.

go to **student's book unit eleven** pp.130–131

narrating

Typical activities include learners telling the story of a book or film, or recalling an anecdote about something that happened to them or someone they know. Learners can also create their own storylines from ideas and pictures, for example in unit eleven, learners develop ideas about a man's life from photos.

go to **student's book unit eleven** p.133

discussion

This takes many forms, but often involves learners in preparing the pros and cons of a particular statement, e.g. Does television have a positive influence on children's education? Questionnaires are also commonly used to promote discussion, as in the questionnaire on men and women in unit ten.

go to **student's book unit ten** p.122

role play

Many classroom role plays are concerned with service encounters, e.g. buying something in a shop, complaining in a hotel, phoning a school or college for information, etc. More elaborate role plays might be job interviews, celebrity interviews, or business meetings.

go to **student's book** (unit twelve) **pairwork** p.145 and 147

presentations

These sometimes form part of an activity, e.g. after a planning activity, each group has to present their results to the rest of the class, as in the **extended speaking** activity in unit two. Or it can be the principal part of an activity, e.g. learners have to prepare a five-minute talk on a topic they have researched.

go to **student's book unit two** p.31

games

Guessing games are very common, e.g. 20 Questions, as are board games, e.g. conversation topics set out in a grid.

Many activities fall into more than one category, e.g. a problem-solving activity will involve group discussion; a role play may include description, etc.

---

think![1]

Look at these free speaking activities. Which category or categories above would you put them in?

a Using pictures and information, learners (in small groups) choose members of a new band, and decide on their image and musical style. They then tell the rest of the class what they have decided and why.

b Learners interview a partner for a voluntary job, and are then interviewed themselves for a different job. At the end, the pairs evaluate the two interviews.

c Learners read a case study about a man who borrowed money from his best friend and didn't pay him back. They discuss who was responsible and how the problems could have been avoided.

---

go to **answer key** p.167

expose learners to a wide range of activities

Different activities make different demands on the learners, so it is vital that the class is exposed to a wide range of activity types for all-round language and skills development. Whatever your students' reasons for learning English, most adults will recognize the need to be able to cope in a range of situations, and to accomplish various communicative tasks, e.g. exchange information, give simple instructions, sequence chronological events, make comparisons between things, marshal thoughts and opinions, etc.

Variety is also important in order to take into account the different personalities and interests within the group. Some learners really enjoy discussion of social issues; others have little to say. Some learners find role play stimulating and fun; others feel uncomfortable unless the territory is very familiar (in general it should be). You will need to weigh up these likes and dislikes so that speaking activities go as far as possible towards meeting the needs and preferences of the group as a whole.

2   What is a good speaking activity?

think!²
Think of a free speaking activity that is generally successful with your learners. (It could be something you have done with different groups, and possibly at different levels.) Now read the section below. Which of the features mentioned does your activity contain?

For a speaking activity to be consistently successful with different groups of learners, it should contain certain features:

- Learners need to be interested in the content / topic of the activity and feel they have something to contribute to it. It doesn't have to be a subject for which they have a burning passion, but it does need to be one they can all relate to, and is not too abstract or removed from their experience.

- The group needs to feel comfortable about what they have to do and to see the aims of the activity as both relevant and appropriate. Learners have a more positive attitude towards activities when they are clear about what they are doing and why.

- The activity benefits from having a very clear goal or outcome – for example, reaching a consensus decision or producing a document co-operatively.

- The activity should be challenging but achievable. If learners lack the necessary language to do an activity, it will be frustrating for them; if they are not linguistically challenged, it may be enjoyable but not truly satisfying. To be successful, therefore, the activity itself should be language rich. It should place demands on the learners that will push them to the limits of their language ability, and won't allow them to fall back on a very narrow use of structure and expression. In other words, a successful activity encourages learners to use new language and experiment.

- The activity itself should be designed so that everyone has an equal opportunity to contribute. That is not to say that everyone will (or even should) participate to the same degree. In any classroom you will have a range of personalities; some will be naturally more extrovert and likely to contribute more than others. The topic will also influence how much each person has to say. The crucial point is to minimize the possibility of it becoming dominated by one or two people in the group. In practice, this isn't easy, and it may be the teacher who can influence this more than the activity itself, either by the way they set up the activity in the first place, or in the way they manage it once it is underway. Every teacher comes across the occasional learner who is extremely shy, and in that case, a minimal contribution, perhaps with a sympathetic partner, may be the most you can hope to achieve.

think!³
This extract comes from recordings made during the piloting of the **extended speaking** activity in unit six. Three learners have read the case study and had time to think individually about the advantages and disadvantages of the second solution.

a   Do you feel the learners are comfortable with the topic and the activity seems relevant?

b   Would you say this is a language-rich activity for these learners, and that they are communicating effectively?

c   Do the participants contribute more or less equally? If not, do you think it is a problem?

2   Rowena could go back to work after the baby is born and be the main **breadwinner**. Andrew could stay at home and look after the baby.

A   OK, number 2. I think that is a good idea. He can be at home and, er, he can do some DIY ... I think he can this do better than his wife.

B   But when they have a baby the living cost will be more, so I'm not sure the salary is enough for each.

A   Oh, but his wife have a good job in the city.

B   Yes, but maybe it's not enough.

C   It is not answer that Rowena could go back to her job after children born.

A   Why not?

C   Same, same job. I think ... she have a problem to get the same job.

A   No, but I think the insurance in the UK is very good for mothers ... she can take a holiday for the birth.

C   But after that?

A   Yes, and afterwards she can go back to the job. In Switzerland it's different, we haven't any insurance for that.

B   Hmm ... but the child is just baby so she need mother.

A   I think for the wife it could be a very good point to work and to do anything in the business. She's maybe happy with, with her job and she will, er, do a career.

B   I agree with you the point, but how about the baby?

C   If her salary is enough for his family, Rowena should go back to her job and he, Andrew should take care of the baby and he should look for, look for his job using one year. One or two years ...

A   Oh, after one or two years?

C Yeah, long thinking time. It's good timing for the baby.

A For a new orientation, for, for looking for a new job.

C Yes, I think if the salary is enough for their family. He should spend a lot time to decide his job.

A They move probably the problem because they would have a second baby and I don't know what then. (laughter)

NB These learners have had no language input for this activity; this recording was made in the research stage of the course, before the units were written.

from **student's book unit six** *pp.78–79*

go to **answer key** *p.167*

3 How can you help to make activities successful?

In free speaking activities you are handing over much of the control to your learners, and no matter how hard you have worked at facilitating the activity, there will be times when it doesn't work out in the way you planned, or the class simply isn't 'in the mood'. Nevertheless, there are various things you can do as a teacher to influence a speaking activity and increase the likelihood of it being successful.

a prepare learners by giving them the necessary language

b set the activity up clearly

c build in time for thinking, planning, and rehearsal

d manage the activity effectively once it is underway

Let's look at these in turn.

a prepare learners by giving them the necessary language

In **natural English**, learners will have studied much of the language they need for the role plays and **extended speaking** activities earlier in the unit. They are also given the opportunity to look back at the language they have already studied before beginning the speaking activity. However, when you are devising your own speaking activities, it will be your job to decide what language the learners will need in order to do the activity successfully. With some activities, you will find it easy to anticipate useful language that you can pre-teach; in others, it may be unpredictable. In this case, there are two useful strategies you can use.

– The first is to anticipate and pre-teach the language you think <u>might</u> be useful and/or necessary for the task. However, when you do the activity, monitor it carefully and take notes. (If the facilities are available, you could record your learners doing the activity in small groups.) At the end you will need to give feedback, and you may well find you are introducing relevant new language arising out of the activity that you hadn't anticipated. This is a very useful source of data for you, and if you keep a record of it with the material you used, you will know what to pre-teach next time you do the same activity.

– Secondly, you could use the **try it out** idea opposite.

try it out a practice run

Do a 'practice run' of the activity with another teacher. It is much better if you can record it, then you will be able to analyze the language used and will therefore be in a better position to select language which is clearly useful for the activity. But remember the significant gap between your English, and your learners' English, and only select language which is relevant to their level.

Alternatively, if you are doing the same activity with several levels, do it with the higher level group first, and note down useful language as an achievable target for lower level groups.

b set the activity up clearly

Do a warmer or some kind of preparation activity at the beginning of the class. Many groups only meet up once or twice a week, so don't expect your learners to arrive in class and go straight into an **extended speaking** activity; it may be two or three days, or even a week since they last spoke in English. Start with one or two activities to get them operating in English, and to get them in the mood.

Group size and the composition of the group can be a very important factor in the success of an activity. Consider exactly how you will divide the class in order to achieve the best group dynamics and to avoid one member of a group dominating too much. It sometimes helps to put the most dominant learners together in one group.

At the beginning of the activity, tell the learners what they're going to do. In the early stages of a course, you may also need or want to explain why you are asking them to do something. Decide exactly what and how much you need to tell them at each stage. This is a difficult balance: explaining everything before they start could be an information overload and may not mean very much; say too little, and your learners may feel they are operating in the dark.

c build in time for thinking, planning, and rehearsal

think![4]

Imagine you are living in another country and learning the language. You're at about intermediate level. Look at these two situations. Which of the things below would you do in each situation?

1 Your teacher tells you that tomorrow you have to give a short talk (about five minutes) to the rest of the class about public transport in your country.

2 At your accommodation you have a number of problems, including a faulty shower and a horrible smell in a cupboard in your room. You also want to delay paying your accommodation fees for a few days until your money arrives from home. You are going to talk to your landlord or landlady about these things.

– do it completely unplanned and unrehearsed
– plan what to say and in what order
– write some notes
– check vocabulary you don't know in a dictionary
– ask a friend / native speaker / teacher for words and phrases

- practise in your head
- rehearse what you're going to say with a friend / native speaker / teacher
- record what you're going to say onto a tape and then listen to it
- other?

Thinking and planning time is now much more widely recognized as a useful language learning strategy both for the classroom and the real world. During the piloting of the **extended speaking** activities, our data showed that learners did benefit considerably from planning and rehearsal time. As a result, we included the **Think!** instruction at relevant points in the units, and staged the role plays and **extended speaking** activities to include a number of preparation activities. We have found that these help to reduce some of the following problems that all teachers will have experienced at some point in their teaching:

- learners feeling inhibited about speaking in English
- learners having nothing to say in discussion activities
- learners experiencing frustration at not being able to express ideas satisfactorily, and quite often, resorting to the mother tongue.

Thinking time helps learners to feel more in control of what they have to do – crucial for the psychological well-being of most adults – and this in turn builds confidence. It won't solve all your problems, but it is one way of making a challenging task more achievable. Conversely, of course, if you want to make an activity more difficult or challenging, you can do it by limiting the thinking time!

preparing for activities

Learners can prepare for activities in a number of ways.

- They can think up ideas and consider reasons, examples, or justifications for what they plan to say. This allows them to extend their interactions considerably and frees them to respond more spontaneously.
- They can think about how to express the more complex ideas, and if necessary find the words or phrases they don't know (by using a dictionary, other learners, or the teacher).
- They can brainstorm or prepare ideas with a partner.
- In a role play, they can talk through the role they are going to play with a learner who will play the same role. They can discuss / prepare what they are going to say.
- They can rehearse more challenging activities with a partner before doing a more public performance to a group, e.g. recounting an anecdote.

How much preparation time learners need for an activity will clearly depend on the nature of the task. For example, if you want them to think about how they would react in a number of everyday situations, they may only need a minute. However, the planning and rehearsal which is necessary in order to make a success of an extended speaking activity (like those in **natural English**) will take more time. Clearly, only part of that preparation will be silent thinking time.

A final point about devising your own speaking activities is that learners usually benefit from having a clear framework or structure to help their preparation. You will find these

throughout **natural English** in **it's your turn!** and in all the **extended speaking** activities.

go to **student's book unit seven** p.87

d manage the activity effectively once it is under way

It is obviously important to check that learners are doing the activity appropriately. Move briefly round all the pairs / groups to check this is happening, before embarking on more detailed monitoring and data collection. If you realize that the majority of the class have not fully understood the instructions and so the activity is not proceeding correctly, it is better to stop the activity as soon as possible and clarify the instructions to the whole class rather than trying to explain it to each group in turn. An important issue for you is how you manage their time; allow too little time for an activity and learners may become frustrated, allow too much time and the lesson loses momentum. If you give groups a time limit and regular time checks, it can help them to use their time effectively, and they will know when to wind down. If a pair or group finishes early, you will need to have a short activity up your sleeve to keep them busy, or ask them to listen to other groups. At the end, round up the activity with feedback.

Want to know more? Go to **how to ...** monitor and give feedback pp.156–161.

monitoring the use of L1

For teachers with monolingual groups, the use of the mother tongue is obviously a concern in free speaking activities. Is <u>any</u> use of the mother tongue justifiable, or is it better to impose a veto on its use? And if it is justifiable, how much use is acceptable?

Your approach with your learners may be either consultative or authoritative, depending on the context.

- Many teachers find it works to have a rational discussion with their groups about when use of the mother tongue is acceptable, and then agree certain 'ground rules'.
- Other teachers may record learners doing activities so that learners can see for themselves how much they are using L1, and whether this is reasonable. Learners are sometimes quite surprised to see how much they do in the mother tongue that they could easily do in English.

Want to know more? Go to Mark Hancock's article for a suggested procedure.

go to **follow up** p.167

- Some teachers appoint 'monitors' to listen in to pair and group activities to police the use of English. This procedure can be employed in a more subtle way by sometimes including a learner in each group who is an observer with a monitoring task – not so much connected with the accurate use of English as with the degree to which the communicative goals were achieved. The effect of having a listener tends to add to a sense of 'performance' and can encourage more consistent use of English.

Want to know more? Go to **how to ...** monitor and give feedback (try it out) p.159.

4 Role play issues

In **natural English**, you will find a number of 'service encounter' role plays, both in the **how to ...** lessons and in the **extended speaking** activities. For this reason we feel it is worth considering some of the issues specific to this kind of activity.

There are a number of good reasons for including service encounter role plays (in shops, hotels, railway stations, etc.).

- Role plays of this type often create a need for specific functional exponents and lexis which might not otherwise be covered in other speaking activities, e.g. buying clothes in a shop or asking for information at a railway station.
- When they go well, they are usually very popular with both learners and teachers.
- From the teacher's point of view, they provide variety through a different activity type.
- For learners, they are practising language in a context they recognize as relevant and familiar.

This last point is worth emphasizing. One of the dangers of role play is that learners think they are being placed in a situation where they have to pretend to be someone else and start acting. In truth this is rarely the case. In most role plays, learners are effectively being themselves in common 'service encounter' situations, e.g. in a shop, railway station, tourist information office, etc. Even if they are taking the part of the shop assistant, receptionist, etc. these are still roles which are familiar to them and should not be difficult to handle.

problems with role play activities

As soon as role plays become more removed from the learners' own experience, there is the danger that less confident members within the group may feel uncomfortable or at a loss what to say. You just have to use your own judgement here. You know your class better than anyone, so you are in the best position to select or create roles which will bring out their full potential, and reject activities which learners may find threatening.

Ironically, the familiarity of many role play situations can be their downfall. It is very easy to assume that everyone will know what to do and what to say, and so to assume that planning and preparation time is not necessary to the same extent. This is not the case, as you will see in the example role cards below.

One final practical difficulty with role play, particularly with service encounters, is that they can be unbalanced with one participant having more to say than the other. This results in a problem of class management; the person with more to say in the role play probably needs more time to prepare than their partner. How do you cater for this in the planning time?

designing an effective role play

You can combat most of these problems by the way the role play is devised and staged.

think![5]

Look at the role cards below. How long do you think this activity would last with an intermediate group? Why? What problems might arise during the role play?

A You need a doctor's appointment. Ring the receptionist, explain what your problem is, which doctor you would like to see, and arrange a day and time to see them.

B You are a doctor's receptionist. Your job is to fix up appointments for patients. You answer the phone.

Unless your learners are unusually imaginative, this exchange probably won't last long at all. There is nothing very challenging here, little unpredictability, and not even much in the way of information exchange. Student A will need a couple of minutes to think about what the problem is and which doctor they want to see, while there is very little for the receptionist to think about. This illustrates the class management problem mentioned above. With so little information on the role cards, you also run the risk that one in the pair may start to create a more imaginative scenario which their partner is not aware of, and this can end up in misunderstandings and confusion. In execution, the role play is also likely to be dominated by one person, i.e. the patient.

Now look at these role cards.

A You want to make a doctor's appointment for today or tomorrow.

(What's wrong with you? Why can't you wait any longer?)

You can't go this afternoon, however. You've got another appointment at 3.15.

(You decide what it is).

You want to see Dr. Brown (a 40 year-old female doctor).

(Why do you want to see her in particular?)

You know there is also Dr Elliott, an older male doctor, and there is also a new doctor, but you don't know anything about them.

B You're a receptionist at a doctors' surgery which is very busy at the moment.

(Why is it so busy? Why do you only have a few free appointments? You decide.)

People ring you to make appointments with different doctors:

Dr Brown – female, 40 years old (busy for the next two days)

Dr Elliot – male, early sixties (free tomorrow at 10.00)

Dr Caswell – female, young (free this afternoon at 3.00)

There is a problem with transport / the roads around the surgery at the moment.

(What is it? You'll need to warn the patients.)

These role cards differ from the first set in a number of ways.

- Both participants have some information in common. This shared knowledge gives the context a solid foundation around which they can negotiate.

- Both participants have a sufficient amount of information to absorb and exchange; at the very least, this should ensure the activity lasts a certain amount of time.

- Both participants have roughly the same amount of information to process; this avoids the problem of unequal preparation time.

- Both participants have to think up a certain amount of information for themselves. This helps to personalize the activity for the learners, and introduces an element of unpredictability into the situation. Neither knows exactly what to expect, and this immediately raises the level of challenge.

For the teacher, there is the added bonus that different pairs may have different solutions; something you can exploit in feedback. For extra support, learners with the same role card could prepare their part together before they do the role play with a new partner.

exploiting role play

In **natural English** you will often find that there are two sets of role cards for an activity. This allows learners to play different roles and practise different language. If you encourage learners to talk about how their first role play went, they can learn from it and improve on it in the second role play. If you are doing a role play where the roles are unequal, you can always ask learners to swap roles.

As the teacher, you can exploit the fact that different pairs in a class will perform the same role play in different ways. If one pair finishes early, you can tell them to listen to another pair to see how the 'conflict' was resolved in their case. Alternatively, at the end you can put pairs into fours, and each pair does their version of the role play for the other pair. You can then ask the class whether the situation was resolved in the same way by each pair.

conclusion

In this chapter we have discussed:

- a variety of free speaking activities, and the importance of exposing learners to a wide range of activity types

- the criteria for devising a good free speaking activity

- the ways in which you can help make a success of these activities, by, for example, preparing learners appropriately and giving them sufficient thinking and planning time

- issues and problems specific to role plays, particularly service encounter role plays, and how to solve or avoid these problems when you devise role plays for your learners.

Free speaking activities form an integral part of the learners' classroom experience at this level; but to be successful, they will require just as much planning and preparation on your part as any other skill or part of the syllabus.

answer key

think![1] *p.156*

a planning and creating; presentation

b role play; discussion

c problem solving; discussion

think![3] *p.158* suggested answers

a We feel the learners have plenty to say; they have had a stimulus which works and they have come up with a number of relevant points in discussion. They seem to be relating well to the topic.

b They are using quite a wide range of language for this level. They are communicating well; they are listening and responding to each other, and are not just concerned with their own contribution.

c A has more turns than C, and C has more turns than B. However, we don't feel that one learner is excessively dominant. (A is a Swiss man, B is a Japanese woman, and C is a Japanese man.)

follow up

Parrott M 1993 *Tasks for Language Teachers* Cambridge University Press (discussion tasks 20–21)

Nolasco R & Nolasco L 1987 *Conversation* Oxford University Press

Porter Ladousse G 1987 *Role Play* Oxford University Press

Hancock M 2000 *Roleplaying Roleplaying* in English Teaching Professional (issue 15)

Nettle M 1997 *Making the Most of Roleplay* in English Teaching Professional (issue 2)

how to ... teach phonemic script

1 Why teach phonemic script?

think!¹

Do you ever teach phonemic script to your learners?

If <u>yes</u>, cover box B. Read box A, then think of two or three reasons why teachers don't do it.

If <u>no</u>, cover box A. Read box B, then think of two or three reasons why teachers do it.

A why I teach phonemic script

- Sound-spelling relationships are difficult in English; phonemic script is a useful guide.
- Learners can work on pronunciation independently through dictionaries.
- Learners can keep a written record of the pronunciation of new words.
- It's a useful tool to highlight differences between sounds e.g. /ɪ/ and /iː/.
- It's very useful for correction.

B why I don't teach phonemic script

- I don't feel very confident about what the symbols mean.
- It's too time-consuming for learners.
- Learners have enough to worry about without learning a new script.
- Pronunciation is best learnt through oral models – they're less confusing.
- The way I pronounce the phonemic symbols is different from the dictionary.

In **natural English**, we have included phonemic transcriptions of many new or difficult vocabulary items as we feel the advantages of learning the script greatly outweigh the disadvantages. Some teachers may lack confidence when they start using phonemic symbols, but they are not as daunting as they may at first appear, and it takes surprisingly little time to learn and feel confident using them, especially as the phonemic symbols for many consonant sounds are the same as their orthographic form. If you introduce phonemics to your learners 'little and often', you will learn them yourself, and you may even be surprised to discover how much fun they can be. Many speakers of English, whether native speakers with regional variations or non-native speakers, may pronounce the phonemic symbols slightly differently from the standard pronunciation. If this is the case for you, you need to be aware of any differences, but you should only point them out to your learners if it creates any kind of conflict with the material you are using.

think!²

Write the words below in the correct columns, according to the sound of the underlined syllables. Would people learning the language of the country where you teach have similar problems with sounds and spelling?

t<u>oe</u>   thr<u>ew</u>   tr<u>u</u>th   c<u>u</u>p   th<u>ough</u>
bl<u>oo</u>d   thr<u>ow</u>   en<u>ou</u>gh   s<u>ew</u>   l<u>o</u>se
b<u>oo</u>t   h<u>o</u>ney   thr<u>ou</u>gh c<u>ou</u>rage kn<u>ow</u>

/əʊ/	/uː/	/ʌ/

go to **answer key** *p.171*

2   The phonemic chart

The phonemic chart on the back cover of the **listening booklet** was designed by Adrian Underhill. You'll notice that it is divided into three main sections:

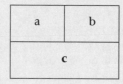

Section **a** contains vowel sounds, **b** contains diphthongs, i.e. compound vowel sounds, and **c** has consonants and approximants, /r/, /w/, and /j/. (The sounds /w/ and /j/ are sometimes called semi-vowels.)

a the vowels

The organization of the vowels demonstrates three different factors involved in producing the sounds:

- whether the lips are stretched or rounded
- whether the jaw is closed or open
- the position of the tongue.

iː	ɪ	ʊ	uː
e	ə	ɜː	ɔː
æ	ʌ	ɑː	ɒ

Try saying the sounds on the top line in order from /ɪ/ to /uː/. Notice the position of your tongue, and how your lips go from a stretched position to a rounded one. Then say the first three vertical sounds, i.e. /ɪː/ to /ae/. Put your hand under your chin, and feel your jaw gradually opening. Your tongue should remain more or less in the same position.

b the diphthongs

The diphthongs are organized into three groups based on the second sound in each case.

/ə/	/ɪ/	/ʊ/
ɪə	eɪ	
ʊə	ɔɪ	əʊ
eə	aɪ	aʊ

c the consonants

The consonants in the two top rows are organized in voiceless and voiced pairs, e.g. /p/ (voiceless) / /b/ (voiced). The consonants to the left of the row are produced at the front of the mouth, e.g. /p/ and /b/ (they are both produced by closing the lips). As you go along the row, the production of the sounds takes place further back in the mouth, until /k/ and /g/, at the end of the row, which are produced right at the back of the mouth ('velar' sounds). The bottom line contains the nasal sounds /m/, /n/, and /ŋ/, the consonants /h/ and /l/, and the approximants /r/, /w/, and /j/.

Want to know more? Read **Sound Foundations** by Adrian Underhill

go to **follow up** p.171

3 How can I approach the phonemic chart in class?

First of all, you need to show your learners how a knowledge of phonemic symbols can help them. You could explain this to them, but the best way is probably through illustration. Write these words on the board:

turn   heard   skirt   colonel

Ask learners how to pronounce them. They may (or may not) give you a fair approximation for the first three, but they will almost certainly mispronounce *colonel*. You can then write a phonemic transcription of the first three, highlighting the common /ɜː/ sound in each one, and invite learners to find the correct pronunciation of *colonel* using dictionaries, i.e. /ˈkɜːnl/. They will quickly see that phonemic symbols in the dictionary give them instant access to the correct pronunciation of words; and you can point out that they can do this independently of a teacher, in their own time. If they then write down the words and phonemic transcriptions, they have an accurate written record of the pronunciation – in case they forget.

how to teach the symbols

Some teachers like to teach all the symbols in one go, but we feel it is more practical and less daunting to organize the symbols into small groups, and introduce them in five- to ten-minute slots – often as a break from other activities – over a series of lessons. For teaching purposes, it is sensible to divide them into pairs or groups of sounds that are close together and often a source of confusion. You can start with some of the sound-spelling relationships that are classic problems, e.g. pronouncing the letter *o* as /ɒ/ (as it is in many other languages), when in English, the pronunciation may be /ʌ/ as in *some*, or /əʊ/ as in *don't*.

how to group the sounds

Here is one way of grouping the sounds over a series of lessons, although the groupings and order are very much up to you, and may depend on the nationality you are teaching.

schwa

The schwa /ə/ is the most common sound in English as it often represents the letters *a*, *o*, and *e* in unstressed syllables.

vowels

/ɪ/ (bit) and /iː/ (beat)

/ɒ/ (not) and /əʊ/ (know) and /aʊ/ (now)

/ʌ/ (run) and /ʊ/ (put) and /uː/ (blue)

/æ/ (hat) and /ɑː/ (arm) and /ɔː/ (fall)

/eɪ/ (wait) and /aɪ/ (white)

/ɪə/ (ear) and /eə/ (hair) and /ʊə/ (pure)

/e/ (bed) and /ɜː/ (burn) and /ɔɪ/ (boil)

consonants

/ð/ (this) and /θ/ (think)

/s/ (see) and /ʃ/ (sure) and /z/ (lose) and /ʒ/ (measure)

/dʒ/ (due) and /tʃ/ (chew)

There are other consonant sounds that may be problematic for certain nationalities, e.g. /d/ and /ð/ for Spanish speakers, /f/ and /h/ for Japanese speakers, or /p/ and /b/ for Arabic speakers.

how to introduce the sounds

To introduce these groups of sounds, it helps if you have a large copy of the chart on the wall. If you don't have one, write the relevant sounds on the board. Here are some simple techniques to get started.

- Point to two sounds, e.g. /ɪ/ and /iː/, and model them for learners to repeat.
- Point to a sound e.g. /e/, and elicit it from the class.
- Point to a sound and model it 'silently', showing the position of your lips and jaw, e.g. /ɔː/ or /aː/. Then elicit it from the learners.
- Once you have established a sound, elicit simple words containing the sounds, e.g. /ɜː/ *bird*, *turn*.
- Tap out on the chart a simple word using 'easy' consonant phonemes for learners to say, e.g. point to /b/ + /ɪ/ + /t/ = *bit*; /iː/ + /t/ = *eat*.
- As you teach new sounds, also revise familiar ones.

how to help learners see progress

One approach which can help to give learners a sense of progress is for them to make a blank copy of the phonemic chart on the back of the listening booklet. Each time they learn a new symbol, they write it in the correct square on their chart, until finally they have a completed copy. Using your wallchart, you can do quick revision activities during the lesson. For example, point to different symbols and ask learners to give you the sound, or a word containing that sound. You can ask learners to take the role of teacher, and come out and do the same, praising or correcting where necessary. Alternatively, tap out some words you taught recently and see if learners can remember them, e.g. /r/ + /aʊ/ = *row*.

4 Phoneme activities

spot the schwa

Teach the schwa symbol /ə/ and sound. Then choose a paragraph from a simple text, or part of a dialogue, e.g. the Bretécher cartoon in unit 1, and ask learners in pairs to circle all the instances of /ə/. Go over the text or play the dialogue with pauses to check their answers. Learners then practise reading in pairs.

which sound?

Give learners a group of words (or a set of flashcards) to sort into groups, according to the pronunciation of the underlined sound, e.g.

/e/ or /eɪ/ ?			
br<u>ea</u>k	br<u>ea</u>kfast	br<u>ea</u>d	st<u>ea</u>k
f<u>a</u>mous	m<u>a</u>ny	p<u>ai</u>d	s<u>ai</u>d

odd one out

Give learners a handout with groups of four words. Each group contains the same letter or combination of letters, e.g. *h<u>ou</u>se, l<u>ou</u>d, c<u>ou</u>rage, ar<u>ou</u>nd*. Ask learners to identify the odd one out in each group (in terms of pronunciation), and provide the two phonemic symbols, i.e. *courage* /ʌ/ is the odd one out; the others are all pronounced /aʊ/. They could go on and construct their own groups of words for other learners to work on.

how many letters? how many sounds?

This is a useful way to distinguish silent letters, e.g. cupboard, and to deal with consonant clusters, e.g. al<u>th</u>ough.

word	how many letters?	how many sounds?	what sound(s)?
cu<u>pb</u>oard	2	1	/b/
an<u>sw</u>er			
ar<u>ch</u>itect			
al<u>th</u>ough			
lan<u>gu</u>age			
wei<u>gh</u>t			
furni<u>t</u>ure			

five things

Give learners two sounds, e.g. /ɪ/ and /iː/ and put them into pairs. They have to think of five things to eat or drink with each sound, e.g. *fish*, /ɪ/ *cheese* /iː/. You can adapt it to different sounds and different topics – as long as you can find the answers yourself!

phonemic quiz

When learners have covered a number of phonemic symbols, you can do this as a warmer. On a handout, write five suitable general knowledge questions in phonemic script, e.g.

1 /wen wɒz ðə laːst əlɪmpɪk geɪmz/ (When was the last Olympic Games?)

2 /huː wʌn ðə wɜːld kʌp in tuː θaʊzənd ənd tuː/ (Who won the World Cup in two thousand and two?)

In pairs, learners have to read them, then write the answers (in Roman script) as quickly as possible.

---

try it out phonemic bingo

1 Give each learner a copy of the table below. Alone, they circle <u>one</u> word in each box in pencil (so that they can rub it out later).

2 You then read out one of the two words in the first box. Tick the word you say. If a learner has circled the word you said, they put a tick next to it.

3 Read one word from the next box, and so on to the last box. Then go back and repeat the procedure, reading the other words. When a learner has ticked all the words they circled, they shout 'bingo!'

4 Now check the learner's answers against the ones you read out. If there is a mistake, continue the game with the rest of the class till you get a winner. You can then ask learners to write out the words in Roman script.

5 Put learners in small groups of four or five. They can play the game, with one learner in the group as the teacher.

You can adapt this game to include typical pronunciation problems for learners in your teaching environment.

wɔːk wɜːk	ʃɪp ʃiːp	pæk paːk
riːd red	kʌp kæp	fjuː vjuː
weɪt waɪt	suːp səʊp	wɒtʃ wɒʃ
bæk bæg	paːθ paːs	wʊd gʊd

dictionary race

Give learners a list of ten words they regularly mispronounce. (This will vary from country to country, but the ones suggested are very common to many nationalities.) Tell learners to work in pairs. They look up the phonemic transcriptions in dictionaries and say the words to each other to make sure they can pronounce them correctly. The first pair to finish should say the words to the class. If they are confident with the words and symbols, you could suggest they record only the phonemic transcriptions of the words in their notebooks to test themselves on the correct pronunciation at a later date.

comfortable	headache	dangerous	interesting	oranges
vegetable	women	science	mountain	usually

homophones

Give learners the words in phonemic script below, and ask them to find two different spellings for each one, using dictionaries if necessary.

example /blu:/ blue blew

/əlaʊd/ (aloud, allowed); /weɪt/ (wait, weight); /tu:/ (too, two); /ðeə/ (there, their); /weɪ/ (way, weigh); /weist/ (waste, waist); /flu:/ (flew, flu); /wi:k/ (weak, week).

homonyms

Give learners the words below, and they use dictionaries to find out the two ways the words are pronounced, and what each one means.

row	tear	lead	wind	wound

conclusion

In this chapter, we have looked at:

- the reasons why teachers may or may not teach phonemic script
- ways of organizing and introducing the phonemic chart
- a range of discrete phoneme activities which make excellent warmers, revision activities, or can be introduced at different points in a lesson to provide a change of focus or pace.

If you have never used the phonemic script with your classes before, this chapter gives you a basic introduction, and we hope that you will experiment with it.

answer key

think![2] *p.168*

/əʊ/ – toe, though, throw, sew, know
/u:/ – threw, truth, lose, boot, through
/ʌ/ – cup, blood, enough, honey, courage

follow up

background reading

Underhill A 1994 *Sound Foundations* Heinemann

Kenworthy J 1987 *Teaching English Pronunciation* Longman

Roach P 1983 *English Phonemics and Phonology* Cambridge University Press

Newton C 1999 *Phonemic script: the pros and cons* in English Teaching Professional (issue 12)

classroom activities

Hancock M 1995 *Pronunciation Games* Cambridge University Press

Hewings M 1993 *Pronunciation Tasks* Cambridge University Press

Haycraft B 1993–4 *English Aloud 1 and 2* Heinemann

Fletcher C 1989 *Sounds English* Longman

language reference key

unit one

1.1 1 When is he leaving?
2 Where does she live?
3 Can he speak German?
4 Did he come to see you?
5 Are they married?

1.2 *sample answers*
1 How far is it?
2 How often do you visit him?
3 How many CDs have you got?
4 How old is your brother?
5 What sort of car is it?
6 How many people were there?
7 What time did you get home?
8 How long have you known her?
9 How much milk do you need?
10 How long have you had your car?

1.3 *sample answers*
1 What happened?
2 Which bag was it?
3 Where did you last see it?
4 When did this happen?
5 Who found it?

1.4 1 to
2 for
3 to
4 about
5 for

1.5 1 have they
2 can he
3 isn't she
4 don't you
5 isn't he
6 didn't you
7 aren't we
8 should they
9 doesn't he
10 did she

1.6 1 never
2 before
3 never
4 ever
5 before

1.7 1 Have you seen this man before?
2 Sue has never driven a car.
3 Have they ever used this software?
4 Harry and Pam have never met.
5 Has he ever told you about it?

1.8 1 This is the first time I've tried yoga.
2 This is the third time we've travelled to India.
3 Is this the first time you've been to the Taj Mahal?
4 It's the only time he's ever been angry.
5 This isn't the fist time I've seen this film.

1.9 1 Haven't you finished yet?
2 I've just had lunch.
3 Ben has already seen that film.
4 It's hasn't stopped snowing yet.
5 Oh, no! I've just broken a glass.

1.10 1 ✓ I went to Holland last year.
2 ✓ It's the first time I've been to Rome.
3 ✓ I saw James at the wedding.

1.11 1 Julie has been to Egypt. = Julie went to Egypt and now she's back.
2 Mike's gone to the shops. = Mike is at the shops now.

1.12 1 What are you going to wear?
2 Where are you going to put it?
3 How is he going to get to work?
4 How are we going to celebrate?
5 What is she going to do with it?

1.13 1 I'm hoping to go to France.
2 I'm planning to travel round Europe.
3 I'm thinking of going to the cinema this evening.

1.14 1 ✗ What a fantastic day!
2 ✗ What a pity!
3 ✓
4 ✗ What terrible weather!
5 ✓
6 ✓
7 ✗ What a fascinating book!
8 ✗ What beautiful flowers!
9 ✓
10 ✓

unit two

2.1 1 bigger / the biggest
2 easier / the easiest
3 stronger / the strongest
4 nicer / the nicest
5 cheaper / the cheapest
6 happier / the happiest
7 hotter / the hottest
8 later / the latest
9 lazier / the laziest
10 narrower / the narrowest

2.2 1 better
2 than
3 most
4 more
5 further

2.3 1 Pat is slightly taller than me.
2 I am far older than you are. / You are far older than I am.
3 Liz is much more reliable than I thought.
4 The house is a bit further away.
5 It is a lot more expensive than it should be.

2.4 1 a bit / a little / slightly
2 much / far / a lot
3 much / far / a lot
4 much / far / a lot
5 much / far / a lot

2.5 1 c, 2 a, 3 a, 4 b, 5 b, 6 c, 7 b, 8 c, 9 c, 10 c

2.6 1 'm working
2 's writing
3 'm taking
4 'm sleeping
5 's watching

2.7 *sample answers*
1 traffic lights / traffic jam / traffic warden
2 snack bar
3 coffee cup / coffee bar / coffee break
4 writing paper / writing desk

5 toothpaste / toothbrush / toothpick
6 sunglasses / sunblock / sunburn
7 bus stop / bus driver / bus depot
8 bedroom / bathroom / living room
9 postman / post office
10 shoe shop / shoe laces / shoe polish

unit three

3.1 1 I've lived here since for three years.
2 She's bought that car three years ago.
3 I've been went / was in Paris last weekend. / I've been in to Paris since last weekend.
4 I didn't see haven't seen Mark since Monday. / I didn't see Mark since on Monday.
5 I wasn't haven't been there since last year. / I wasn't there since last year.
6 Jane has worked here since for a month.
7 Mike's been went / was on holiday last week. / Mike's been on holiday since last week.
8 I didn't see haven't seen Jason since last year.
9 I enjoyed tennis when I've been was a child.
10 We've seen saw our friends yesterday.

3.2 1 for
2 since
3 since

3.3 *sample answers*
1 How long have you known him?
2 How long have you been working here?
3 How long have you had your car?
4 How long did you live in France?
5 How long have you been blonde?

1 friend
2 sorry
3 play
4 take
5 missed

3.5 1 I used to play tennis a lot.
2 We used to go to Spain every year.
3 Patrick never used to like Maths at school.
4 Anne used to have long hair.
5 You never used to / didn't use to go to the gym.

3.6 1 ✓
2 ✗ I went to Rome twice for a holiday.
3 ✓
4 ✗ I don't play football these days.
5 ✓

unit four

4.1 1 go
2 leaving / to leave
3 live
4 getting up / to get up
5 travelling / to travel

4.2
1 might
2 could
3 would
4 might
5 wouldn't
6 might
7 Would
8 might
9 would
10 could

4.3 1 c, 2 a, 3 b

unit five

5.1
1 He doesn't sound very pleased.
2 She made a very bad mistake.
3 We had delicious food but the room was terrible.
4 The prize made them very happy.
5 That soup smells lovely.

5.2
1 hopefully
2 hard
3 well
4 simply
5 easily
6 late
7 fast
8 incredibly
9 nicely
10 horribly

5.3
1 fast
2 well
3 badly / terribly
4 carefully
5 hard

5.4
1 mustn't
2 don't have to
3 doesn't have to
4 mustn't
5 don't have to

5.5
1 mustn't
2 must / have to
3 must
4 don't have to
5 must / have to
6 don't have to
7 must
8 must / have to
9 Do (you) have to
10 mustn't

5.6
1 You shouldn't park here.
2 You aren't / 're not allowed to park here.
3 You aren't / 're not allowed to smoke in this room.
4 You shouldn't wait here.
5 You should eat less salt.

unit six

6.1
1 0
2 1
3 1
4 0
5 1

6.2 *sample answer*
1 c, 2 d, 3 e, 4 a, 5 b

6.3
1 Unless
2 I'll get up
3 if

6.4
1 when
2 If
3 when / if
4 if
5 when

6.5
1 before taking
2 of working
3 After leaving
4 of cooking
5 without falling

unit seven

7.1
1 Adam said told me he was leaving tonight. / Adam said me he was leaving tonight.
2 I want Peter to go now.
3 Ella told me that she felt ill. / Ella told said that she felt ill.
4 Guy advised me to put the money in the bank.
5 My brother explained to me that it was difficult. / My brother explained told me that it was difficult.

7.2 Students' own answers.

7.3
1 are having
2 are discussing
3 interrupts
4 tells
5 is lying

7.4 Students' own answers.

7.5
1 This is a postman's uniform.
2 Those are policemen's uniforms.
3 Peter and John are Jenny's sons.
4 The student's test results were so bad he had to retake it.
5 This is the girls' changing room. Where are the children's clothes.
7 I'm going to the doctor's later.
8 Let's go over to Ann's tonight.
9 Is this the women's fashion department?
10 Could you buy two steaks at the butcher's, please?

7.6
1 the result of the match
2 Peter's
3 the top of the mountain
4 Paul's car
5 the end of the road

unit eight

8.1 1 ✓, 2 ✗, 3 ✗, 4 ✓, 5 ✓

8.2 Students' own answers.

8.3
1 I think she will find the course very difficult.
2 ✗
3 ✗
4 They say the economy won't improve until next year.
5 I'm sure he will be here soon.

8.4
1 It will probably rain / It's probably going to rain on my birthday. It usually does.
2 Look at that blue sky! It's going to be a nice day.
3 Be careful! You're going to fall off that ladder.
4 In 2035 I'll be seventy. / In 2035 I'm going to be seventy.
5 I'm sure she's going to win. / I'm sure she'll win. She's playing really well.

8.5
1 Yes
2 Yes
3 No

8.6
1 the
2 singular
3 can't

8.7
1 some advice / some information
2 the news
3 some research
4 the furniture
5 the information

unit nine

9.1
1 If you knew the answer, you could help me.
2 She might get angry if you told her that now.
3 If I were you, I wouldn't accept that job.
4 If I had lots of money, I'd give up work.
5 If you were me, what would you do?

9.2 *sample answers*
1 If I had a timetable, I could check the train times.
2 If he spoke some English, it wouldn't be so difficult to communicate.
3 If he didn't have a bad cold, he could go out.
4 If the journey wasn't so long, she would go.
5 If I was ambitious, I would get promoted.

9.3 Students' own answers.

9.4
1 impolite
2 inconvenient
3 unpack
4 illegal
5 disappear
6 unlock
7 inefficient
8 disagree
9 immoral
10 irrational

9.5
1 always
2 never / hardly ever
3 hardly ever
4 hardly ever / seldom / rarely
5 normally / usually / almost always

9.6
1 I always go to bed before midnight.
2 We often take the dog to the woods.
3 Do you normally drive so fast?
4 I have occasionally written articles about it.
5 His films are seldom entertaining.

9.7
1 There is usually a good film on Sunday evenings. / Usually, there is a good film on Sunday evenings.
2 I sometimes wonder what life is all about. / Sometimes I wonder what life is all about.
3 I quite often forget to lock my front door. / Quite often, I forget to lock my front door.
4 We normally have friends round for a meal at the weekend. / Normally, we have friends round for a meal at the weekend.
5 You see foxes at the bottom of the garden occasionally. / Occasionally, you see foxes at the bottom of the garden. / You occasionally see foxes at the bottom of the garden.

unit ten

10.1 1 The Love is the most important thing in life.
2 I think the money is the problem with society.
3 Generally girls are more mature than the boys.
4 The Oranges are good for you: they're full of vitamins.
5 I'm very happy with the life at the moment.

10.2 1 a, 2 an, 3 a, 4 a, 5 a, 6 The, 7 the, 8 a, 9 the, 10 the

10.3 *sample answers*
1 I ate all my apples
2 Most of the children we invited came to the party.
3 They ate some of the sandwiches.
4 They all turned up for judo class today.
5 Some of the people arrived late.

10.4 1 which / that
2 who / that
3 which / that
4 who / that
5 which / that

10.5 1 I bought a ring which / that cost over £200.
2 I took the medicine which / that the doctor recommended.
3 I rang the man who / whom / that I met at the party.
4 I work for a company which / that makes microchips.
5 I spoke to the people who / that live next door.

10.6 1 modesty
2 weakness
3 education
4 confidence
5 punctuality
6 importance
7 popularity
8 arrangement
9 sadness
10 patience

10.7 1 dangerous
2 musical
3 creative
4 democratic
5 thoughtful

unit eleven

11.1 1 (He) took his son to the station.
2 Tom was bitten by (a dog.)
3 I was woken by (the baby) crying.
4 (The train) pulled out of the station.
5 By six o'clock, (we) were travelling down the motorway.
6 (Someone) broke into the museum.
7 The rings were stolen by (the burglars.)
8 (The volcano) erupted last night.
9 The village was covered by (the lava.)
10 This book is published by (Oxford University Press.)

11.2 1 At the moment all the phone lines are being used.
2 This floor has just been cleaned but it still looks dirty.

3 The announcement will be made tomorrow.
4 Most of our products are exported.
5 The house was sold last week.

11.3 1 The robber was arrested.
2 The town centre has been cleaned up.
3 The books are printed in Hong Kong.
4 A photo has been taken of the murder scene. / The murder scene has been photographed.
5 The Prime Minister was shown round the hospital.

11.4 1 They don't look very happily happy, do they?
2 She looks like beautiful.
3 It looks as if they are going to a party.
4 They looks look like a group of tourists.
5 He looks as like a rich man.

11.5 1 must
2 might
3 can't
4 can't
5 might

unit twelve

12.1 1 A, 2 B, 3 B

12.2 1 I couldn't go to the restaurant because I had spent all my money.
2 When I arrived, the others had already left.
3 ✓
4 When the film started, I realized I had seen it a year ago.
5 ✓

12.3 1 stand
2 sit
3 tidy
4 Hurry
5 saving

12.4 1 Please take off your helmet before coming into the bank.
2 I went back to the post office with the parcel.
3 We have to fill in this questionnaire.
4 It was midnight but I carried on working.
5 I'll pick you up from the station.

12.5 1 ✓, 2 ✗, 3 ✓, 4 ✓, 5 ✗

12.6 1 scissors
2 are
3 are
4 isn't
5 were
6 are
7 pair of shorts
8 has
9 are
10 some

OXFORD
UNIVERSITY PRESS

Great Clarendon Street, Oxford OX2 6DP

Oxford University Press is a department of the University of Oxford. It furthers the University's objective of excellence in research, scholarship, and education by publishing worldwide in

Oxford New York

Auckland Bangkok Buenos Aires Cape Town Chennai Dar es Salaam Delhi Hong Kong Istanbul Karachi Kolkata Kuala Lumpur Madrid Melbourne Mexico City Mumbai Nairobi São Paulo Shanghai Taipei Tokyo Toronto

Oxford and Oxford English are registered trade marks of Oxford University Press in the UK and in certain other countries

ISBN 0 19 437329 0
Edited by Theresa Clementson

Printed and bound by Grafiasa S.A. in Portugal

Acknowledgements

The Publisher and Authors would like to thank the following for permission to reproduce photographs:
Getty images: cover and throughout (Uwe Krejci/2 people); 146, 152 (Rutz Manfred/ear)